PORTFOLIO / PENGUIN

THE 100 BEST BUSINESS BOOKS OF ALL TIME

JACK COVERT is the president and founder of 800-CEO-READ, a specialty business book retailer that began as a subsidiary of the Harry W. Schwartz Bookshops. Jack lives in Milwaukee, Wisconsin, with his wife of forty-plus years, many granddaughters, and three cats.

TODD SATTERSTEN is the founder of BizBookLab, a company that identifies, develops, and launches business books around the world. He lives in Portland, Oregon, with his wife and three children.

Visit www.100bestbiz.com

The 100 Best Business

Books of All Time

What They Say, Why They Matter, and How They Can Help You

JACK COVERT AND TODD SATTERSTEN

PORTFOLIO / PENGUIN

PORTFOLIO / PENGUIN
Published by the Penguin Group
Penguin Group (USA) Inc., 375 Hudson Street, New York, New York 10014, U.S.A.
Penguin Group (Canada), 90 Eglinton Avenue East, Suite 700, Toronto, Ontario,
Canada M4P 2Y3 (a division of Pearson Penguin Canada Inc.)
Penguin Books Ltd, 80 Strand, London WC2R 0RL, England
Penguin Ireland, 25 St. Stephen's Green, Dublin 2, Ireland (a division of Penguin Books Ltd)
Penguin Books Australia Ltd, 250 Camberwell Road, Camberwell,Victoria 3124, Australia
(a division of Pearson Australia Group Pty Ltd)
Penguin Books India Pvt Ltd, 11 Community Centre, Panchsheel Park,
New Delhi – 110 017, India
Penguin Group (NZ), 67 Apollo Drive, Rosedale, Auckland 0632, New Zealand
(a division of Pearson New Zealand Ltd)
Penguin Books (South Africa) (Pty) Ltd, 24 Sturdee Avenue,
Rosebank, Johannesburg 2196, South Africa

Penguin Books Ltd, Registered Offices: 80 Strand, London WC2R 0RL, England

First published in the United States of America by Portfolio, a member of
Penguin Group (USA) Inc. 2009

This paperback edition with new material and revisions published 2011

10 9 8 7 6 5 4 3 2 1

THE LIBRARY OF CONGRESS HAS CATALOGED THE HARDCOVER EDITION AS FOLLOWS:
Covert, Jack.
The 100 best business books of all time : what they say, why they matter, and how they can help you / by Jack Covert and Todd Sattersten.
p. cm.
Includes bibliographical references and index.
ISBN 978-1-59184-240-8 (hc.)
ISBN 978-1-59184-446-4 (pbk.)
1. Business—Bibliography. 2. Management—Bibliography. 3. Businesspersons—Books and reading—United States. 4. Executives—Books and reading—United States. 5. Best books—United States. I. Sattersten, Todd. II. Title. III. Title: One hundred best business books of all time : what they say, why they matter, and how they can help you.
Z7164.C81C85 2009
[HF1008]
016.65—dc22 2008036664

Printed in the United States of America
Designed by Joy Panos Stauber

I dedicate this book to A. David Schwartz, who saw something in me that I didn't, and who is either really proud or is rolling over in his grave. Either way, thanks!

Jack Covert

To Eric and Sue Sattersten—For your love and support from the very beginning.

Todd Sattersten

CONTENTS

NARRATIVES page 251

INNOVATION AND CREATIVITY page 279

BIG IDEAS page 301

PREFACE TO THE PAPERBACK EDITION

WRITING *The 100 Best Business Books of All Time* was the culmination of my twenty-five years of reading, reviewing, and recommending business books. It thrills me that the book has continued to sell consistently and has been reprinted in ten languages. Of course, over the past years, we've gotten some pointed questions and concerns about our choices, which we expected when we placed this stake in the ground, and the business book world has changed quite a bit in the intervening years. But I am happy to say that as we updated the material for this paperback, I am still excited by every book, every nugget of information we've included here.

Since publishing *The 100 Best*, it would be an understatement to say that a lot has changed in the world. Economically, we have survived a worldwide financial tsunami and continue to struggle amid its aftermath. Globally, we have watched as countries were smashed by real tsunamis and other environmental disasters. On a smaller scale, the publishing industry has faced the wave of e-books and e-readers as its "tipping point" (read Malcolm Gladwell, page 139) has clearly been reached. The digital book will continue to radically change the way people get information and will continue to mold the look of the publishing industry in the future. Our small company has felt the impact of these swells. We have reacted to these changing times by staying lean and differentiating ourselves through our customer service and ability to customize. In order to adapt, we've applied many lessons learned from the books recommended here.

The trends in business books are also shaped by the economy, by necessity, by the demands of busy readers who can download business information immediately. Over the past few years, the number of big-thinking, investigative books about the economy has soared. Books encouraging entrepreneurs to venture out independently and create something new (as Todd has done, leaving the company in 2009 and founding BizBookLab in Portland, Oregon) are incredibly popular. Social media books now come in every flavor. While we still believe *The 100 Best* is a definitive list, among these recent trends, there have been many worthy and meritorious books published. We created the 800-CEO-READ Business Book of the Year award to celebrate them. (View the archive here: 800ceoread.com/page/show/book_award_winners.)

For this paperback edition, Todd and I have expanded the book reviews we originally included in the final chapter of the hardcover called "Takeaways" and moved those deserving books and their reviews into their respective chapters. We have updated the sidebars to keep them timely. And we have added new pieces of writing that we hope are helpful and insightful. This new material includes the answers to such questions as why 1982 was such a critical year in business books, which books will help you learn how to make better choices, why sometimes pictures work better than words, and how to read a business book.

Thank you for reading,

Jack Covert, Founder and President of 800-CEO-READ

The 100 Best Business Books of All Time

INTRODUCTION

11,000. That was the number of business books published in the United States in 2007. Placed one on top of another, the stack would stand as tall as a ninety-story building. And the 880 million words in that ninety-story pile would take six and a half years to read. Locked somewhere in this tower of paper is the solution to your current business problem.

In fact, a book publisher recently shared research with us that showed the number one reason people buy business books is to find solutions to problems. Sitting at the educational crossroads of "I know nothing about this" and "Let's hire a consultant," good business books contain a high-value proposition for thirty dollars and two hours of your attention.

But it is more than that. Business books can change you, if you let them. *The Lexus and the Olive Tree* will lead you to a paradigm shift from local to global. *Now, Discover Your Strengths* quizzes you, then encourages an exploration of your talents, not your weaknesses. And *Moneyball* shows that any industry is ripe for reinvention.

It is difficult to find those gems, though. The endless stream of new books requires a filter to help discern the good and the better from the absolute best. The solution to *that* problem is this book, *The 100 Best Business Books of All Time*.

Recommending the best in business books is in our company's DNA. In the early days of 800-CEO-READ, Jack manually compiled a new acquisitions list every week to keep customers informed of the latest releases. This weekly list evolved into a set of monthly reviews called "Jack Covert Selects." When Todd joined the company in 2004, the recommendations were further expanded to include a daily weblog, a semiweekly podcast, and the monthly publication of essays on ChangeThis (changethis.com). The latest additions are the annual 800-CEO-READ Business Book Awards and the publication *In the Books*, both of which highlight the best of the year in business books.

After sifting through "the new and the now" of business books for a quarter-century, we decided it was time to bring together the books that are most deserving of your attention.

OF ALL TIME?

Our choices for the one hundred best business books of all time will certainly find detractors. So early on we want to make clear our criteria for selecting these books. First, the most important criterion was the quality of the idea. Recognizing that judgment of quality is subjective, we found the only route to choosing the best was to ask of each book the same set of questions: Is the author making a good argument? Is there something new to what he or she is presenting? Does the idea align or contradict with what we intrinsically know about business? Can we use this idea to make our business better? After asking these questions of thousands of books, we found ample candidates. However, a good idea was not the only consideration in selecting the *100 Best*.

The second factor in choosing these books was the applicability of the idea for someone working in business today. We dismissed books that described dated theories that have since been replaced or those containing anecdotes for success about companies that no longer exist. For example, Frederick Taylor's turn-of-the-century view that laborers were merely replaceable cogs in some organizational machine has been largely replaced by a more humanistic view that individuals bring the diversity of their strengths to the work they do. The selections in our book represent a more contemporary (and thus, more applicable) point of view and in this way diverge from other "best of" lists.

Finally, the books needed to be accessible. A good idea is indecipherable when conveyed using cryptic language, and worthwhile messages get lost when surrounded by pointless filler. For all the love we have for Adam Smith, we didn't select *The Wealth of Nations* and its nine hundred-plus pages because of the sheer magnitude of the undertaking. We suggest Geoffrey Moore's *Crossing the Chasm* as a more accessible substitute for Everett Rogers's *Diffusion of Innovations*. In this sense, we champion the reader's need for clear access to whatever idea the author is selling.

HOW TO USE THE BOOK

This book contains twelve sections, organized by category. We start with the most important subject of all: you. Then, leadership, strategy, and sales and marketing follow. We include a short section on rules and scorekeeping, after which you'll find sections devoted to management, biographies, and entrepreneurship. We close with narratives and books on innovation and creativity and big ideas.

In the reviews themselves, we aimed to stay true to the promise of our subtitle, "What They Say, Why They Matter, and How They Can Help You." This was an ambitious task in the 500 to 1,000 words we allotted for each book, but the effort resulted in reviews that are an amalgamation of a summary of the book, our own stories, the context for the ideas presented by the authors, and our take on how the book might best be used. Since we divided the task of reviewing the books, we've identified the reviewer (Jack or Todd) at the beginning of each entry.

We were as careful with the design of this book as we were with the selection of the books included. We drew on a wide variety of inspirations to create the layout that makes it something different. The browse-friendly style of magazines inspired our use of highlighted quotes, large headings, and rich illustrations. We mimicked the Choose Your Own Adventure children's book series by giving readers the opportunity to choose their own path through the listings. And finally, scattered throughout *The 100 Best* are sidebars that stand independent from the reviews, taking the reader beyond business books, suggesting movies, novels, and even children's books that offer equally relevant insights.

We truly hope you enjoy the book and use it to find solutions to your business problems. We'd love to hear whether you agree or disagree with our choices, and of any successes that resulted from reading one of the recommended books. Jack is available at jack@800ceoread.com, and Todd is at Todd.Sattersten@gmail.com. You can also find more material online at 100bestbiz.com.

YOU

Yes, you! How about spending some time on you for once?
You have things to do.
You have some habits to break and some new ones to form.
You have a life you want to live.
You need to start by reading this chapter.

Flow

MIHALY CSIKSZENTMIHALYI

Reviewed by Jack

The pursuit of happiness has been contemplated by many thinkers over the ages, from Aristotle to Thomas Jefferson to Viktor Frankl, and the conversation continues today. No matter how much society has evolved in physical comforts or cultural achievements, happiness remains elusive. We talk about it, we write books about it, and yet we barely recognize it.

But we have all experienced it. Happiness comes in those moments of effortless concentration when minutes, even hours, seem to pass without so much as a glance at the clock. It's the point guard unconsciously dropping three-pointers in the big game. It's the writer sitting at her keyboard while the story writes itself. In those moments, we have experienced what Mihaly Csikszentmihalyi calls *flow*, when we are totally focused and completely un-self-conscious. This achievement of flow captures that longed-for state of happiness.

These moments appear to us as fleeting and unpredictable, though Csikszentmihalyi's research shows otherwise. Certain pursuits and activities lend themselves to reaching a state of flow. Csikszentmihalyi describes the common characteristics of these activities as including "a sense that one's skills are adequate to cope with the challenges at hand, in a goal-directed, rule-bound action system that provides clear clues as to how well one is performing." Games, in the broadest sense of the word, contain those elements. Rules provide boundaries. Practice builds skills. And scoring systems offer immediate feedback on your performance.

If jobs were constructed like games, Csikszentmihalyi posits, flow would be reached more often at work. He offers surgeons as an example of workers who reliably achieve flow. A surgeon's goal is clear: fix what is broken. The feedback is immediate and continual: check heartbeat monitor. The intense challenge is recurring, though no surgery is the same. The operating room itself is designed to block out distractions. And because the risk is so great, a surgeon is in a state of concentration "so intense that there is no attention left over to think about anything irrelevant, or to worry about problems. Self-consciousness disappears, and the sense of time becomes distorted." All of these features create an emotional rush for a surgeon. The only time a surgeon loses that level of engagement is when he or she gets into a position of rote repetition and the game becomes predictable.

Flow is "the state in which people are so involved in an activity that nothing else seems to matter; the experience itself is so enjoyable that people will do it even at great cost, for the sheer sake of doing it."

The premise of this book is based on an experience we have all had: those precious moments when time flies and we find we have accomplished a great deal. I have included *Flow* here at the beginning of this section as a starting point, a broad discussion about our mental approach to accomplishing tasks. But the significance of these optimal experiences extends beyond productivity and lies in their ability to provide us with periods of happiness. I *know* the feeling of flow, the kind of high it gives, and as with all good things, I want to learn how to tap into that feeling more often. There seems to be no more worthwhile endeavor. **JC**

Flow: The Psychology of Optimal Experience, Harper Perennial, Paperback 1991, ISBN 9780060920432

WHERE TO NEXT? » Page 295 for **the art of possibility** » Page 54 for **the art of leadership** » Page 313 for **the art of self-awareness** | EVEN MORE: *Man's Search for Meaning* by Viktor E. Frankl; *The Pursuit of Happiness* by David G. Myers; *Group Genius* by Keith Sawyer

Getting Things Done

DAVID ALLEN
Reviewed by Todd

Most efforts to get organized fail. Even given one's diligent use of a FranklinCovey planner or PDA, tasks change hourly based on priorities of the corporate moment. Calendars capture but a fraction of our total responsibilities, and simple to-do lists prove, as author David Allen puts it, "inadequate to deal with the volume and variable nature of the average professional's workload."

In *Getting Things Done*, Allen suggests productivity comes from a quiet state of mental being. Distractions easily disrupt conscious thought. Poorly defined to-do's force the brain into repeating loops of infinite alternatives. *Getting Things Done* shifts the focus from the commonly defined problems of time, information, and priorities, to action with a capital A. By defining and managing actions, ambiguous tasks are turned into clear next steps. And once those actions are captured using a reliable system, the mental noise clears, allowing space for more substantive thought.

"The big problem is that your mind keeps reminding you of things when you can't *do* anything about them."

Allen introduces a "workflow method" made up of five distinct stages. Everything that commands attention—unread e-mails, a pile of magazines, the never-ending list of household projects—is collected and processed, and decisions are made about subsequent actions. The results are organized into lists, calendars, or projects. The overall flow is reviewed weekly, allowing a wide-angle view of the progress. The final step is doing: writing the e-mail, returning the call, buying the groceries. As Allen

THE FIVE STAGES OF MANAGING WORKFLOW

We . . .

1. *collect* things that command our attention
2. *process* what they mean and what to do about them
3. *organize* the results
4. *review* as options for what we choose to . . .
5. *do*

says, despite most people's declaration that there is just not enough time in the day, time is not the issue; clarifying the actions needed is where people fall down.

The modularity of Allen's system makes it attractive to all people looking to be more productive. While the highest possible Getting Things Done mind-set is achieved with devotion to all five interlocking steps, adopting a single discipline or stand-alone technique can bring measurable benefit. For example, Allen suggests using a tickler folder to hold items that can be dealt with at a later date. I recently took his advice and started an electronic tickler folder (as opposed to the physical folder system he recommends), and I'm happy to report that the simple benefit of a reliable system for follow-up calls and forthcoming business books clears a perceivable portion of my personal RAM.

To say *Getting Things Done* has a following would be an understatement. Programmers and technology enthusiasts were early adopters, attracted to its simple but methodical approach to eliminating mental clutter. These same individuals tested and experimented with the most effective use of software, often writing their own code to create a solution that best fit their unique needs. Several dozen stand-alone applications have been brought to market, as well as supplements for industry standards like Microsoft Outlook. New *Getting Things Done* converts can do a simple Google search to discover forums, blog posts, and vendors of all sizes to help with their organizational metamorphoses.

High-level athletes train for years to perfect the smallest aspects of their performance. Allen is suggesting the same in *Getting Things Done*. Mental loose ends and overflowing in-boxes sap our ability to perform. By implementing processes and focusing on action, businesspeople share with athletes the same benefits of a clear mind and forward momentum. **TS**

Getting Things Done: The Art of Stress-Free Productivity, Penguin Books, Paperback 2001, ISBN 9780142000281

WHERE TO NEXT? » Page 18 for **personal effectiveness** » Page 32 for **early effectiveness** » Page 95 for **organizational effectiveness** | EVEN MORE: *Ready for Anything* by David Allen; *Mind Hacks* by Tom Stafford and Matt Webb; *Lifehacker* by Gina Trapani

Jack Covert Selects

Karen Sherlock, Milwaukee Journal Sentinel, 1995

"Jack Covert Selects" book reviews morphed out of a memo I produced each week in the late 1980s called the "New Acquisitions List." Every Saturday I typed up the new book titles (yup, on a typewriter) from that week along with twenty-five to fifty words directly from the books' flyleaf copy. I would then mail the list to my customers, mainly corporate librarians and the rare dedicated business-book reader. This piece filled an information void until Amazon arrived in 1995 and made reviews on specific genres, like business books, more readily available. My customers also changed during that time; corporate purchasing began to go the way of the woolly mammoth due to easy access to new information through the Internet.

For the new millennium, David Schwartz, my mentor and owner of the Harry W. Schwartz Bookshops, from which 800-CEO-READ originated, suggested that we grow the "New Acquisitions List" into a monthly review of recommended books—reviews that would consist of *my* words, not those of the publishers. The reviews would continue the conversation with our customers about good books while differentiating our suggested titles from the information available online. "Jack Covert Selects" was our first step toward branding our company as the arbiter of good business books. My reviews have become a cornerstone of the wide range of information products we offer to all avid business book readers.

Through the years, we have reviewed over 350 books. Eighteen titles featured in this book were originally featured in "Jack Covert Selects."

Written by Jack Covert

*Books reviewed in *The 100 Best* that appeared in "Jack Covert Selects":

The Effective Executive

PETER F. DRUCKER
Reviewed by Todd

Peter Drucker's theories and arguments always start at the most basic level, assuming little or no previous knowledge of a topic on the part of the reader. The premise of *The Effective Executive* is no different. Drucker starts by asking: if the ultimate measurement of manual labor is efficiency, what is the corollary measurement for knowledge workers? Drucker argues that rather than *doing things right*, knowledge workers must strive for effectiveness by *doing the right things*. This powerful insight into how individuals need to work led to this book's inclusion in *The 100 Best*.

"Nothing else, perhaps, distinguishes effective executives as much as their tender loving care of time," Drucker begins. In his classic style of driving to the core of an issue, Drucker quotes studies that show how humans have a poor perception of time and are worse at remembering how they spend their time. Because the typical executive is at the mercy of those he serves, the issue of time becomes more acute. Drucker suggests keeping a log, and if more than one-half of an executive's time is being dictated by others, it is time to wrestle back control. Three common time sponges that need to be considered include: doing things that don't need to be done, doing things that could be better done by others, and doing things that require others to do unnecessary things.

Effective executives use the strengths of individuals in an organization. Drucker talks about the importance of strengths in this book, almost thirty-five years before Gallup's popular theory was discussed in *Now, Discover Your Strengths*. In leveraging extraordinary strengths, however, you must also put up with weaknesses. Drucker has no qualms about hiring the prima donnas and geniuses, saying any managerial discomfort is simply a part of the deal. Contribution is the only measurement of success that matters.

To that point, Drucker spends a whole chapter on contribution, asserting that this type of measurement provides focus for the effective executive. At the organizational level, an eye on contribution shifts attention from downward and inward to upward and outward, toward clients, customers, and constituents. "To ask, 'What can I contribute?' is to look at the unused potential in the job," Drucker writes. He believes that communication, teamwork, self-improvement, and development of others all become natural extensions of contribution.

Contribution itself comes only with concentration. Drucker felt this was the one true secret to effectiveness, and his statement, "Effective executives do first things first and they do one thing at a time," foreshadows the rise of David Allen's *Getting Things Done* philosophy. With a focus on singular activity, executives ask important questions about abandoning often benign initiatives and programs, especially ones that have never met expectations. Leaving the past is central to progress. The very nature of an executive's job is to make decisions about committing resources to the possibilities of tomorrow.

"Effectiveness is, after all, not a 'subject,' but a self-discipline."

Decision making is Drucker's final practice of effectiveness. Effective executives solve problems once. They look at problems as generic to begin with, and try to solve them with rules that will be simple and easy to follow for everyone, not just those involved in the current issue. Decision makers also understand that doing nothing is an acceptable option as well. Effective executives know that a decision is not complete until it is put into action. Simple solutions that everyone in the organization can understand improve the likelihood of their adoption. We hear echoes of Bossidy and Charan's *Execution* here as Drucker emphasizes the idea that a decision is merely intent if it is not a part of someone's responsibilities.

Time. Strengths. Contribution. Concentration. Decision making. Each of these subjects has been covered in myriad works since Drucker first addressed them in *The Effective Executive*, but his book stands alone as an indispensable handbook for the leader, covering the topics at just the right level of detail and from just the right perspective to enable action.

The book can serve as both a starting point for the novice and a firm reminder for the experienced that our labor is not about doing things, but rather doing the right things. **TS**

The Effective Executive: The Definitive Guide to Getting the Right Things Done, HarperCollins, Paperback 2006, ISBN 9780060833459

WHERE TO NEXT? » Page 183 for **building strengths** « Page 9 for **narrowing your focus** » Page 95 for **turning decisions into actions** | EVEN MORE: *Managing for Results* by Peter F. Drucker; "What Makes an Effective Executive" by Peter F. Drucker, *Harvard Business Review* in June 2004 (also included as the introduction to the 2006 edition of *The Effective Executive*)

How to Be a Star at Work

ROBERT E. KELLEY
Reviewed by Jack

To excel in business you need to rise above your peers and be noticed for all the right reasons. *How to Be a Star at Work* is the book that will show you how to accomplish that feat without selling your soul to the god of hubris.

The core concepts of this book revolve around research compiled from Bell Labs during the mid-1980s and after the breakup of "Ma Bell." For twenty-four months, Robert E. Kelley and his team worked as consultants to management at Bell Labs to discover what separates a star performer from all the rest. First, they surveyed senior and middle managers, asking what they thought was the difference between star performers and average performers. The managerial responses were what you would expect: stars would be smarter, better problem solvers, more driven, more outgoing, and greater risk takers. The company then gave multiple tests to a number of stars and average performers. The results were surprising. The researchers found no measurable difference. For Bell, this was a good news/bad news situation. It was bad news in that there wasn't one trait management could look for to provide a shortcut to finding stars. The good news was the realization that all employees can be shown the elements needed to become stars and then escorted down that path by aware managers.

Kelley presents nine strategies one can learn to reach "star-hood." One of the nine points he delineates is "Organizational Savvy":

> What average performers think it is: The talent for brownnosing and schmoozing in the workplace to help me get noticed by the right people. What star producers know it to be: A work strategy that enables me to navigate the competing interests in an organization, to promote cooperation, address conflicts, and get things done.

To help readers gain organizational savvy, Kelley offers a six-step approach that is wholly doable: find a mentor; understand the "real" organizational

THE NINE WORK STRATEGIES

1. **Initiative: Blazing Trails in the Organization's White Spaces**
2. **Networking: Knowing Who Knows by Plugging into the Knowledge Network**
3. **Self-Management: Managing Your Whole Life at Work**
4. **Perspective: Getting the Big Picture**
5. **Followership: Checking Your Ego at the Door to Lead in Assists**
6. **Teamwork: Getting Real about Teams**
7. **Leadership: Doing Small-L Leadership in a Big-L World**
8. **Organizational Savvy: Using Street Smarts in the Corporate Power Zone**
9. **Show-and-Tell: Persuading Your Audience with the Right Message**

chart, not the one in the annual report; master relationship building; learn to manage conflict; create a niche; develop credibility.

Another of Kelley's strategies is "Initiative," which he describes as: "Blazing Trails in the Organization's White Spaces." Kelley gives examples of people who have taken initiative with some amazing results. He tells about a state bureaucrat who was afraid of losing her job during a potential downsizing within her department. In an effort to establish her value to the organization, she took all the Medicare and federal funding manuals home to study and found an accounting "wrinkle" between the way the state and the Feds calculated hospital costs and income. As a result, the state was getting much less from the federal government than was deserved. In the end, the state got a check for $489 million and our bureaucrat kept her job. Kelley believes that stars show initiative when they: "Seek out responsibility above and beyond the expected job description," "Undertake extra efforts for the benefit of coworkers or the larger group," "Stick tenaciously to an idea or project and follow it through to successful implementation," and "Willingly assume some personal risk in taking on new responsibilities." In the author's research, 60 to 80 percent of average performers in the workforce don't have inherent initiative and are resistant to the extra effort because they view it as doing somebody else's work.

"Stars are made, not born."

Interestingly, Kelley's research helped some groups succeed even more, the details of which he added in a chapter in the revised paperback edition. For instance, he discovered that women and minorities sometimes had difficulty with three of the strategies—initiative, networking, and teamwork—due to a history of discrimination in the workplace. While Kelley found that, generally, when all employees incorporated the star strategy into their day-to-day routine the company's productivity rate increased an average of 100 percent, he also discovered that when women and minorities incorporated this strategy, productivity rates rose to over 400 percent.

Kelly clearly comes down on the nurture side of the nature-versus-nurture debate, concluding that performance can be nurtured even in large organizations. That speaks well enough for the effectiveness of the strategies in this book. *How to Be a Star at Work* is a practical book needed by both employees and employers to move to the next level. **JC**

How to Be a Star at Work: 9 Breakthrough Strategies You Need to Succeed, Three Rivers Press, Paperback 1999, ISBN 9780812931693

WHERE TO NEXT? » Page 154 for **what the boss expects** » Page 127 for **how to network better** » Page 316 for **how people are programmed** | EVEN MORE: *Sink or Swim* by Milo Sindell and Thuy Sindell; *You're in Charge, Now What?* by Thomas J. Neff and James M. Citrin; *Know-How* by Ram Charan

The 7 Habits of Highly Effective People

STEPHEN R. COVEY
Reviewed by Todd

The 7 Habits of Highly Effective People is the outcome of Stephen Covey's doctoral research into personal development literature. He studied two hundred years' worth of self-help, popular psychology, and self-improvement writings, and identified two distinct philosophies of self-improvement. The first is what we identify with principles found in the works of early-American visionaries like Benjamin Franklin: principles such as integrity, industry, humility, and simplicity. Covey calls this the "Character Ethic," and it was the dominant philosophy in American success literature until the early twentieth century. But Covey found the literature changed significantly after World War I, with a shift in emphasis from quality of character to improvement of personality, behavior, and attitude: the Personality Ethic. He takes aim at books, though not by name, like *How to Win Friends and Influence People*, *Think and Grow Rich*, and *The Power of Positive Thinking*, saying at best these books focus on secondary traits and at worst teach deception using a quick-fix mentality.

Covey divides the first six habits equally between habits of private victory and habits of public victory. The first private habit, "Be Proactive," describes the freedom of choice one has between stimulus and response, between loss of a job and loss of self-worth. The initiative to learn a new skill is a simple incarnation of "Let's look at the alternatives" versus "There's nothing I can do."

"Management is efficiency in climbing the ladder of success; leadership determines whether the ladder is leaning against the right wall."

THE SEVEN HABITS

1. Be Proactive
2. Begin with the End in Mind
3. Put First Things First
4. Think Win/Win
5. Seek First to Understand . . . Then to Be Understood
6. Synergize
7. Sharpen the Saw

Then, his second habit, "Begin with the End in Mind," encourages the use of imagination to envision a set of creative choices about the future, the same energies employed in leadership. Covey advocates the development of personal mission statements to codify the varying roles and responsibilities of home, work, and community. "Put First Things First" takes that newly defined identity derived from the mission statements and matches up tasks and priorities to ensure alignment. When Covey asked readers which habit was the most difficult to adopt, this management process ranked number one, and he wrote another book, *First Things First*, to further explore the challenges.

"Self-mastery and self-discipline are the foundation of good relationships with others," Covey writes, and then moves forward with his three public habits: "Think Win/Win," "Seek First to Understand . . . Then to Be Understood," and "Synergize." All are based on relationships. "Think Win/Win" is interpersonal leadership that creates mutual benefits for all parties. The classic negotiation book *Getting to Yes* uses the same philosophy, calling for individuals to use an abundance mentality in their interactions and look past the confining paradigm of the zero-sum game.

Being a good listener is a skill that is helpful in any relationship and sits at the core of "Seek First to Understand . . . Then to Be Understood." When someone is speaking to us, our natural response is to listen autobiographically: agreeing or disagreeing, asking questions from our point of view, giving advice based on our own experiences, trying to figure out what is making someone feel the way they do based on how we would react. Covey spends much of the chapter on an extended example of a conversation between a disillusioned son and well-intentioned father. Covey replays the conversation a number of times showing how ineffective listening with our biases can be. When listening, the author writes, "*rephrase the content and reflect the feeling.*" Then he shows how the conversation completely changes. The second half of the discussion of this habit is about presenting ideas, and Covey returns to Aristotle's rhetorical philosophy of *ethos* (character), *pathos* (emotion), and *logos* (logic).

"Synergize" encapsulates the entire Seven Habits process. When people join together, the whole is greater than the sum of the parts, and greater insights and previously unseen results are achieved. Covey suggests synergy is the third alternative to "my way or the wrong way." All relationships grow when trust and cooperation grow.

The seventh habit, "Sharpen the Saw," returns to the individual but "will renew the first six and will make you truly independent and capable of effective interdependence." Covey believes we all have four dimensions that need continual renewal: the physical, the mental, the spiritual, and the social/emotional. He suggests spending an hour working on the first three every day. Find time for a cardiovascular workout. Read the classics. Keep a journal. Meditate or pray. It is only through recharging that we have the energies to succeed in the other aspects of our lives. **TS**

The 7 Habits of Highly Effective People: Powerful Lessons in Personal Change, Free Press, Paperback 2004, ISBN 9780743269513

WHERE TO NEXT? » Page 21 for **the philosophy Covey takes to task** » Page 313 for **more on empathic listening** » Page 38 for **keeping the end in mind** | EVEN MORE: *Man's Search for Meaning* by Viktor E. Frankl; *First Things First* by Stephen R. Covey; *Eat That Frog!* by Brian Tracy

How to Win Friends and Influence People

DALE CARNEGIE

Reviewed by Todd

"Hello, 800-CEO-READ. This is Meg. How can I help you?"

"This is Jane Doe from Any Company. My order hasn't arrived and I needed it today."

This is the call every service company hates to get. The customer didn't get what they needed and now there is a relationship to fix. It is the same as being late for dinner when your spouse cooks your favorite dish: an expectation was not met and someone's feelings are now hurt. Whether you are a customer service representative, a division president, or a loving spouse, a set of skills is needed to mend the emotional break and maximize the potential in every relationship.

How to Win Friends & Influence People is often touted as *the* text for the hard-core personal development crowd. The title itself implies backslapping, sweaty handshakes, and always a friendly word for a new networking acquaintance. As a result, many readers react instinctively with skepticism to Carnegie's message. Even Carnegie admits that after relating a story of complimenting a post office clerk on his fine head of hair, the listener asked him, "What did you want to get out of him?" Yet Carnegie refutes such a cynical interpretation and quotes psychologist Alfred Adler to convey the lens through which the book must be read: "It is the individual who is not interested in his fellow men who has the greatest difficulties in life and provides the greatest injury to others. It is from among such individuals that all human failures spring."

When complimenting the man at the post office, Carnegie was obeying what he believes to be the most important law of human contact: always make the other person feel important. "Please," "Thank you," and "Would you mind . . . ?" are simple extensions of the precept. "Make the other person feel important . . ." is the common wisdom, but how Carnegie ends the statement frames the whole book: ". . . and do it sincerely."

Carnegie divides the book into four main sections. In the first section, he explains the three main tenets of relating to people. Next, he takes six short chapters to describe how to make people like you. In the third section, he shows how to win people to your way of thinking with twelve principles. And in the final section, Carnegie takes on the topic of leadership, with headings like "Talk about Your Own Mistakes First" and "Give a Dog a Good Name."

"Always make the other person feel important."

Regardless of whether you are dealing with a missed shipment or a missed dinner date, Carnegie provides several tools to smooth the stormy waters. Start by using the person's name and state how sorry you are for the misstep. Admit the mistake and let the crossed individual air his or her grievances. And—the final token of sincerity—say, "I don't blame you one iota for feeling as you do. If I were you I would undoubtedly feel just as you do."

Over seventy years and fifteen million copies later, people are still reading *How to Win Friends and Influence People* because there are simple truths found throughout Carnegie's book. Over time his principles have been criticized with claims that the anecdotes are too dated for the new century, but, truly, the book delivers the ever-needed reminder that all we have are the relationships with those around us, and there is always a better way to manage those relationships. **TS**

How to Win Friends and Influence People, Pocket Books, Paperback Special Anniversary Edition 1998, ISBN 9780671027032

WHERE TO NEXT? « Page 18 for **Covey's rebuke of Carnegie** » Page 201 to **read about one of Carnegie's examples** » Page 208 to **see our list of classics** | EVEN MORE: *Think and Grow Rich* by Napoleon Hill and Arthur Pell; *The Power of Positive Thinking* by Norman Vincent Peale

GLOBALIZATION OF MANNERS

In 1990, Roger Axtell wrote *Do's and Taboos Around the World,* the best-selling guide to international behavior, inspired by the experiences of more than 500 international travelers. Today, the need to understand the diverse cultures of the countries with which we do business has increased due to globalization.

Did you know? Singapore prides itself on being the most corruption-free country in Asia. Consequently, it has strict laws against bribery, so Government employees may not accept any gifts at all. (From *Kiss, Bow, or Shake Hands: Asia,* by Terri Morrison and Wayne A. Conaway)

Did you know? In the Middle East, a deal is not done even after the terms have been agreed upon. Negotiation continues until the signing of the contract. (From *Multicultural Manners: Essential Rules of Etiquette for the 21st Century,* by Norine Dresser)

Did you know? In traditional negotiations, Chileans consider feelings more important than facts. The truth is considered to be subjective and personal. (From *Kiss, Bow, or Shake Hands: Latin America,* by Terri Morrison and Wayne A. Conaway)

HERE ARE SOME TITLES TO CHECK OUT:

Do's and Taboos Around The World

Multicultural Manners—Essential Rules of Etiquette for the 21st Century

An American's Guide to Doing Business in China

Kiss, Bow, or Shake Hands: How to Do Business in Sixty Countries

Cultural Intelligence: A Guide to Working with People from Other Cultures

Written by Aaron Schleicher

Swim with the Sharks Without Being Eaten Alive

HARVEY B. MACKAY
Reviewed by Jack

Harvey Mackay has always been a "can-do" guy. After college, Mackay took an entry-level job at a local envelope company and worked up into sales. Three years later, he bought a different small envelope company and turned it into a $100 million business. He now is a best-selling business book author who has sold over four million copies in thirty-five languages of this debut book. But his reach stretches past the sphere of his own personal accomplishments. He helped organize a campaign to keep the Minnesota Twins baseball team in Minneapolis, raised the money needed to build the Metrodome there, and has also raised money for cancer research for the University of Minnesota. There is much about Harvey Mackay to be inspired by, including this classic motivational book about how to handle yourself in business situations, surviving and thriving amid the "sharks" who are out to eat your lunch.

The original edition of this book was published in 1988, but the 2005 paperback has an "author's note" in which Mackay talks about the changes that have taken place between these publications. In the updated version, he has added material on how to apply technology to save time and reach out to others more efficiently. The new material is proof positive that, like Mackay claims, "sharks change," and staying up to date with all the assets that are available is key to your continued success. But the real meat in this book is the everlasting original content.

Swim with the Sharks is divided into four sections: sales, management, negotiations, and a final section called "Quickies." With almost 90 chapters in this 250-page book, you will find succinct lessons that are easy to absorb. For example, Lesson 9 in the sales section, "Create Your Own Private Club," was eye opening to me because I recognized that I have been on the receiving end of this lesson when visiting publishers in New York City. Mackay explains how you don't need to have a fancy club membership to impress a client. He offers step-by-step instructions on how to call the best restaurant in town and know what to ask for so that when you walk in, you are greeted personally, and when the meal is complete, you just walk out, because everything is prepaid. End result? You've given your client the impression that you are a big shot and deserving of his business. Lesson 19, "Show Me a Guy Who Thinks He's a Self-Made Man and I'll Show You the Easiest Sell in the World," is a concise chapter containing only this insight: "All you have to do is make him think it's his idea." Simple yet effective, with just the right amount of real-world boldness to know that Mackay means business.

Other examples of Mackay's wisdom are counterintuitive. From the Management section comes Lesson 64, "The Acid Test for Hiring": "Ask yourself, How would you feel having this same person working for your competition instead of for you?" From the same section is Lesson 44, "Your Best People May Spend Their Most Productive Time Staring at the Walls": "If you discover one of your executives looking at the wall . . . instead of filling out a report, go over and congratulate him or her. . . . They're thinking. It's the hardest, most valuable task any person performs." These are certainly obvious concepts—hiring good people and supporting a creative environment—but Mackay comes at these insights with an alternate perspective that enables us to internalize the lessons because they are so unexpected.

"I used to say that networking is the most underrated management skill. Now I believe *it may be the most important management skill, bar none.*"

In his final section, called "Quickies," he includes an amusing story titled, "How to Get to Know a Celebrity." When Mackay was set to meet Castro, he did a little research and found that Castro enjoyed bowling. Upon meeting the man, Mackay asked him how he kept in such good shape. Castro, who supposedly didn't understand English, replied before the translator translated, "Bowling." Mackay told Castro that he was a three-time bowling champion in college and . . . suddenly Castro and Mackay were communicating in English. Mackay believes that to connect with celebrities, you need to avoid the "fan syndrome" and instead talk to them about their interests.

There are books that break new ground and then there are books that show you a new way to think about the basics. Harvey Mackay has written a classic version of the second type of book, with the added imperative that your survival is on the line. The information offered here is truly timeless, presented with humor, and will be around to save many business lives for years to come. **JC**

Swim with the Sharks without Being Eaten Alive: Outsell, Outmanage, Outmotivate, and Outnegotiate Your Competition, Collins Business, Paperback 2005, ISBN 9780060742812

WHERE TO NEXT? » Page 98 for **more irreverence** » Page 143 for **more quick quotes** » Page 136 for **another animal** | EVEN MORE: *Fish!* by Stephen C. Lundin, Harry Paul, and John Christensen; *Eating the Big Fish* by Adam Morgan; *It's Not the Big That Eat the Small . . . It's the Fast That Eat the Slow* by Jason Jennings and Laurence Haughton; *What They Don't Teach You at Harvard Business School* by Mark H. McCormick

The Power of Intuition

GARY KLEIN
Reviewed by Todd

Stories of a fake Greek statue at the Getty Museum and John Gottman's "Love Lab" at the University of Washington turned Malcolm Gladwell's sophomore effort, *Blink*, into a best seller and brought the topic of intuition to the forefront of cocktail conversation in 2005. Tucked into one of Gladwell's key stories, however, was a man named Gary Klein. The Ohio-based PhD has been studying decision making for three decades and is well known in the field for his work with professionals in high-intensity occupations.

Klein found that firefighters, U.S. Marine lance corporals, and neonatal nurses don't make a conscious effort to consider all the options before taking action; instead, they quickly gather information and act. As more information becomes available, these specialists reassess and change course if needed. When asked how they came to such quick decisions, Klein's subjects used vague, mystical references like ""The Force" and "ESP" to describe their abilities. Klein, unsatisfied, probed deeper.

As you read *The Power of Intuition*, the deconstruction of split-second decision making feels disorienting. How often do you think about how you think? We all can reflect to when we were faced with such life-changing decisions as moving to the big city or deciding whether to take a new job, but the vague hunches we receive from our cavemanlike brains are difficult to articulate, often harder to act on. Studies show that professionals in fields ranging from naval command to offshore oil platform management use intuition 90 percent of the time in their decision making. By choosing individuals whose own lives, and others', depend on the accuracy of their intuition, Klein found subjects who were attuned to this unconscious mental process. He delineates the process to develop a teachable framework.

Klein's decision model is illustrated in a loop that starts with the situation as a whole. First, we look for cues: a firefighter searches for the heat source or an account rep looks for common threads in prior sales proposals. Those cues lead to the recognition of patterns, whether dangerously unknown or comfortably familiar. And then our brains start running "action scripts," in which we simulate an effort and evaluate each potential action singularly until we find a satisfactory answer. With a decision made, we act and start the process over again.

Recognizing the process gives you the chance to improve your intuition, and Klein suggests a variety of ways. Throughout the book, he provides a wide array of decision games. These are simple stories which drop the reader into murky hypothetical situations. In one case, the president of your company asks you to lead a new product development effort with workers idled by weak revenue. Klein then presents twenty-six pieces of information that appear as the project progresses, ranging from coworker gossip to company-wide e-mails, and asks you to note your reaction to each and its impact on your project. This exercise squarely focuses on developing the early skills of the model: filtering cues and seeing developing patterns.

"I define intuition as *the way we translate our experience into action.*"

Intuition is not some magical power or extraordinary mental attribute that some have and others don't. Improved intuition comes from recognition of this unconscious routine and the accumulation of real-world experience. While the stakes are clearly higher in the lives of Klein's research subjects, the world of business shares the need for quick and accurate decision making. And *The Power of Intuition* shows you how to trust your gut and improve your own sixth sense. **TS**

The Power of Intuition: How to Use Your Gut Feelings to Make Better Decisions at Work, Currency/Doubleday, Paperback 2004, ISBN 9780385502894

WHERE TO NEXT? » Page 105 for **what else influences our decisions** » Page 322 for **how crowds make decisions** » Page 29 for **making decisions about your life** | EVEN MORE: *Blink* by Malcolm Gladwell; *Sources of Power* by Gary Klein; *Decision Traps* by J. Edward Russo and Paul J. H. Schoemaker

What Should I Do with My Life?

PO BRONSON
Reviewed by Jack

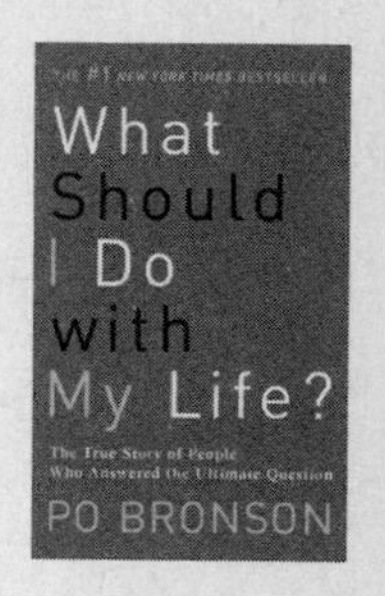

Po Bronson was at a turning point in his life. His job as a TV screenwriter had dissolved when the series he wrote for was canceled. He was unemployed with his first child on the way. Not succumbing to the worry over getting his next paycheck, Bronson instead asked himself the universal question, "What should I do with my life?" His introspection made him curious about how other people were able to envision a new kind of future or identity for themselves when standing at that same career crossroads. So, he decided to investigate, determining to "travel the country tracking down the people whose stories spoke to me." The stories he collected here in *What Should I Do with My Life?* are about regular people, some with families, some with little education, some with money—all everyday folks from whom we can learn a great deal.

What Should I Do with My Life? was published in 2002, during what Bronson describes as "a time when we were losing our respect for corporate leaders, we no longer believed new technology would make our lives better, and the attack on our freedom made life precious and weighty. People were reassessing what mattered to them and what they believed in." What he presents here are stories about the ghosts and stumbling blocks that prevent us all from pursuing what Bronson names "our true calling."

The organization of this material is unconventional. Eight sections are aligned with just what ghost the person is struggling with or the obstacle they have succeeded in clearing. There is something rich and satisfying about this interpersonal way of grouping stories. For example, in explaining why he featured people who have demonstrated patience and persistence, Bronson writes: "I include them not to admonish the young and urgent, but to respect the Big Picture. Most of us take the slow road, no shortcuts." Bronson relates to his subjects so intimately that it is impossible to not become engaged in their stories yourself.

Bronson interviewed individuals from every social strata. His willing subjects bared their souls and took confession with the writer. Bronson makes no attempt to distance himself, serving as subject and scribe. While that is sometimes a sign of an author's ego, here it feels natural and integral to the subject matter. Bronson has lived a fascinating life, suffered through much the same uncertainty; his own stories add connective tissue to the chapters.

"The most common question I'd get asked was, 'So is your book about life, or about careers?' And I'd laugh, and warn them not to get trapped by semantics, and answer, 'It's about people who've dared to be honest with themselves.' "

In the opening section, Bronson shares a story about a seventeen-year-old Phoenix boy who receives a letter from the Dalai Lama, who instructs the teenager to go to India and fulfill his destiny as the reincarnation of an ancient Tibetan warrior. The boy agrees and begins a twelve-year journey to becoming a monk. In another case, a PR executive in England passes on a plum promotion that would double her salary, and instead pursues a degree as a landscape designer. Both of these stories have in common an unexpected decision, a choice to take the road less traveled. Guided by an internal compass, the actions of these two people exemplify what Bronson calls "rightness." Many times we make decisions to change the course of our lives by following a hunch stemming only from passion, a direction not based in real-world experience but one that satisfies some unfulfilled need.

Po Bronson hopes this book will give us the courage to step out of our comfortable nests armed with the inspirational stories of regular folks who have taken the leap before us. For himself, he learned a valuable lesson that he shares with us: "I used to think life presented a five-page menu of choices. Now I think the choice is in whether to be honest, to ourselves and others, and the rest is more of an uncovering, a peeling away of layers, discovering talents we assumed we didn't have." JC

What Should I Do with My Life? The True Story of People Who Answered the Ultimate Question, Ballantine Books, Paperback 2005, ISBN 9780345485922

WHERE TO NEXT? » **For inspiration, read one of the biographies reviewed in this book. Start on page 199. »** | EVEN MORE: *I Could Do Anything If I Only Knew What It Was* by Barbara Sher with Barbara Smith; *I Don't Know What I Want, But I Know It's Not This* by Julie Jansen; *Free Agent Nation* by Daniel H. Pink; *What Color Is Your Parachute?* by Richard Nelson Bolles

The First 90 Days

MICHAEL WATKINS

Reviewed by Todd

"The President Gets 100 Days to Prove Himself—You Get 90."

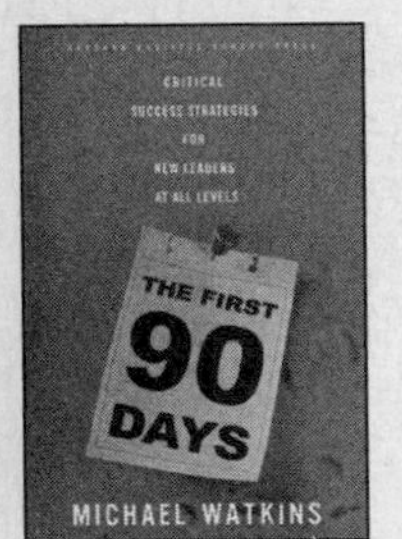

That's the first line in *The First 90 Days*, and while that certainly creates a sense of urgency, I think another quote by Michael Watkins makes the best case for why you should read this book: "When a new leader fails, it is a severe, perhaps career-ending blow to the individual." A little more personal, isn't it?

Now think about the sort of training corporations provide. Have you ever attended a class on how to successfully start a new job? Probably not. And to make matters worse, the finite number of transitions in one's career makes it difficult to accumulate the experience needed to ensure success at these critical junctures. Just because you succeeded at your previous position and that success paved the way for your move upward, that same skill set will not guarantee success with each increasing step of responsibility, new set of employees to manage, or new global challenges to face. This is a primary reason *The First 90 Days* should be required reading for anyone starting a new job.

The emphasis of the book, apparent in its title, is on speed. If you have only ninety days to learn the ropes, then, Watkins advises, you must accelerate your learning in the early days by talking with people both inside and outside the company. Secure early wins to establish credibility and create momentum. Conversations need to take place with your manager to set the proper expectations for timing, resources, and results.

The further you move up, the more your success depends on others. Spend time early in those ninety days evaluating your reports against the challenges you have identified and make the necessary adjustments. Develop relationships beyond your workgroup and build coalitions to help you accomplish your goals. Finding allies brings more support, more momentum, and continues to build upon them.

Bottom line: understand that you have a new job. Even if you just moved from another cubicle across the hall. Watkins tells readers to "Promote Yourself." This may sound like a call to create a press release announcing your arrival, but what Watkins really wants you to do is understand the requirements of your new role, and this means abandoning the tried-and-true. Don't coast on your previous successes. Prepare for early missteps and be ready to learn from those mistakes. Rebuild your set of advisors with individuals who can continue to help you grow. And be aware of peers who don't want to recognize you and your new responsibilities.

The First 90 Days is the book to read before your next job transition; let it take the responsibility for figuring out what you should do when. Then just follow the directions, quickly, to ensure your highest approval ratings. TS

The First 90 Days: Critical Success Strategies for New Leaders at All Levels, Harvard Business School Press, Hardcover 2003, ISBN 9781591391104

WHERE TO NEXT? « Page 29 for **why you first should know what you want to do with your life** » Page 154 for **what the CEO wants you to know in those first three months** | EVEN MORE: *From Bud to Boss* by Kevin Eikenberry and Guy Harris; *The 5 Patterns of Extraordinary Careers* by James M. Citrin and Richard A. Smith; *Talent Is Overrated* by Geoff Colvin

Oh, the Places You'll Go!

DR. SEUSS/THEODORE GEISEL
Reviewed by Todd

A number of years ago we got a substantial order for *Oh, the Places You'll Go!* from one of our corporate customers. When we received subsequent orders, we became curious. What would an international manufacturer need with such a supply of Dr. Seuss books? A call to the company's HR department revealed to us that they were using the book in their new-employee orientation.

While your employer may never have presented you with a copy, perhaps you received the book as a graduation present or at a baby shower. And perhaps you are wondering what on earth *Oh, the Places You'll Go!* is doing on a list of must-read business books. If you haven't cracked open your copy for a while, take this opportunity to pull it from the bottom shelf of your bookcase, where it is probably wedged between an old geometry textbook and a dog-eared atlas. Here's why.

Oh, the Places You'll Go! was published in 1990 and was Theodore Geisel's (aka Dr. Seuss) last book. The book spent its first two years on the *New York Times* best-seller list, and Geisel remarked, "This proves it. I no longer write books for children. I write books for people."

It is this book's broad appeal and keen effectiveness that demands its mention here. Jack and I often say that we have seen the same book regurgitated dozens of times, just between different covers. To watch how many times a subject has been covered or a cliché has been reanimated can be disheartening. What keeps you coming back to some, however, is the magic that's created when an idea and the way it is packaged conveys new (and true) meaning.

Oh, the Places You'll Go! is self-help at its finest—self-help in the same way that Thoreau and Emerson championed self-improvement on the individual level. The book couldn't begin on a more positive note:

Congratulations!
Today is your day.
You're off to Great Places!
You're off and away!

At just under six hundred words, the book covers the gamut of human experience. Our unnamed young man is told that choice is within his power and that all he has to do is decide. But deciding requires judgment and is not without consequence. Seuss points him to the less-traveled path because "there things can happen and frequently do."

It is the reality of the negatives that makes the book so believable and motivating. Confusion, loneliness, and procrastination all make appearances. Each is a challenge, but Seuss never doubts that our little man will get through his difficulties. Geisel said the only thing all of his books had in common was hope, and *Oh, the Places You'll Go!* will provide you with a healthy dose to face each new experience or disappointment that lies on your path.

**"And will you succeed?
Yes! You will, indeed!
(98 and ¾ percent guaranteed.)"**

Many nights I find myself reading this book to my children. I am not sure if its frequent appearance at bedtime is for them or for me. I do know that this book taps into the ideal that we can all be better people and help make the world a better place for us and for our children. Every book should deliver on such a promise. **TS**

Oh, the Places You'll Go!, Random House, Hardcover 1990, ISBN 9780679805274

WHERE TO NEXT? » See the next page for **more business books for all ages.**

Business Books for Kids of All Ages

Sometimes to think outside the box you have to draw outside the lines. Draw inspiration, that is, from unlikely sources. "All grown-ups were children first," wrote Antoine de Saint-Exupéry. Whether it's time to reevaluate, rejuvenate, or simply escape the demands of our busy lives, we recommend returning to the stories and lessons that were most impressive to us as children. The truths you'll find there are timeless. Here are a few stories in which we find inspiration again and again.

Le petit prince, or *The Little Prince*, is Antoine de Saint-Exupéry's classic novella about a small, extraterrestrial boy who changes a grown man's life by reminding him of simple truths too often forgotten with age: Children learn by asking questions. Flowers bloom when they are nurtured. Work is futile when it lacks purpose. You must experience the world to appreciate it. There is still time to make friends. And, perhaps most profoundly, "*On ne voit bien qu'avec le cœur, l'essentiel est invisible pour les yeux*"—"It is only with the heart that one sees rightly; what is essential is invisible to the eyes." *The Little Prince* will put you in a renewed frame of mind; you might even look up at the stars tonight.

Based on a short story by Leo Tolstoy, Jon J. Muth's *The Three Questions* follows a small boy, Nikolai, as he searches for answers to three questions: "When is the best time to do things?" "Who is the most important one?" and "What is the right thing to do?" As Nikolai visits his animal friends and helps a few in need, he learns—with a little help from an old turtle named Leo—that he already possesses the answers. Muth's concise prose and serene watercolors make *The Three Questions* a contemplative read for children and adults alike.

Kevin Carroll's *Rules of the Red Rubber Ball* is a creative little book with a big message for people of all ages: no matter what you do, pursue that which makes you most happy . . . and pursue it with abandon. For the young Carroll growing up on the streets of Philadelphia, the playground was his refuge and passion. *Rules of the Red Rubber Ball* is both his remarkable story of chasing that red rubber ball for the rest of his life, and also a powerful charge to dream big, take chances, and make time for play in everything you do.

In *Walk On! A Guide for Babies of All Ages*, Marla Frazee uses Baby's experience of learning to walk as a metaphor for knowing how to get out of a rut, take chances, overcome obstacles, and determine who and what to trust. It's the earliest "try, try again" experience we have as humans. With its universal observation, "See how different everything looks from here?" *Walk On!* reminds us that sometimes you have to stand on your own two feet to find a new perspective on the world.

Written by Rebecca Schlei

Chasing Daylight

EUGENE O'KELLY

Reviewed by Jack

An advance review copy of this book had been sitting on my office table for three weeks, untouched—one of many review copies I receive from publishers. I was clearing off the table for a new delivery of books when I finally read the back cover:

> On May 24, 2005, Eugene O'Kelly stepped into his doctor's office with a full calendar and a lifetime of plans on his mind. Six days later he would resign as CEO of KPMG. His lifetime of plans dwindled to 100 days, leaving him just enough time to say goodbye.

I closed my office door, forwarded my telephone calls, and read this amazing little book, *Chasing Daylight*, in one afternoon. I am not ashamed to admit that tears flowed.

The book details the three and a half months between the diagnosis of O'Kelly's terminal brain cancer and his death. His haunting yet extraordinarily hopeful voice narrates the book and reminds us to embrace the fragile, fleeting moments of our lives—the time we have with our family, our friends, and even ourselves. O'Kelly is totally honest about his fears. But what really moved me was his simple yet profound writing style. For example, consider this brief passage:

> The business of dying is hard. The wrapping up. The paperwork, the legal work. The stuff that's boring and maddening about life when life is going well. Of course, the other stuff that's happening when dying—the physical stuff and the huge emotional stuff—can be unspeakably awful. But if paperwork is enough to break your spirit—and it is—then how can you have anything left?

The impact of those few sentences continues to move me no matter how many times I read them. He could be writing about anything: selling a house or making plans for a trip. But it becomes clear that he is talking about courage, about leaving this earth the right way.

Just imagine you are the CEO of a major accounting firm, where you started your career as an assistant accountant in 1973. You are only fifty-three years old and still have so much of your life in front of you. Or at the very least, a tempting retirement plan. But then you learn that you have inoperable brain cancer. It is the end of life as you planned it. *Chasing Daylight* speaks to us simply because we are human. Perhaps this book moved me because I am of the same generation as O'Kelly. Or perhaps it is because I had lost a good friend, a mentor, the year before to lung cancer, and was still shaken by the loss. But for anyone reading *Chasing Daylight*, it is a singular insight into the mind of a man who knows he is going to die—simply a part of the human condition met early and thus, greatly feared.

"I was blessed. I was told I had three months to live."

I was concerned that the author would tell a story of spiritual enlightenment, or, as with many end-of-life memoirs, spend the book listing his regrets—maudlin passages about his young daughter and loving family. Not that there isn't room for some of that, but those are songs we've heard sung. And that wasn't in O'Kelly's nature. When he discovers the seriousness of his disease, he does what he was trained to do as an accountant—he makes lists: "1. leave my job, and 2. choose a medical protocol that allowed me to . . . 3. make the time remaining the best of my life, and as good as it could possibly be for those most affected by my situation." Next, he creates a to-do list for his final days: "*Get legal and financial affairs in order, *'Unwind' relationships, *Simplify, *Live in the moment, *Create (but also be open to) great moments, 'perfect moments,' *Begin transition to next state, *Plan funeral." A bean counter to the end.

The title of the book comes from O'Kelly's routine of playing golf with his wife after getting home from work—playing golf throughout that summer, chasing daylight. His love of his family is deep, and the end of the book is truly staggering. His wife writes the last chapter, telling the story of how he died. She also corrects his reporting of his final days since his brain cancer was spreading and *his* reality was not reality.

Chasing Daylight is an eloquent confirmation that our lives and the people in them are temporary joys, but the time we spend enjoying them is never lost. And if we conquer our fears—even the fear of facing the end of our lives and leaving those we love—we can conquer anything. This was my favorite book of 2006 and will remain one of my favorites for all time. I urge you to read *Chasing Daylight*: this book will change your life. **JC**

Chasing Daylight: How My Forthcoming Death Transformed My Life, McGraw-Hill, Paperback 2008, ISBN 9780071499934

WHERE TO NEXT? » Put this book down and spend some time with the people you care about. | EVEN MORE: *Not Fade Away* by Laurence Shames and Peter Barton; *The Year of Magical Thinking* by Joan Didion; *The Last Lecture* by Randy Pausch and Jeffrey Zaslow

LEADERSHIP is this seemingly unidentifiable quality we all wish for in politicians, chief executive officers, and—whether we admit it or not—parents. This section proves there is nothing elusive about what it takes to lead people. All of these authors take different routes to the same destination: everyone wants a leader to define what the future will be and take them there.

On Becoming a Leader

WARREN BENNIS

Reviewed by Todd

Warren Bennis postulates that leadership cannot be taught: "[M]ore leaders have been made by accident, circumstance, sheer grit, or will than have been made by all the leadership courses put together. Leadership courses can only teach skills. . . . Developing character and vision is the way leaders invent themselves." Interviews with almost thirty leaders from all walks of life, and Bennis's own experience as leader, academic, and consultant (advising even U.S. presidents), give *On Becoming a Leader* incredible depth. The evergreen interest in this title reflects its unique prescriptions for leadership. The book also addresses beautifully the timeless search for meaning in one's own life and how that can affect your success as a leader.

Successful leaders are those who can access and then express their true selves, Bennis says—a nod to his belief in humanistic psychology. Developed by Abraham Maslow, this branch of psychology concerns specifically what it means to be human; its main goal for the individual is self-actualization. What might sound like some mystical Eastern path to enlightenment is instead a philosophy central to Maslow's hierarchy of needs. You may have come across this philosophy more recently in Gallup's strengths-based tools. Let me put it another way: to be successful you must figure out what you are good at and do it.

"No leader sets out to be a leader," Bennis says. "People set out to live their lives, expressing themselves fully. When that expression is of value, they become leaders." Bennis asks us to consider, then, our lives and how family, friends, and school have shaped our beliefs, stressing that those relationships and experiences don't define us but rather provide the material to discover or reflect upon a true and unique self. Though the logical left brain often competes with the emotional right, instinct serves a leader well only if he or she can listen to a balanced inner voice. To do so, we must examine our motives and strive for healthy expressions of value while abandoning selfish pursuits.

There is no direct path to personal enlightenment, and the structure of *On Becoming a Leader* seems to mimic the anfractuous course we must all take. The chapters, with provocative titles such as "Knowing Yourself" and "Operating on Instinct," provide a loose framework. Bennis then draws from a wide range of sources and interviews that lend the book a conversational tone. On page after page, wisdom from multiple sources challenges readers to consider leadership from diverse perspectives. For example, the late film director Sydney Pollack observes that "Driving a car, flying an airplane—you can reduce those things to a series of maneuvers that are always executed in the same way. But with something like leadership, just as with art, you reinvent the wheel every single time you apply the principle." This extra content provides another point of contrast with the more commonplace and neatly packaged how-to type of leadership guides.

"[M]ore leaders have been made by accident, circumstance, sheer grit, or will than have been made by all the leadership courses put together."

In *On Becoming a Leader*, Bennis treats leadership with a certain gravitas that is perspective changing. He references a scientist from the University of Michigan who asserts that after nuclear war and worldwide epidemic, the greatest risk to society is the quality of leadership in our institutions. Then Bennis follows with a challenge to his readers: "Our quality of life depends on the quality of our leaders. And since no one else seems to be volunteering, it's up to you. If you've ever had dreams of leadership, now is the time, this is the place, and you're it. We need you." TS

On Becoming a Leader: The Leadership Classic, Basic Books, Paperback updated and expanded 2003, ISBN 9780738208176

WHERE TO NEXT? » Page 306 on **how to lead during uncertain times** » Page 54 for **another leadership book with the same vibe** « Page 29 for **help figuring out what you should do** | EVEN MORE: *Judgment* by Noel M. Tichy and Warren Bennis; *Organizing Genius* by Warren Bennis and Patricia Ward Biederman; *The Maslow Business Reader* by Abraham H. Maslow and Deborah C. Stephens

Up the Organization

ROBERT TOWNSEND

Reviewed by Jack

The late sixties was one of the more intense periods of societal change in our country. Huge public demonstrations for equal rights and against the Vietnam War commingled dynamically with some of the most exciting creations in the arts. But the world of business was still stuck in the "gray flannel suit" era of the fifties. On the horizon, however, were some glimmers of change. Robert Townsend wrote this revolutionary book, *Up the Organization*, in 1970, which, along with *The Peter Principle* in 1972, showed people that business books didn't have to be academic to teach and motivate. Instead, even serious business books could be short, irreverent, and fun to read.

Robert Townsend took a small car rental company and created Avis Rent A Car, famous for its slogan, "We try harder." Townsend's approach to his own business was to concentrate on innovation, abolish hierarchy, and encourage decision making from all employees up and down the line. *Up the Organization* came ten years before *In Search of Excellence*, which is often regarded as the first book to break through a more regimented approach to management, but this book shows that Townsend had already put humanistic management to work.

A relatively young executive at fifty when he wrote this book, Townsend's youthful energy is evident in every word. Some chapters are as short as one paragraph, and all are in alphabetical order with simple chapter headings like: Budgets, Decisions, and No-No's. These titles may appear pedestrian, but the effectiveness of the book is a direct result of this straightforward, commonsense handling of critical business advice. Consider *Up the Organization* an alphabetical primer summarizing the basics of running a business.

These selections from the short chapters show a precision of thought and strategy that cannot be disregarded despite their simplicity:

Reorganizing: Should be undergone about as often as major surgery. And should be as well planned and as swiftly executed.

Thanks: A really neglected form of compensation.

Titles Are Handy Tools: There is a trade-off here. In one way, titles are a form of psychic compensation, and if too many titles are distributed, the currency is depreciated. But a title is also a tool. If our salesman is a vice president and yours is a sales rep, and both are in a waiting room, guess who gets in first and gets the most attention.

There are many editions of *Up the Organization*, but in 2007 the book was reissued as part of the Warren Bennis series by Jossey-Bass. I chose to review that edition because there are numerous add-ins that make it even more satisfying than the original, including essays by Townsend's original editor from Alfred A. Knopf, Robert Gottlieb, and other leadership heavyweights, a transcript from a Townsend speech, and a story from Warren Bennis about meeting Townsend. The publisher also omitted Townsend's "Guerrilla Guide for Working Women," from the 1971 edition. There are still outmoded references to the girls in the steno pool and a chapter on mistresses that is certainly antiquated, but the value to be found in Townsend's book is still high, and I hope that new readers don't throw the baby out with the obviously unenlightened bathwater.

When we go back to the masters, we have the opportunity to see where contemporary thought originates. Without *Up the Organization*, books like *Swim with the Sharks* would be different, less relatable, and, I am sure, much less fun to read. JC

Up the Organization: How to Stop the Corporation from Stifling People and Strangling Profits, Commemorative Edition, Hardcover 2007, ISBN 9780787987756

WHERE TO NEXT? « Page 24 for **surviving and thriving in the corporate world**
» Page 204 for **the inner workings of a large organization** | EVEN MORE: *The Peter Principle* by Dr. Lawrence J. Peter and Raymond Hull; *The No Asshole Rule* by Robert I. Sutton, Ph.D.; *The Daily Drucker* by Peter F. Drucker

The Leadership Moment

MICHAEL USEEM

Reviewed by Jack

On August 5, 1949, Wagner Dodge and his team of fifteen firefighters were called to parachute into Montana's Mann Gulch to fight a grass and forest fire. In the language of "smoke jumpers," it was a ten o'clock fire, one that they would fight through the night and have under control by the next morning. As they fought the flames, the wind unexpectedly spread the fire, and their escape to the river at the base of the gulch was blocked. Dodge and his team abandoned their attempts to fight the fire and simply tried to escape, but found themselves cornered by the advancing blaze. In the chaos, Dodge stopped, lit a match, and threw it into the prairie grass. With this counterintuitive move, he hoped to create a fire within the fire to protect him and his men. But by this point, he had lost the confidence of his crew. They ignored his emphatic motioning for them to join him, and instead sought their own route to safety. For thirteen of Dodge's men, this proved to be a fatal choice. In his book, *The Leadership Moment*, Wharton School professor Michael Useem uses this story, along with a series of others, to illustrate the singular moments that leaders face.

Useem uses masterful storytelling, focusing on real people who experienced a leadership moment to teach nine leadership principles. He defines this moment as a time when our credibility and reputation is on the line, when the fate or fortune of others depends on what we do. Leadership at such moments is best when "the vision is strategic, the voice persuasive, the results tangible." Useem draws from a wide range of occupations and incidents, showing what real leaders do, or don't do, when the chips are down. This sweeping perspective results in an inspiring work that broadens the definition of what it means to be a leader.

Useem starts each chapter with captivating episodes, but then dissects the actions taken and, in some cases, the mistakes made in order to emphasize the underlying lesson. During the Mann Gulch fire, Dodge's first mistake came earlier that day when he instructed his crew to advance without him toward the fire while he returned to get supplies from the drop site. Upon his return, the fire was much further developed and their only option was to flee. At that time, Dodge commits another error, telling his crew to drop all their tools. Useem says the use of this command was the equivilent of Dodge "ordering his soldiers to shed their uniforms." Both decisions were the right reactions to the set of circumstances Dodge faced, but Useem believes there is an additional, less apparent, reason his crew lost faith in him. Dodge's style of communication was quiet and instructive, and over time he had not established a rapport with the men. When he presented an uncommon solution in an unexpected environment, his crew had no reference point from which to trust him.

"Leadership is at its best when the vision is strategic, the voice persuasive, the results tangible."

Other leadership moments happen when a decision is made to serve a greater good. Useem tells the hopeful story of Roy Vagelos, Merck & Co., and his mission to combat a pervasive disease called river blindness. In 1988, over 20 million people worldwide, most of them poor, had the disease; one-third went blind. The disease is caused by a waterborne parasitic worm. Merck chemists had discovered that a drug for heartworm in animals could also kill the parasite. As the head of research, Vagelos was presented with these findings and left in a quandary: a new product with no profit potential, since the recipients had no money to pay for the treatment. Also, the transfer of drugs from animal use to human use frequently failed, and given the nature of the disease, those inflicted would need annual doses for up to fourteen years to completely eradicate the parasite. Despite those significant drawbacks, Vagelos green-lighted the project and the trials showed immediate success. When the time came to make the decision to commercialize the product, Vagelos, by then CEO of Merck, decided again to support the project, but this time he was supporting a project that flew in the face of his fiscal responsibility to shareholders. Vagelos took the heat and supported the initiative despite the outcries, showing that doing the right thing is leadership at its best.

Although much of the material included in *The Leadership Moment* relates incidents from outside traditional business, Useem's wealth of knowledge from his position at Wharton allows him to draw parallels to the challenges contemporary business leaders face throughout their careers. The story format provides the reader vivid access to the high level of intensity withstood by leaders in all situations, and inspiration for how to make the most out of every leadership moment. **JC**

The Leadership Moment: Nine True Stories of Triumph and Disaster and Their Lessons for Us All, Three Rivers Press, Paperback 1998, ISBN 9780812932300

WHERE TO NEXT? » Page 70 for **another leader in history** » Page 89 for **a great leadership moment** » Page 264 for **a poor leadership moment** | EVEN MORE: *The Killer Angels* by Michael Shaara; *Leading at the Edge* by Dennis N.T. Perkins; *It's Your Ship* by Michael Abrashoff

Leadership

in Movies

A movie can be pure entertainment, or it can influence what you do in your everyday life. While few of us will ever need to learn how to defuse a booby trap while leading shipwrecked survivors on a quest for lost treasure, many of us face challenges of leadership at the office. For inspiration and even some ideas about leadership, here is a guide to films that depict leadership at its finest.

12 Angry Men [1957]

Starring Jack Klugman, Jack Warden, Henry Fonda, and Ed Begley. Directed by Sidney Lumet. Nominated for three Oscars and four Golden Globes. | On almost every critic's "must see" list, *12 Angry Men* exemplifies the leadership, drive, and negotiation skills needed by many managers and CEOs. It revolves around a court case and the twelve-man jury that debates the fate of an accused man. All but one of the jurors believes the accused is guilty, and what follows is a tense and dramatic debate that reveals in depth the character of each of the twelve men. Within the story, important tools of persuasion and dealing with confrontation are available for the attentive viewer.

Apollo 13 [1995]

Starring Tom Hanks, Bill Paxton, Kevin Bacon, and Gary Sinise. Directed by Ron Howard. Nominated for nine Oscars (won two) and nominated for four Golden Globes. | In 1970, three astronauts set out to put a man on the moon. Though not one of them stepped on the moon, the mission was deemed a "successful failure." An explosion during liftoff left them with a deteriorating spacecraft and the astronauts' survival in jeopardy. On Earth, Flight Director Eugene Kranz pushed the NASA crew beyond its creative limits to find a solution that would bring the astronauts home alive. In space, Commander James Lovell kept his team focused on the task, working together, and, given the circumstances, optimistic. The extraordinary leadership displayed by these two men is, like the mission, legendary.

A Midwinter's Tale [1995]

Starring Michael Maloney, Joan Collins, Jennifer Saunders, and Julia Sawalha. Directed by Kenneth Branagh. Winner of the Golden Osella and nominated for the Golden Lion. | *A Midwinter's Tale* is the old "Hey, let's put on a show!" motif that appears often in literature. Here, it is a community group that aims to put on a production of Hamlet in order to save a church. Whether a stage show or a new idea in the boardroom, one person always owns it, directs the plan of action, and works hard to implement it. Certainly not all of these shows run smoothly. But in real life, the skills needed to get everyone pulling on the same oar are critical for success. Some conflict inevitably arises, and employees (in this case, the actors in the play) aren't motivated or don't grasp the bigger picture. It takes a great leader to clarify the main objective, keep each member motivated and on task, and maintain a level of intensity that will ultimately culminate in something quite meaningful.

Additional Leadership Movies:

Aliens [1986]

Dead Poet's Society [1989]

Elizabeth [1998]

The Leadership Challenge

JAMES M. KOUZES AND BARRY Z. POSNER

Reviewed by Todd

To begin their research for *The Leadership Challenge*, Jim Kouzes and Barry Posner asked people of all backgrounds this open-ended question: "'What values, personality traits, or characteristics do you look for and admire in a leader?'" Twenty characteristics captured the wide range of responses, and four of them came up consistently: *honest, forward-looking, inspiring,* and *competent*. The findings correspond to what communication experts call "source credibility." Successful newscasters, salespeople, and politicians all exhibit these qualities, but it is particularly the ability to be forward-looking that lifts someone from being credible to being a leader.

The authors continued their research, studying individual leaders to determine how they work when they are performing at their best. After gathering several hundred case studies (now several thousand) on personal-best leadership moments and searching for common themes in those experiences, Kouzes and Posner developed five governing practices: Model the Way, Inspire a Shared Vision, Challenge the Process, Enable Others to Act, and Encourage the Heart. When they found parallels between their initial research into what followers valued in a leader and the common themes underlying leadership's best, the authors knew they were on to something. They further tested the validity of their research by correlating those leadership behaviors with external measurements such as increased financial performance and team satisfaction.

To see how Kouzes and Posner's copious research was then applied, consider the leadership characteristic *forward-looking* aligned with the authors' second leadership principle, "Inspire a Shared Vision." Leaders imagine what is possible; as one interviewee said, "'I'm my organization's futures department.'" Yet senior managers say they spend only 3 percent of their time looking forward. Those who operate on the front lines, the authors claim, should be spending five times that, and even more time with each step they take closer to the executive suite. The authors suggest reading publications to spur inspiration; *The Futurist* and *Popular Science* come to mind.

Another trick the authors recommend, labeled the "Janus Effect," is to widen your time horizon. Start with the past, thinking about where you and your company have been . . . and then think about the future. Professor Omar El Sawy is referenced here, having found that starting with history allows prognosticators to see twice as far into the future. Then, to truly bring vision to life, the vision must be "shared," enlisting others in the process.

Due in part to the appeal of the authors' extensive research and to their practical approach, *The Leadership Challenge* has sold over 1.5 million copies since 1987 and was recently published in its fourth edition. But the book is not the end of the road for readers interested in applying the authors' lessons. A unique variety of supplements gives *The Leadership Challenge* added depth. For example, three million people have taken the thirty-question Leadership Practices Inventory and helped evaluate the hundreds of thousands of leaders they work with. The Leadership Challenge Workshop provides a kit which gives corporate trainers and independent facilitators the tools to share the principles with groups of all sizes. Workbooks, videos, and worldwide seminars further emphasize that leadership is a skill set that anyone can learn.

"Leadership is not a gene and it's not an inheritance. Leadership is an identifiable set of skills and abilities that are available to all of us."

The book and its additional resources provide a framework for seeing how leadership fits together with all aspects of business. Jim Kouzes refers to *The Leadership Challenge* as a Christmas tree: businesspeople have all sorts of thoughts and ideas about how they and their companies should operate, much like shiny ornaments and strings of bright lights just waiting for a tree on which to be hung. **TS**

The Leadership Challenge, Jossey-Bass, Hardcover fourth edition 2007, ISBN 9780787984915

WHERE TO NEXT? « Page 9 for **a strategy on getting organized** » Page 326 for **a strategy on making ideas "sticky"** » Page 78 for **a strategy on strategy** | EVEN MORE: *The Offsite* by Robert H. Thompson; *The Leadership Challenge Workbook* by James M. Kouzes and Barry Z. Posner; *Christian Reflection on* The Leadership Challenge by John C. Maxwell, James M. Kouzes, and Barry Z. Posner

Leadership Is an Art

MAX DE PREE
Reviewed by Jack

Art has always been an integral part of the success of Herman Miller, Inc. From the beginning, the Michigan-based manufacturer of modern furniture collaborated with some of the century's greatest designers, such as George Nelson and Charles and Ray Eames, to create icons of industrial design. These collaborations deeply influenced the values of the company. Today, Herman Miller continues to align its goals of innovative design with innovative leadership practices. In *Leadership Is an Art*, Max De Pree, former CEO of Herman Miller, describes this art of leadership as "liberating people to do what is required of them, in the most effective and humane way possible." De Pree conveys this message through stories and ideas rather than practices and rules.

In the early days, Herman Miller's factory used a central driveshaft to run the machines. The millwright supervised this system and was a key person within the factory. One day the millwright died. De Pree's father, founder of the company, visited the widow to give his condolences. While he was there she read him some poetry. The elder De Pree asked who wrote the poems and she told him that her husband, the millwright, had. Now, sixty years after that revelation, Max De Pree wonders: "Was he a poet who did millwright's work, or was he a millwright who wrote poetry?"

The younger De Pree seems saddened by the lost opportunity. The secret poet could have been the public copywriter. "When we think about leaders and the variety of gifts people bring to corporations and institutions, we see that the art of leadership lies in polishing and liberating and enabling those gifts." Doing this eliminates the separation between the life we lead at home and that which we lead at the office.

Even with such a people-first perspective, a leader must be able to put theory into practice. One practice De Pree advocates is "roving leadership." He writes that in many organizations there are two kinds of leaders—the traditionally hierarchical and the roving. The rovers are the people who step up and take charge or ownership of a situation, regardless of their position or assignment. He tells the moving story of a person who passes out at church and is helped when the roving leaders swiftly take charge of the crisis. I spent some time reflecting on my own and my employees' ability to be roving leaders, and it was refreshing to see that I had created a corporate culture that attracted and retained just such people. Particularly in a small company like mine, where employees' duties tend to ebb and flow depending on what is essential to the company at any given time, roving leaders are crucial to making every project a success.

"Understanding and accepting diversity enables us to see that each of us is needed."

De Pree fills his book with compelling and heartfelt passages about what it truly means to guide a company and its employees: "The first responsibility of a leader is to define reality. The last is to say thank you. In between the two, the leader must become a servant and a debtor. That sums up the progress of an artful leader." It is never too late to pick up *Leadership Is an Art* and find yourself, or the leader you wish to become, within its pages. **JC**

Leadership Is an Art, Currency/Doubleday, Paperback 2004, ISBN 9780385512466

WHERE TO NEXT? » Page 179 for **proof that listening helps** » Page 240 for **business by trial and error** » Page 92 for **the other companies with soul** | EVEN MORE: *Servant Leadership* by Robert K. Greenleaf; *Synchronicity* by Joseph Jaworski; *Stewardship* by Peter Block

The Radical Leap

STEVE FARBER
Reviewed by Jack

Fables and parables take complicated ideas and, as part of well-written stories, deliver easily comprehendible lessons. The use of storytelling enables the reader to internalize the message the author is communicating. And when the right combination of characters, plot, message, and conclusion collide, magic can happen. Steve Farber has accomplished this synergistic coming-together marvelously with his enjoyable 160-page parable, *The Radical Leap*.

The Radical Leap offers more than a few plot twists. In a story that takes place during a single week, Steve Farber plays himself, and, as with most business parables, he is searching for an answer. A management consultant, Steve is called by a friend who is in an untenable situation at a company she really loves. Janice is the SVP of marketing who has become the de facto second in command when the charismatic president suddenly disappears and is replaced by a real bean counter, Bob Jeffers. This new guy has no people skills. Janice is so upset about the change in her company that she is thinking of quitting and turns to Steve for help with that decision. She also asks Steve to try and find the president who had left. She was very close to him and wants his counsel.

Luckily for Steve, earlier that week he had gone out for a cup of coffee and found himself in a conversation with a person who looked like a beach bum. Edg, one of the most colorful characters in business fiction, becomes Steve's guide. Edg explains to Steve that leadership is "'always substantive and rarely fashionable. It is intensely personal and intrinsically scary, and it requires us to live the ideas we espouse—in irrefutable ways—every day of our lives, up to and beyond the point of fear.'" To deal with this fear, Edg advocates "extreme leadership." Edg's advice helps Steve determine how to help Janice.

Extreme leadership is living in pursuit of the OS!M, a catchy acronym for an "Oh Sh*t! Moment." Edg defines OS!M as the "'natural, built-in human indicator that you are doing—or about to do—something truly significant, and you are—rightfully so—scared out of your gourd.' " Edg also teaches Steve about LEAP, which stands for: cultivate Love, generate Energy, inspire Audacity, and provide Proof.

For many business practitioners, the individual aspects of LEAP can be a bit hard to swallow on first read. Love and energy are not considered "real" business practices by most businesspeople and may seem a little touchy-feely. But when you think about work that you were really passionate about and how you just loved getting up and doing that job . . . this is the love and energy Edg talks to Steve about. It is an intense passion that can actually end up "changing the world." Big-picture thoughts can and will inspire audacity, and, in the end, you will end up providing the proof, or results.

" 'Do what you love in the service of people who love what you do.' "

I am not going to give away how this story ends. But trust me, this is a special book. It shows that extreme leadership is the best and most successful way of leading. *The Radical Leap* is also special because it stands on its own as a work of fiction. The characters are fun, easy to get to know, and the plot has many twists and turns. As a result, you will be invested in the characters' attempts to solve problems, and, in turn, be inspired to take a LEAP and radicalize your own leadership. **JC**

The Radical Leap: A Personal Lesson in Extreme Leadership, Dearborn (Kaplan), Hardcover 2004, ISBN 9780793185689

WHERE TO NEXT? « Page 51 to **meet Farber's friends** » Page 173 to **read a great novel on management** | EVEN MORE: *The Radical Edge* by Steve Farber; *Leadership and Self-Deception* by the Arbinger Institute; *The Fred Factor* by Mark Sanborn

Control Your Destiny or Someone Else Will

NOEL M. TICHY AND STRATFORD SHERMAN
Reviewed by Todd

In 1994, I accepted a position with General Electric in their Manufacturing Management Program, one of several training programs used to groom college graduates. It was sometime in that first year that I received my first copy of *Control Your Destiny or Someone Else Will*. The book had been published the year prior and was being warmly received within the company. Noel Tichy was instrumental in redeveloping the leadership training programs at GE, and the book, written with Strat Sherman, opened the doors to show the evolution of the conglomerate under CEO Jack Welch.

Control Your Destiny came out before the accolades, before Jack Welch was named "Manager of the Century" by *Fortune* magazine, before the company's market capitalization reached $450 billion. Professors and pundits now can easily look back and call Welch's twenty-year turnaround remarkable, but Tichy and Sherman were the first to recognize and write about it. Though GE fell short of the financial metrics needed for recognition in Jim Collins's seminal work *Good to Great*, read *Control Your Destiny or Someone Else Will* to see how Jack Welch took an organization from good to great.

The situation Jack Welch inherited when he became CEO in 1981 was one of the toughest for any leader: life at GE was good, but he believed it could be better. Not exactly a situation that encourages a change-oriented agenda, and the new leader had 420,000 employees to convince that a new course was needed. To spur change, in 1982 Welch made his now-famous declaration that every GE business would be number one or number two in their markets and vowed to "'fix, close, or sell'" any business that did not meet those standards." The incumbent managerial class yawned; "same story, different leader" was their reaction.

Over the next ten years, Welch made good on his declaration. He sold 125 businesses in the first four years alone, including many consumer-based brands central to the company's long-standing identity. In that first decade, 300,000 people left GE through the sale of laggard divisions or company-encouraged means. "I think one of the jobs of a businessperson is to get away from the slugfests and into niches where you can prevail," Welch said, and by 1993, every part of GE held one of the top two rungs in each of their markets. Welch referred to this time as "getting the hardware right," building the business engine that has allowed GE to succeed as a conglomerate.

Welch knew there was a limit to gaining through reduction, and in the second half of his tenure, the focus shifted to "the software." Welch pumped money into the revitalization of Crotonville, the company's New York–based facility that would train 10,000 employees yearly and "indoctrinate managers in the new principles." He quickly realized those direct efforts would only reach a fraction of the workforce and that something more than the typical videotaped messages and company newsletters were needed. The new values needed to be experienced at GE's manufacturing plants and office buildings around the world.

"Peter Drucker . . . greatly influenced [Jack] Welch by writing, 'If you weren't already in the business, would you enter it today?' "

This insight served as the seed for Work-Out, town hall–style meetings where thirty to one hundred employees, over the course of a few days, would discuss "their common problems." Bosses were not allowed to attend until the final hours when they were forced to make on-the-spot, yes-or-no decisions on the groups' compiled action items. In a five-year period, more than 200,000 GE employees, or 85 percent of the company's workforce, experienced a Work-Out session. This cultural breakthrough empowered employees to take the steps required to eliminate unnecessary work, and built trust across pay grades and business functions, an effort Harvard Business School professor Len Schlesinger called "one of the biggest planned efforts to alter people's behavior since Mao's Cultural Revolution."

The current version of *Control Your Destiny* is quite daunting at 694 pages, but do not let the heft scare you away. The first half is a narrative about Welch and the company he started with, while the second half details the challenges and associated initiatives Welch took on, ranging

Questions from a Jack Welch Business Review:

- **What does your global competitive environment look like?**
- **In the last three years, what have your competitors done to you?**
- **In the same period, what have you done to them?**
- **How might they attack you in the future?**
- **What are your plans to leapfrog them?**

Source: "It's All in the Sauce," *Fortune*, April 4, 2005

from globalization to speed. In 2001, as Welch was leaving his post, a revised edition included over 160 new pages of his letters from twenty years of annual reports. A second revision was published in 2005 that again revised material and added a new opening note from Sherman and an afterword from Tichy. The last bit of heft comes in the form of a seventy-page "Handbook for Revolutionaries," written by Tichy, that delivers a challenge to leaders to assess their organizations against the radical change GE went through.

I count myself lucky to have been employed by GE, and I will personally vouch for the impact, the absolute culture change, engendered by Jack Welch's actions at General Electric. I never met Welch, but the knowledge and experience that I gained in my six years at the company will likely never be matched. While GE may build aircraft engines and issue credit cards, its true core product is creating world-class managers. All of GE's CEOs have come from within the organization, and Boeing, Chrysler, and Intuit are just a few of the companies now run by former GE executives. Tichy and Sherman's portrait of Jack Welch gives leaders everywhere a strong example of leadership at its best. TS

Control Your Destiny or Someone Else Will, Collins Business Essentials Edition, Paperback 2005, ISBN 9780060753832

WHERE TO NEXT? » Page 186 for **another take on changing knowing to doing** » Page 89 for **another great corporate turnaround** » Page 78 to **see which companies Jim Collins did recognize** | EVEN MORE: *The Cycle of Leadership* by Noel M. Tichy; *Winning* by Jack and Suzy Welch; *If Harry Potter Ran General Electric* by Tom Morris

Leading Change

JOHN P. KOTTER

Reviewed by Jack

After 9/11, our business hit a speed bump, as did many others. The shake-up altered the typically positive atmosphere of our book company; at the same time, there wasn't much we could do to fight the slowdown in the market. I brought in a consultant to introduce a change initiative that would get us all working together again. The change initiative failed to catch on, however, despite being embraced by the employees in its initial push. John Kotter's *Leading Change* reveals why. A change initiative is like redirecting a river. Build a wall of rocks on the riverbed and still the water will rush around and over—and eventually through—it, determined to continue on its natural path. Thus, to change the course of a river requires constant maintenance. The payoff from this book is that Kotter shows us how to change the course of a company permanently.

Kotter named the book *Leading Change* because he believes that for change initiatives to succeed, a company needs leaders, not managers. In fact, he asserts that successful change requires 70 to 90 percent leadership and 10 to 30 percent management. Many organizations don't have enough leadership bandwidth for this to work. Contemporary organizations have institutionalized management at the expense of leadership, which only adds to the change woes. Reflecting on my company's dilemma, I can now easily see that while I knew change was imperative—and indeed, I was the one who called for it—I regarded it as a managerial mandate and didn't realize that I needed to lead the change, to be the first to put change into action.

The book is built around "The Eight-Stage Change Process." The first process is "Establishing a Sense of Urgency." Sounds simple enough, but as Kotter states: "In an organization of 100 employees, at least two dozen must go far beyond the normal call of duty to produce significant change. In a firm of 100,000 employees, the same might be required of 15,000 or more." Because my company uses open-book management, I felt that showing our employees the numbers was enough to inspire such urgency, but the numbers, nebulous "factoids" for most employees, were not enough to jolt us out of our complacency.

Kotter's discourse on complacency reveals how the "but" in a conversation about change dooms any change initiative. His chart of ways to raise the urgency level is loaded with practical examples on how to motivate people. With suggestions that include setting targets so high that success can't be reached by conducting business as usual, and sending more data about customer satisfaction and financial performance to more employees—especially information that demonstrates weakness vis-à-vis the competition—Kotter shows how to help people understand the seriousness of the problem management faces. I am quite aware now that I missed an opportunity to make the company's challenges real for my employees.

"Enterprises everywhere will be presented with even more terrible hazards and wonderful opportunities, driven by the globalization of the economy along with related technology and social trends."

"Creating the Guiding Coalition" is another process Kotter advocates, asserting that the solo CEO is destined to fail in promoting change because the initiative needs a well-rounded team for success. Kotter suggests characteristics needed for the guiding coalition: position power, expertise, credibility, and leadership, with trust and sincerity as the glue to keep the team together. He emphasizes that "[y]ou need both management and leadership skills on the guiding coalition, and they must work in tandem, teamwork style. The former keeps the whole process under control, while the latter drives the change." In our case, I was struggling to maintain the change against the stronger current of complacency and had not created a solid team to continue the push toward making the change habitual.

As I have learned, change is easy to start, difficult to grow, and really hard to sustain over the long haul. Whether you are trying to energize a company, save a failed strategy, or reorganize teams, you'll find value in what Kotter has done in *Leading Change*, presenting ways to redirect the river by providing us with sandbags and step-by-step instructions on where to place them for maximum, lasting effect. **JC**

Leading Change, Harvard Business School Press, Hardcover 1996, ISBN 9780875847474

WHERE TO NEXT? » Page 98 for **how the future is all about change** » Page 86 for **a zealot's version of change** » Page 192 to **choose your approach to change** | EVEN MORE: *Our Iceberg Is Melting* by John P. Kotter; *Managing at the Speed of Change* by Daryl R. Conner; *Managing Transitions* by William Bridges

The Economist

The Only Magazine You Need to Read

There isn't always time to read a book, so if you can find time to read only one business publication a week, make it *The Economist.*

The Economist has been at the nexus of business, politics, and community since British hatmaker James Wilson founded it in 1843. The mission of the weekly paper was to promote free trade and oppose the protectionist trade policies of the British Parliament.

The now-worldwide publication continues to advocate for free trade. And because of the strong devotion to that mission, *The Economist* staff is not confined to reporting only on the business community, but covers all aspects of contemporary life—political movements and trends, government policy, international debates, science, and culture—that may affect that community. These aspects include how its members go to work, do business, and interact with others.

This approach serves the business community well, for business is intricately tied to these forces—the political and social landscapes surrounding it.

Whereas magazines like *Forbes* and *Fortune* focus more narrowly on following American politics and financial markets, and tend to be influenced by Wall Street, *The Economist* examines and reports on the larger context in which those markets exist. Staff members are anonymous when they write for *The Economist,* which lends the periodical an objective credibility and turns the spotlight on the issue at hand rather than on an individual writer's perspective.

Every issue of *The Economist* offers in-depth coverage of the week's events with sections devoted specifically to the United States, the Americas, Asia, the Middle East and Africa, Europe, and its native country, Great Britain. Its content includes analysis and insight on the overall business and political climate, sections devoted to books and the arts, and quarterly reports on science and technology.

Written by Todd Sattersten with Dylan Schleicher

Questions of Character

JOSEPH L. BADARACCO JR.

Reviewed by Todd

Stories play a central role in business books. Whether it is the tale of how Richard Branson created his Virgin companies or the investigation of Ken Lay and Jeff Skilling's shell games at Enron, stories convey powerful lessons. However, when the episodes of a business leader's career are recounted via a journalist's profile, a formal case study, or a reflective autobiography, we the readers often wonder if the events are "true" or distorted by time or even intentional misdirection. Former Hewlett-Packard CEO Carly Fiorina and board member Tom Perkins clearly have different perspectives on the events surrounding Ms. Fiorina's departure from the company, and such differing perspectives can lead to alternate but completely plausible conclusions, making the lessons to be learned unclear.

Instead of wrestling with the inevitable complexities of real-life business studies, professor of business ethics at Harvard Business School Joseph Badaracco felt fiction could be used as a learning tool. Fictional stories have the unique advantage of not being tied to reality. This provides, ironically, a more reliable view into the thoughts, motivations, and actions of the characters, either directly or via a narrator. Badaracco searched extensively for classic works of fiction that specifically address the challenges and nuances of leadership, and he developed a course at the Harvard Business School around this idea. *Questions of Character* is the hardcover version of that curriculum.

Each chapter addresses one of eight questions about leadership through a concise summary of a fictional work, followed by a careful reflection of the protagonist's struggles. The first four stories focus on situations one might face early in a career, while the final four illuminate the challenges a leader with growing responsibilities faces.

To consider the question "How Flexible Is My Moral Code?" Badaracco recounts the lessons learned in Chinua Achebe's *Things Fall Apart*. Okonkwo, the story's African tribal leader, works hard as a young man, eventually earning wealth (along with the associated respect) and becoming the tribe's leader. His village and its way of life are challenged physically and morally by the arrival of white colonists, but Okonkwo is unable to react to the siege, confined by his ritualistic, inflexible moral code. Badaracco contrasts this with a moral code that is like an "old, weathered tree"—one that has deep, value-based roots and tall branches that sway or even bend to the surrounding environment.

The stories that Badaracco uses effectively move us past the rote rules most business books offer and more realistically reflect life's variability. Willy Loman from Arthur Miller's *Death of a Salesman* embodies the very real consequences dreams can have on their holders in Badaracco's chapter: "Do You Have a Good Dream?" The captain in Joseph Conrad's *The Secret Sharer* shows how difficult it is to truly know the answer to the question "Am I Ready to *Take* Responsibility?"

"[S]erious fiction gives us a unique, inside view of leadership."

In each example, Badaracco challenges readers to slip into the shoes of the protagonist and ask him- or herself, "What would I do?" In this unique approach to the business book, Badaracco engages the reader's imagination and forces each of us to ask questions of our own character. **TS**

Questions of Character: Illuminating the Heart of Leadership Through Literature, Harvard Business School Press, Hardcover 2006, ISBN 9781591399681

WHERE TO NEXT? » Page 67 for **how to use stories as a leader** » Page 264 for **serious questions of character** » Page 268 for **more subtle questions of character** | EVEN MORE: *Things Fall Apart* by Chinua Achebe; *The Love of the Last Tycoon* by F. Scott Fitzgerald; *I Come as a Thief* by Louis Auchincloss; *A Man for All Seasons* by Robert Bolt; *Antigone* by Sophocles

The Story Factor

ANNETTE SIMMONS

Reviewed by Jack

Storytelling has long been a valued method of communication for many people and in many cultures. The effectiveness of this art is difficult to quantify and even more difficult to apply to business. And yet, Annette Simmons, president of Group Process Consulting, contends that storytelling is the best way for leaders to persuade and motivate their people. But for many leaders, storytelling does not come naturally and is hard to learn because of its amorphous nature. Simmons explains: "Breaking storytelling down into pieces, parts, and priorities destroys it. There are some truths that we just know, we can't prove it but we know them to be true. Storytelling moves us into the place where we trust what we know, even if it can't be measured, packaged, or validated empirically."

Most businesspeople, Simmons contends, have had their ability to storytell trained out of them; facts, research, and PowerPoint skills are favored over the art of storytelling. Yet Simmons warns that because people have easy access to too much information, they don't want or need—and perhaps may distrust—facts. Facts can be manipulative and limiting. People want to believe in what a leader has to say, to have faith. "It is faith that moves mountains, not facts," she says. And only stories, Simmons believes, can tap into this desire. In *The Story Factor*, Simmons presents a convincing argument for the unique power of the story to inspire and influence, and offers advice on improving your storytelling skills to garner the best response from your audience.

To help us rediscover our innate talent for storytelling, Simmons presents six different types of stories that have the power to influence others: Who I Am; Why I Am Here; the Vision; Teaching; Values-in-Action; and I Know What You Are Thinking. She gives examples of each type along with instructions on how to create your own story. For example, in the beginning of any story, you must tell people who you are and why you are speaking to them. Personal stories work best to explain your motivation and allow you to explain your position before your audience can draw assumptions.

When you have a significant point to make to an audience—whether you are a new leader coming onboard an organization or an activist detailing the effects of poverty—"you need to see it, feel it, smell it, hear it . . . to 'go there' in your mind. The difference in your delivery will be dramatic. Most people hold back. They hang on so tightly to 'here' they don't go 'there' where their story is." But Simmons believes that most leaders are afraid to open themselves up to such an approach for two main reasons: "The first reason is that they are afraid they will look stupid, corny, manipulative, or 'unprofessional.'" Our image of the professional is of someone who is straightforward, gets to the facts, and refrains from being too emotional. But, Simmons warns, when that happens our delivery becomes cold and ultimately fails to influence listeners.

"Values are meaningless without stories to bring them to life and engage us on a personal level."

The second reason people hold back is that "we are a bunch of control freaks. Losing yourself in the telling of your story means you are not as 'in control' as when you are reading bullet points off slides or reading from notes." Take Tom Peters, for example, who's often lauded as a brilliant presenter and storyteller. Anybody who has seen a great presenter like Peters knows that staying to the facts and refraining from using emotion aren't Tom's traits. When he is done with an all-day seminar, he has given us everything he has to give, and he has really "gone there" with the attendees.

It is one thing to be like Peters and present your stories to an audience that is paying for the opportunity to listen, but trying to influence the unwilling takes some special handling, and Simmons offers a chapter on that subject. She suggests that storytelling offers a real advantage in high-risk circumstances. In this case, you can't lose. You may not win, but you can't lose. When you are in the middle of serious negotiations and dealing only with facts or rational thinking, you are actually drawing a line in the sand. This gives your opponent the opportunity to say no, to disagree, to prove you wrong. When you use stories, you can sometimes move around that obstacle, and even if you can't move around it, you can revisit the subject because there is no clear "no."

In delving into the do's and don'ts of storytelling, Simmons emphasizes that we need to use this influential tool for good. An accomplished storyteller herself, Simmons explains:

> Storytelling is like any other art. It can be done well. It can be done badly. And sometimes the ones who do it really well get the big head and fly too close to the sun. Power is power. When you tell a powerful story of influence you will feel this rush of power. You will look out at a sea of faces or even into the eyes of one enraptured face and know that you are *inside* the head of the person listening to you. You have gained access to a secret place where their imagination paints new realities and draws new conclusions based on the stories played there. Although you might not control the whole show, you are one of the stars.

This passage speaks to how intimate a relationship between storyteller and audience member can become, how there must be trust in that intimacy. A storyteller should never betray that trust.

Simmons uses various stories and parables as examples throughout the book, along with practical advice on becoming a better communicator. As a leader, knowing how to influence a situation or group of people is a valuable—no, essential—asset, and *The Story Factor* is the book to help you hone your skills. **JC**

The Story Factor: Inspiration, Influence, and Persuasion Through the Art of Storytelling, Basic Books, Paperback 2006, ISBN 9780465078073

WHERE TO NEXT? » Page 189 for **a story about teams** « Page 56 for **a story about leadership** » Page 173 for **a story about constraints** | EVEN MORE: *The Hero with a Thousand Faces* by Joseph Campbell; *The Leader's Guide to Storytelling* by Stephen Denning; *What's Your Story?* by Craig Wortmann

Never Give In!

SPEECHES BY WINSTON CHURCHILL,
SELECTED BY HIS GRANDSON, WINSTON S. CHURCHILL

Reviewed by Jack

Here's the scene: Your organization is being attacked by the same competition that has beaten you badly in the past. Your organization is on its own, much like an island, without many options for escape or for immediate help. The board has tried to negotiate with this competitor and reached an agreement that was quickly broken. The board decides to dump the CEO and bring back an old guy out of retirement to try and rally the people. This guy is known for unconventional management methods, but is a great communicator; in fact, he is arguably the greatest communicator of the twentieth century.

If you haven't guessed by now, this hypothetical organization is actually the United Kingdom in 1940 and the reinstated CEO is Winston Churchill.

Churchill was presented the ultimate turnaround situation . . . only his company happened to be the United Kingdom, not the United Motors Company. Consider June 1940: The Germans kicked the British army off the European continent. It was one of the worst defeats in modern warfare and ended just off the coast of England at Dunkirk. The United States was not prepared to help Britain defend herself, so she was on her own. Enter a sixty-six-year-old man who proved to be history's greatest turnaround artist.

The similarities between Churchill's position and that of a modern-day CEO are compelling. Communication and motivation are crucial to any change, the hallmarks of good leadership. To turn around the country, Winston Churchill called upon his innate talents as one of the great orators of modern times. *Never Give In!* is a collection of Churchill's speeches selected by his grandson. The speeches in this volume range in time from his first speech, delivered in 1897 at the age of twenty-two to the Primrose League, called "The Dried-Up Drainpipe of Radicalism," to a 1963 address at the age of eighty-eight at the White House after receiving his honorary United States citizenship. These selections are only representative of his work, as a complete collection of his speeches would run eight volumes.

Each selection begins with a short preface to put the featured speech into historical context. For example, the preface to Churchill's speech after the evacuation of Dunkirk explains: "National rejoicing verged on euphoria, which Churchill was anxious to dampen down." This setting of the scene prepares the reader for what follows in the speech. In this case, Churchill, after many minutes of desperately needed upbeat and positive statements about the evacuation, added, "We must be very careful not to assign to this deliverance the attributes of a victory. *Wars are not won by evacuations.* But there was a victory inside this deliverance, which should be noted. It was gained by the Air Force" (emphasis added). Churchill was careful not to depress his audience, and yet he remained committed to portraying a realistic picture. Many times a leader's first reaction is to counter the opinion of the masses with a large dose of reality, but, in truth, the ability to choose a milder tone or first acknowledge the emotions of the majority can help spread the message more convincingly than a heavy hand.

"I would say to the House, as I said to those who have joined this Government: 'I have nothing to offer but blood, toil, tears and sweat.' "

In his final speech to the House of Commons in 1955, Churchill advised the English people, "The day may dawn when fair play, love of one's fellow-men, respect for justice and freedom, will enable tormented generations to march forth serene and triumphant from the hideous epoch in which we have to dwell. Meanwhile, never flinch, never weary, never despair." Clearly, Churchill's oratory and writing talents were manna considering the historic circumstances in which he found himself. And while few if any of us may be brought out of retirement to save a country at war, each day we have the opportunity to lead.

Never Give In! is a book that should be on your bookshelf, ready to serve as a motivator the next time you must present your best self. **JC**

Never Give In! The Best of Winston Churchill's Speeches, Hyperion, Paperback 2003, ISBN 9780786888702

WHERE TO NEXT? » Page 114 for **more on selling the invisible** » Page 105 for **the psychology of persuasion** » Page 326 for **why we still read Churchill today** |
EVEN MORE: *The Second World War* by Winston S. Churchill; *The Lost Art of the Great Speech* by Richard Dowis; *Churchill on Leadership* by Steven F. Hayward; *The Wit and Wisdom of Winston Churchill* by James C. Humes

STRATEGY is the sum of all a company does to compete in the marketplace. Decisions range from whether or not to offer free shipping to determining if Omaha is the best place for the new plant. Are you going to thrust or feint? There are an infinite number of ways to put the pieces together, and these books show that some combinations are better than others.

In Search of Excellence

THOMAS J. PETERS AND ROBERT H. WATERMAN JR.

Reviewed by Todd

In Search of Excellence marked a turning point in the evolution of business books, and so it makes the appropriate starting point for our recommended books on strategy. Prior to its 1982 release, historians and academics controlled the discussion about the organization of business, and to no one's surprise, their reportings were often dry and outdated. With this book, Tom Peters and Robert Waterman popularized the exploration of organizational success and created a contemporary conversation that was accessible to a wider audience. The importance of this title in the narrative arc of business thought, as well as the findings themselves, cannot be overstated.

Peters and Waterman first write a capsule history of organizational theory on their way to making a broader case for how organizations must be designed. The arc starts at the turn of the century with political economist Max Weber and mechanical engineer Frederick Taylor. Most are familiar with Taylor for his popularization of time studies and the 1911 publication of *The Principles of Scientific Management*, but it was Weber who suggested bureaucracy as the optimal form for human organization. Then, in *Strategy and Structure* (1962), Alfred Chandler presented the idea that businesses should organize themselves in response to the strictures of the marketplace.

In writing *In Search of Excellence*, Peters and Waterman arrived at a conclusion about the success of an organization that couldn't be more different from those early theories on business organization: *people are irrational and the structures that organize them must account for that.* This argument was 180 degrees counter to the historical modeling of business organizations after the military approach, in which managers fixated on the control of their homogenous teams while following the established five-year strategic plan. Instead, Peters and Waterman advocate humanistic values, including meaning, a small amount of control, and positive reinforcement as a postmilitaristic model. The conclusion is that the soft stuff matters. Culture matters. People matter.

Through this lens, Peters and Waterman spent five years researching such stalwart companies as Boeing, HP, and 3M, which engaged their employees as vital contributors to the success of the company and not simply as rank and file. The second half of *In Search of Excellence* reveals eight principles of organizational behavior gleaned from conversations with these companies:

1. A Bias for Action
2. Stay Close to the Customer
3. Autonomy and Entrepreneurship
4. Productivity through People
5. Hands-On, Value Driven
6. Stick to the Knitting
7. Simple Form, Lean Staff
8. Simultaneous Loose-Tight Properties

Over the twenty-five years since this book was released, others have taken on the challenge of finding the magical model for business success, and as a result, these ideas may look familiar. However, they deserve to be looked at, without preconceptions, as trailblazing concepts providing a prescription for business excellence, and for how surprisingly seldom they are adopted.

"In observing the excellent companies, and specifically the way they interact with customers, what we found most striking was the consistent presence of *obsession.* This characteristically occurred as a seemingly unjustifiable overcommitment to some form of quality, reliability, or service."

In contrast to earlier management texts, *In Search of Excellence* provides a reading experience to be enjoyed, not slogged through. Peters and Waterman write from the viewpoint of passionate observers, and the result is the near-equivalent to sitting in a conference room and listening to these executives recount their tales. The enthusiasm is contagious. (Try listening to the audio sometime with Peters narrating if you really want contagious enthusiasm.) This quality imparts a certain realism to the book that will inspire immediate new behaviors. The book has acquired a historical level of interest, like reading from the journal of an industrial archaeologist. It reported on Wal-Mart fifteen years before its emergence into retail dominance; it talks about the HP Way as a cultural positive; and, before Google, 3M was held up as the company that encouraged employees to spend a portion of their time pursing their passions.

In Search of Excellence advances a timeless vision of business organization: employees—with all of their irrational quirks and natural craziness—are embraced for those very same characteristics. Peters and Waterman posit a truism that has only become more established with time—that the human variable is the fuel that runs the organization. **TS**

In Search of Excellence: Lessons from America's Best-Run Companies, Collins Business Essentials Edition, Hardcover 2006, ISBN 9780060548780

WHERE TO NEXT? » Page 78 for **a structured view of strategy** « Page 70 for **an example of great leadership** « Page 56 for **taking a leadership leap** | EVEN MORE: *Re-Imagine!* **by Tom Peters;** *Give Your Speech, Change the World* **by Nick Morgan;** *Mavericks at Work* **by William C. Taylor and Polly G. LaBarre**

Good to Great

JIM COLLINS
Reviewed by Todd

No one in the last fifteen years has had a greater impact on the discussion of organizational success than Jim Collins. *Good to Great* has sold over two million copies since its 2001 publication, and when you ask chief executives about the books that made a significant impact on their decision making, this book is referenced more often than any other. With *Good to Great*, Collins introduced a new lexicon into management meetings, using memorable metaphors like "the hedgehog concept" and "the flywheel." Most important, he changed the conversation.

Collins's previous book, *Built to Last*, detailed the habits of century-old institutions that had long since established their reputations. Collins wrote *Good to Great* in response to business leaders who wanted to know if they could alter the course of their average companies and achieve the greatness won by the titans characterized in *Built to Last*. He spent five years searching for the answer . . . and the answer was yes.

Collins and his team looked for companies that showed a period of average (or below-average) market returns followed by a run of sustained success. These good-to-great companies were required to return 300 percent over and above the S&P 500 and to have sustained those results over a fifteen-year period. Only eleven Fortune 500 companies passed Collins's strict criteria.

The good-to-great companies were notable for another reason: they were not notable. The list lacked blue chip stalwarts (and media darlings) like General Electric and Coca-Cola. Missing were firms from fast-growth, high-tech sectors, like Intel. Instead, readers will find a steelmaker, three retailers, a couple of financial services providers, three well-known consumer package goods companies, a health-care product company, and another that sold postal meters. This was exactly the message that leaders wanted to believe: if Pitney-Bowes and Fannie Mae can do it, so can we.

Comparing good-to-great companies with a set of peers, Collins discovered a series of practices that were put in action even before the companies transitioned to greatness. During this time, companies identified and promoted leaders who were ambitious—not about their careers, but rather about the overall success of the company. These modest leaders then spent unusual amounts of time selecting the right team before deciding where to take the company, and may have allowed for limited growth until the right talent could be found. Then, these leaders created an environment that allowed employees to voice opinions and take on responsibility.

When companies finally made the transition, they built upon those preparation practices and brought a focus to their efforts. To bring concreteness to this idea, Collins references the ancient Greek fable "The Hedgehog and the Fox," using essayist Isaiah Berlin's analysis, "The fox knows many things, but the hedgehog knows one big thing." The Hedgehog Concept sits at the center of three intersecting circles:

1. What you can be best in the world at
2. What drives your economic engine
3. What you are deeply passionate about

To illustrate the "Hedgehog Concept" at work in business, Collins points to Walgreens. Pharmacists founded and still run the drugstore chain today, which lends authenticity and passion to its mission. The company altered its measurement for economic success by shifting its focus from profit per store to profit per customer visit, because management had the insight that winning loyal customers was about more than being a chain store and having a brand name. Being the most convenient drugstore was the company's differentiator and what it could be best at in the world. This focus now informs all aspects of Walgreens' strategy, from determining the street intersections for store locations to choosing products that best serve their customers.

"Good is the enemy of great."

All good-to-great companies have just such a deliberate nature. Collins describes a disciplined culture that provides constraints while still letting individuals decide the best course of action. Also, he finds that in these companies, technology is assistive, not a driver. Collins compares these efforts to pushing on a gigantic flywheel; the initial efforts are difficult, but the companies slowly build momentum and the ever-increasing rotations propel them forward. This slow and steady mind-set stands in stark contrast to the Tom Peters technicolor "dream big or go home" view of the world.

The book's rational approach to success finds a welcome home on the bookshelves of accountants, lawyers, MBAs, small-business owners, and entrepreneurs. With never-ending pressure from customers and shareholders, every manager is on a quest to find a path to success, but *Good to Great* offers more than that. Collins writes an inspirational tale that gives readers permission to believe they and their companies can achieve what the limited few can do. **TS**

Good to Great: Why Some Companies Make the Leap . . . and Others Don't, HarperCollins, Hardcover 2001, ISBN 9780066620992

WHERE TO NEXT? « Page 75 for **a supporter of good** » Page 152 for **more strategic methodology** » Page 229 for **how to get started** | EVEN MORE: *Good to Great and the Social Sectors* by Jim Collins; *Built to Last* by Jim Collins and Jerry I. Porras; *Blue Ocean Strategy* by W. Chan Kim and Renée Mauborgne

One of the difficulties in choosing which books to include in this compilation was evaluating the accessibility of the book itself versus the value of the idea contained within. There are many superb ideas that don't translate well into the book form, and there are thousands of books whose ideas never should have been published at that length.

Two books in particular deserve mention for the quality of their ideas, but are ones we cannot recommend in their popular book form. In both cases, the book is dense. The diligent reader is welcome to pursue the original works, but let us suggest more practical routes to accessing their valuable ideas.

The Best Route to an Idea

① Michael Porter's *Five Forces of Strategy*

Porter's defining work on competitive strategy is arguably the most important development of business theory in the last three decades. Business students can recite, from memory, the five forces (now repeat with me: suppliers, customers, competitors, substitutes, and new entrants). Porter's book, *Competitive Strategy,* provides an exhaustive 592-page academic view of the material, inappropriate for the majority of readers.

→ Start instead with Porter's *"The Five Competitive Forces That Shape Strategy,"* the 2008 revised version of the original article he wrote for *Harvard Business Review* in 1979. It encompasses all the basics of competitive strategy in nineteen pages.

② Peter Senge's *Learning Organizations*

Upon cracking open Senge's best-selling *The Fifth Discipline,* the casual reader is seduced by the fluidity of the opening chapter, only to find himself bogged down in the author's impenetrable writing style. Senge's primary insight that organizations compete by learning faster than their counterparts builds on the works of Chris Argyris and bears consideration in the discussion of pinnacle business thought.

→ The way to painlessly access the material is with *The Fifth Discipline Fieldbook* and *The Dance of Change*. Written by Senge and a team of writers, both paperback titles are filled with essays, sidebars, and exercises that make *The Fifth Discipline* concepts a pleasure to absorb.

Written by Todd Sattersten

The Innovator's Dilemma

CLAYTON M. CHRISTENSEN
Reviewed by Todd

Many in book publishing have a romanticized view of the industry's origin, beginning with Johannes Gutenberg and the movable-type printing press he invented in 1453. While that treasured form has changed little in the past five and a half centuries, the way the book is sold and distributed has changed dramatically in the last thirty years. Independent bookstores first struggled against the mall chains of Waldenbooks and B. Dalton, then the big-box retailers such as Barnes & Noble and Borders, and now the online superstore, Amazon. And these retail redistributions pale in comparison to the tectonic shifts that lie ahead in the form of print-on-demand and electronic distribution of books. In *The Innovator's Dilemma*, Clayton Christensen shows how management practices that typically serve executives well fail in the face of just such disruptive innovations.

Christensen begins by drawing a distinction between two types of innovation. In the first, everything from new products to customer service is designed to meet customers' demands. In the normal course of business, customers pay the bills, and writing those checks gives them significant influence over an organization's decision making. New ideas and opportunities, evaluated on the ability to serve existing customers and earn the necessary margins to support the company, are called *sustaining innovations* and are always successful ventures for existing (and dominant) firms.

But sometimes, innovation creates a new technology or reveals a new way to organize a firm's resources. This *disruptive innovation* does not offer the performance needed in the existing market, and entrant companies are forced to find a new set of customers who value innovation on a different set of metrics than those of the traditional market. Existing companies disregard the disruptive innovation because of its lower margins, and the newcomers find a small beachhead outside the existing market, using that market space to develop further. As the performance of disruptive innovations outpaces the sustaining innovations, entrants move into established markets and their lower cost structure forces incumbents further up-market, forfeiting existing profitable markets.

Clayton Christensen provides an array of case studies in *The Innovator's Dilemma*, including how the steel industry is still at the mercy of the disruptive innovation of minimills. Using scrap steel over iron ore, minimills require one-tenth the scale and can produce steel at 15 percent lower cost than traditional integrated steel mills. When minimills first emerged in the 1960s, they were able to produce only low-quality steel whose only market was construction rebar. The integrated mills were happy to cede this low-end, price-sensitive market. What the incumbents missed was the minimills' desire to move further into their markets. With a completely different cost structure and technology that was improving faster than existing methods, minimills began producing structural steel and sheet steel. Minimills now account for 50 percent of the steel made in the United States, and here is the amazing part: at no point did an existing steel company using integrated mills construct a minimill to take advantage of the disruptive innovation.

"To succeed consistently, good managers need to be skilled not just in choosing, training, and motivating the right people for the right job, but in choosing, building, and preparing the right *organization* for the job as well."

To suggest that the integrated steel mills simply hid their heads in the sand would be too easy. Christensen says most markets that serve as the launch point for disruptive innovation are too small for large organizations to concentrate on. These emerging markets lack clear evidence that they will turn out profitable. When disruptive technologies are being developed, the applications for them are unpredictable, and worse, companies are misled when they attempt to use the same tools from their mature markets. In nearly every case of disruptive innovation, a new set of companies rises to dominate the industry.

For disruptive innovation to flourish, says Christensen, companies need to create the right organizational structure. Companies often start by promoting successful managers to lead new efforts, but without addressing the processes and values of the new group, the leadership will start to make decisions the same way it always has. Disruptive innovation requires an autonomous organization with the appropriate cost structure to address the emerging markets. In the 1970s, the motor controls industry was disrupted by programmable logic controllers (PLCs), and the only company to successfully traverse the disruption was Rockwell Automation (then Allen-Bradley). The Milwaukee-based company did so by investing in two smaller companies shortly after commercial introduction of PLCs and combining them into a separate division, which it pitted against its existing electromechanical division. Rockwell showed that it is possible to establish dominance during a period of disruptive innovation while maintaining market leadership in the traditional product.

While the innovator's dilemma stems from uncontrollable external pressures, dealing with it is an internal dilemma. Managers lack the information and experience needed to make confident investments in disruptive technology. The tried and true resource allocation process favors current customers and their needs, starving incubatory projects of needed love and attention. And to survive the innovation pipeline, the disruptive technology needs the marketing leader to find new clients who appreciate its current capabilities. As performance improves, the customers who showed no interest in the initial idea are exactly the ones who will be clamoring for it. **TS**

The Innovator's Dilemma: The Revolutionary Book That Will Change the Way You Do Business, Collins Business Essentials edition, Paperback 2006, ISBN 9780060521998

WHERE TO NEXT? » Page 256 for **the disruptive story of steel** » Page 274 for **the story of global disruption** » Page 189 for **a story of team dysfunction** | EVEN MORE: *The Innovator's Solution* by Clayton M. Christensen and Michael E. Raynor; *Competitive Strategy* by Michael E. Porter; *Innovation and Entrepreneurship* by Peter F. Drucker

Learn From Experience

Case studies are an effective way to show theory in practice. These three Harvard Business School case studies further one's thinking about a business issue, and each is from an author with a book that provides the perfect next step for the reader looking for more depth. Find complete case studies at www.harvardbusiness.com.

Learn how to **establish a unique competitive strategy.**

CASE:

Matching Dell

by Jan W. Rivkin and Michael E. Porter.

Michael Dell has used competitive analysis to become a leader in the PC industry by offering his products where consumers want them most. Shifting between direct and retail trends, Dell found and followed a strategy that is now the industry standard. By focusing on products and services and building an infrastructure to support his strategy, Dell has become the longest-tenured CEO in the PC industry.

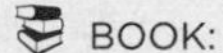

BOOK:

Competitive Strategy: Techniques for Analyzing Industries and Competitors

by Michael E. Porter.

In this landmark book about strategic management, Porter lets readers in on Dell's game plan and offers tools any business can use to succeed in its industry.

Learn about **translating strategy into results.**

CASE:

Boston Lyric Opera

by Robert S. Kaplan.

In late 1992, the Boston Lyric Opera realized that production costs were outweighing income. Under new leadership, it reevaluated its productions and scaled them down while still focusing on quality. After seeing increased membership, the Opera leveraged that loyal community to convert members to donors and solicit volunteer workers and board members, resulting in an engaged audience and a return to profitability.

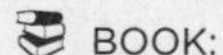

BOOK:

The Balanced Scorecard: Translating Strategy into Action

by Robert S. Kaplan and David P. Norton.

Kaplan's book reinforces the idea of how organizations profit by understanding and comparing both tangible and intangible costs and benefits.

Learn how to **use innovation to your advantage.**

CASE:

Eli Lilly and Company: Innovation in Diabetes Care

by Clayton Christensen.

Eli Lilly had manufactured the highest quality of insulin available since the early 1920s. However, when competitor Novo Nordisk came out with an insulin pen in the early 1990s—a device that provided customers with incredible ease of use, Eli Lilly knew it was in trouble. It responded by creating a similar pen, but one filled with an even better product that closely matched how insulin acted in nondiabetic people.

BOOK:

The Innovator's Dilemma

by Clayton Christensen.

Christensen's book elaborates on how companies such as Eli Lilly can examine their place in the market and leverage creative ideas to move forward.

Written by Jon Mueller

Only the Paranoid Survive

ANDREW S. GROVE
Reviewed by Jack

As one of the founders and a former CEO of Intel, Andy Grove helped create a leading technology business. At first blush, *Only the Paranoid Survive* appears to be an autobiography or business narrative, but the subtitle explains the true focus of the book: *How to Exploit the Crisis Points That Challenge Every Company*. This book is an effective crusade for a method of crisis management, or perhaps crisis identification, that is well served by Grove's wealth of experience in a competitive market.

The cornerstone of Grove's book is the Strategic Inflection Point (SIP). Grove advocates the use of Michael Porter's five-forces model to help determine the competitive well-being of a business. In addition to customers, competitors, suppliers, substitutes, and barriers to entry, Grove suggests a sixth force, "complementors," which are businesses that offer complementary products, like what paper is to ink. A company experiences a strategic inflection point when one of these six forces topples its strategic plan, like a ripple becoming a tsunami, silent movies instantly antiquated by talkies, or what Wal-Mart did to Main Street America. When a monumental change like this happens, management is forced to take alternative actions. "The business responds differently to managerial actions than it did before. We have lost control and don't know how to regain it. Eventually, a new equilibrium in the industry will be reached. Some businesses will be stronger, others will be weaker."

Even in retrospect, the moment an SIP happens can be hard to recognize, but an unattended SIP can be deadly to the future of a company. Grove uses the analogy of a lost hiker. At some point along a hike, the hiker realizes that he is lost but doesn't know when he actually became lost, when his foot first veered off the path. Rarely does he at the same moment realize: " 'Things are different. Something has changed.' " Grove advocates awareness as the main weapon against being defeated by an SIP.

Just as with the hiker, how one reacts to an SIP is key to orienting oneself once an SIP has been recognized and acknowledged.

Grove then offers an example from Intel in the early 1980s, when the Japanese arrived in the memory chip market and ate Intel's lunch because the Japanese companies could make the chips cheaper and more efficiently. Grove emphasizes again just how difficult it is to identify an SIP. He uses the metaphor of "signal vs. noise" for distinguishing whether a threat or problem is the real deal or just a temporary blip on the radar. Grove states that the only way to know whether a market or internal change signals an SIP is through "the process of clarification that comes from broad and intensive debate." Grove admits that in this situation, Intel waited too long to acknowledge that they were facing a real SIP due to significant concern about how Intel's existing customers would react to any change in business as usual. What Intel ultimately did was get out of the memory chip market—which was their main business at the time—and move into making processor chips.

The author's analysis of how the computer industry went from a vertical market built with DEC, Wang, and IBM—who made the hardware and software for their own machines—to a horizontal market consisting of Microsoft, Dell, and HP is valuable. When this SIP ran through the computer business, Novell became a "first mover" in networking in the new horizontal industry. Novell, a small, vertically oriented company doing both hardware and software, literally ran out of money to pay suppliers and had to redesign itself. Within a few years, Novell became a billion-dollar business because it was able to react to the SIP quickly. As Grove points out, it is easier to be the best with a narrow focus like networking than by making the best computers with the best software in a vertical business.

"Managing, especially managing through a crisis, is an extremely personal affair."

The book business I started has had three serious Strategic Inflection Points in its lifetime. The anxiety and stress of feeling lost but not knowing how we took the wrong path, just like Grove's hiker, were low points in my career. No business or market is static, and *Only the Paranoid Survive* will convince you to "look over your shoulder" at the potential incoming train that may be a Strategic Inflection Point, and know whether to jump the track or get on at the next station. **JC**

Only the Paranoid Survive: How to Exploit the Crisis Points That Challenge Every Company, Currency/Doubleday, Paperback 1999, ISBN 9780385483827

WHERE TO NEXT? « Page 81 for **more on Porter's five forces** « Page 61 for **how to lead through an SIP** » Page 256 for **how a company navigated through an SIP** | EVEN MORE: *Andy Grove* by Richard S. Tedlow; *Swimming Across* by Andrew S. Grove; *Direct from Dell* by Michael Dell with Catherine Fredman

Who Says Elephants Can't Dance?

LOUIS V. GERSTNER JR.

Reviewed by Todd

"This is not my autobiography," starts Lou Gerstner in *Who Says Elephants Can't Dance?* As Gerstner's retirement approached, he expected business leaders and bystanders to start asking for his thoughts on the big trends—the economy, globalization, and the like. That was the kind of book he meant to write. Instead, everyone wanted to know how he did it . . . how he turned around IBM. During his tenure from 1993 to 2001, revenues grew from $62.7 billion to $85.9 billion and IBM's stock price grew tenfold. Of course, people were curious; Gerstner believes he had no choice but to write *this* book.

And certainly, to not document the story of how this Long Islander, after stops at McKinsey, American Express, and RJR Nabisco, orchestrated the highest profile turnaround of the twentieth century would have been a travesty. While Jack Welch may have had a tough task reenergizing the still highly successful General Electric, Lou Gerstner gets the top prize for saving Big Blue from near bankruptcy.

When the newly appointed CEO started, rather ominously, on April Fool's Day 1993, he found the company in a shambles. IBM, the pioneer that created the technology industry, had lost half its market share in fewer than ten years. Among competitors, it ranked eleventh in customer satisfaction behind some companies that no longer existed. But Gerstner's gravest concern was IBM's cost position: "On average, our competitors were spending 31 cents to produce $1 of revenue, while we were spending 42 cents for the same end."

To quickly change course, Gerstner made a series of bold decisions. At that time the personal computer was reaching its product zenith and $5 billion were committed to mainframe research and development. Nevertheless, the company-built communications grid was put up for sale. Add to that the abandonment of application development, the decision to sell competitor hardware and software, and a big move into integration services. Thirty-five thousand people were laid off in addition to

TOM WATSON SR.'S BASIC BELIEFS

- Excellence in everything we do.
- Superior customer service.
- Respect for the individual.

the forty-five thousand others who had been let go a year earlier. While these seem like obvious moves in retrospect, Gerstner reflects that, at the time, skepticism filled the pages of business magazines and the halls of IBM office buildings around the world.

But each move was based on a deep strategic view of where IBM and the technology market were headed. The communications network was sold to AT&T for $5 billion as Gerstner saw the coming ubiquity of broadband and IBM's inability to compete with the scale of the existing telecommunication companies. Doubling down on the mainframe business created $19 billion in new revenue, a direct result of hearing the anger of chief information officers and their expectation that IBM defend the role of "big iron" in their transaction-intensive retail, financial, and governmental operations. IBM Global Services went from a rogue arm of the sales function to a $30 billion business that employs one-half of IBM's total workforce.

"Fixing IBM was all about execution. We had to stop looking for people to blame, stop tweaking the internal structure and systems. I wanted no excuses."

After describing the first ten months of his tenure and explaining his strategic moves, Gerstner then digs into the culture of contentment that was pervasive at IBM. Looking back, he believes the root of IBM's problems came from its unparalleled success. The computer giant had for so long been immune to economic cycles and price wars that the company had become insular and unresponsive. Gerstner compares his job of revitalizing the culture to that of "taking a lion raised for all of its life in captivity and suddenly teaching it to survive in the jungle." From abolishing the dress code to sending his executives and their reports out to customers, it was a cultural change made successful by the willingness of hundreds of thousands of employees who believed in Big Blue and in the direction Gerstner was taking the company.

But what about that curious title of this quintessential turnaround story? I'll let Gerstner answer that with a quote that also illuminates just what Gerstner always believed was the potential for IBM:

> Big matters. Size can be leveraged. Breadth and depth allow for greater investment, greater risk taking, and longer patience for future payoffs. It isn't a question of whether elephants can prevail over ants. It's a question of whether a particular elephant can dance. If it can, the ants must leave the dance floor. **TS**

Who Says Elephants Can't Dance? Leading a Great Enterprise through Dramatic Change, HarperBusiness, Paperback 2003, ISBN 9780060523800

WHERE TO NEXT? « Page 58 for **the other great corporate turnaround of the twentieth century** » Page 170 for **why one IBM executive compared reengineering to "starting a fire on your head and putting it out with a hammer"** » Page 224 for **comments from the son of IBM's founder** | EVEN MORE: *The Maverick and His Machine* by Kevin Maney; *Father, Son and Company* by Thomas J. Watson Jr. with Peter Petre; *The Future of Competition* by C.K. Prahalad and Venkat Ramaswamy; *Harvard Business Review on Turnarounds* by Harvard Business Review

Discovering the Soul of Service

LEONARD L. BERRY

Reviewed by Jack

In *Discovering the Soul of Service*, Dr. Leonard Berry discusses fourteen companies that are sustainable businesses with service at their core. Written ten years ago, the featured businesses had an average age of thirty-one years of work, an admirable amount of time in which to develop tried-and-true strategies. The companies Berry studied are not the usual business-media suspects and range from Charles Schwab, The Container Store, and Enterprise Rent-A-Car to the St. Paul Saints minor-league baseball team, all companies whose missions vary widely. I must admit that there is only so much new material to read about Southwest Airlines or Starbucks or Harley-Davidson or Ritz Carlton, those common elite examples of good business, no matter how fascinating their evolution. So, Berry's featured businesses offer a fresh perspective, and include those managing 120 employees to over 35,000, those that are public and those that are private, those that are local, national, or international. I find this range adds a depth to this book absent in many others that focus only on the giants of the service industry.

Despite the differences in companies represented, the one thing they have in common is that they all built their success on sustainable service. Only three of the fourteen have had more than two CEOs in their history. Even now, ten years after Berry wrote the book, most are still run by their original CEOs. Having this kind of stability at the top level allows leaders to build trust and show the integrity and authenticity needed to sustain the success.

These organizations are built on the value of humanity, of treating their employees and customers—or, as the author states, the organization and its partners—humanely, with concern for their well-being and opportunities for development. Value-driven leadership, trust-based relationships, and generosity are three of the nine drivers the author calls out as being essential when establishing a humane organization. These values are remarkably consistent among the companies.

Berry shares with us wisdom from leaders who have faced the challenge of maintaining humane organizations in the face of constant pressure. Restaurateur Drew Nieporent has been very successful in a business that can be very defeating. He has many restaurants scattered around the globe and has won every major restaurant award. He believes that building a values-based business is key to building a sustainable business. " 'Restaurants are like children,' he says. 'They need your attention when they're young. You give them values and principles and hope they grow up strong.' "

"My purpose in this book is to identify, describe, and illustrate the underlying drivers of sustainable success in service businesses."

Yet there are three challenges in sustaining service success. These challenges are made worse when you are creating value for the customer with service: "The more labor-intensive the service, the greater the challenges of: operating effectively while growing rapidly, operating effectively when competing on price, [and] retaining the initial entrepreneurial spirit of the younger, smaller company." Berry then offers the selected companies as examples of successfully avoiding these pitfalls. He talks about Valujet and its rapid growth in the 1990s . . . and its equally rapid decline because of lax controls and a lack of attention to nonfinancial goals. The company that eventually returned as AirTran had not been able to operate effectively during rapid growth.

Age has taught me to lead a quiet and happy life, and has given me the knowledge that the way to achieve such a life is to live it for the right reasons, whether you follow the Ten Commandments or the Golden Rule. For my own life, I place a lot of value on karma (or, what goes around comes around). You do something because it is the right thing to do, not because you are going to get paid for it. *Discovering the Soul of Service* shows that this type of soul-inspired philosophy has been successful in a wide range of organizations, and Berry shows you how to succeed while holding on to the values around which you built your business and live your life. **JC**

Discovering the Soul of Service: The Nine Drivers of Sustainable Business Success, Free Press, Hardcover 1999, ISBN 9780684845111

WHERE TO NEXT? » Page 295 for **discovering more possibilities** « Page 54 for **the soul of leadership** » Page 215 for **another airline with soul** | EVEN MORE: *A Complaint Is a Gift* by Janelle Barlow and Claus Moller; *Minding the Store* by Stanley Marcus; *The Nordstrom Way* by Robert Spector with Patrick D. McCarthy

Execution

LARRY BOSSIDY AND RAM CHARAN

Reviewed by Jack

Over ten years ago I worked with an MBAer who listed himself as a Mensa member on his résumé. He was meant to be the operations guy, the strategy guy, while I concentrated on what I did best: sales and service. During the six years we were partners, I would drive to the finish line on a project at the same pace with which I started it; he, on the other hand, would get all revved up at the start but end up taking the leisurely route, often not completing the project at all. Not a productive pattern for accomplishing operational changes and strategic goals. For a time I thought the problem lay with me. Perhaps I was being slipshod or missing something important. Granted, my end result wasn't always perfect and we would have to go back to review parts, but the task had been completed and the changes made were often minimal. A year after he left the company, this book, *Execution*, arrived on my desk and it revealed to me that the problem wasn't mine but his own inability to take action and follow through—to *execute* the big ideas. For me, *Execution* proved to me that action is necessary—no, paramount—to success. And this message clearly resonates with readers, because we all have experienced a failure of execution during our careers.

The value of getting things done on a personal level is a sound one, but execution is about more than personal performance; a company can surely have the same difficulties making strategic moves and acting on new initiatives. As the authors explain, "Execution is a specific set of behaviors and techniques that companies need to master in order to have competitive advantage." This book offers three perspectives on the problem. Part 1 explains the "discipline" of execution.

- Execution is a discipline, and integral to strategy.
- Execution is the major job of the business leader.
- Execution must be a core element of an organization's culture.

Part 2 presents the "building blocks"; and Part 3, the real "how-to" section of the book, emphasizes the need for action. The authors succeed in making it easy to recognize the areas in which we and our companies need to stretch past our comfort zones.

Reading the book is so thoroughly enjoyable, with its conversational style, that it opens us up to the challenges that lie within. Writing in the first person, Bossidy and Charan take turns sharing experiences, and as a result we get the full benefit of their superstar status in the business world. These first-person sections—an approach that should be used more often in business books—add a human feel to the subject. To shore up their conclusions, Bossidy tells "war stories" from Honeywell, Allied Signal, and GE, and Charan adds views from outside of Bossidy's world and from his thirty-five years of experience as an advisor. This dual perspective lends weight to their conclusions.

"Execution is not only the biggest issue facing business today; it is something nobody has explained satisfactorily."

Despite having sold over one million copies in five years, *Execution* has been criticized since it was first published in 2002. Many have cited the use of failed examples and the authors' personal aggrandizing as detrimental to the message. But the elusive skill of getting things done is an evergreen topic in business literature. Look for a better book on organizational effectiveness and you will spend a lot of time searching. I would ask those same people to suggest an alternative. Drucker's *Managing for Results* covers some of the same ground, but lacks the pointed focus of Bossidy and Charan's argument. Here, the authors map out a blueprint for how leaders can inject a healthy sense of realism into their organizations. *Execution*, no matter how readers or critics choose to interpret it, gets to the basic tenet that business doesn't get done unless things happen. JC

Execution: The Discipline of Getting Things Done, Crown Business, Hardcover 2002, ISBN 9780609610572

WHERE TO NEXT? « Page 12 for **execution at the individual level** « Page 58 for **GE and execution** | EVEN MORE: *Executive Intelligence* by Justin Menkes; *You're in Charge, Now What?* by Thomas J. Neff and James M. Citrin; *The Power of Alignment* by George Labovitz and Victor Rosansky

Competing for the Future

GARY HAMEL AND C. K. PRAHALAD
Reviewed by Todd

Most executives think the competitive fight takes place in the present. Look at how leaders spend the majority of their time—approving yearly budgets, taking global trips to important customers, waiting for the sales number at quarter's close. Gary Hamel and C. K. Prahalad write that the battle, or the war itself, is already lost if business leaders spend all their time on the issues of today. *Competing for the Future* is a fiery rebuke of conventional strategic wisdom, challenging short-term incrementalism as the answer to company growth.

Writing this book in 1994, Hamel and Prahalad were revolting against the vogue of reengineering and "denominator managers" who chose to slash investment and workforce to improve a company's return on investment rather than focus on generating more income with the return they had in hand. At this same time, the authors were seeing a handful of companies redefining their markets with fundamentally new strategies: Wal-Mart, Honda, Canon, Schwab. Getting smaller or better was not the strategy for these mavericks; it was about being different.

Creating strategic differences requires foresight. "If a top management team cannot clearly articulate the five or six fundamental industry trends that most threaten its firm's continued success, it is not in control of the firm's destiny." And the authors say understanding these market forces creates the foresight that allows a company to get to the future first. For those who arrive first, the rewards are plentiful: investment recouped ahead of their foes, early adopters pining for the new with their open checkbooks, and the rule book waiting to be written.

Predicting the exact nature of an industry five or ten years from now is not the end goal, but understanding the forces at play and making an educated guess about direction creates foresight. Hamel and Prahalad's example of the future of a record store illustrates that exact challenge. They write about the advantages of a retail store's knowledgeable staff, immediately available product, and reasonable proximity. However, despite these positives, they go on to describe a future (remember, this was 1994) that sounds eerily like today's iTunes: "10,000 pieces of music," "listen to a 90-second sample," "selections downloaded onto a digital recording device." While it is amazingly accurate in one aspect, completely missing from the description is the emergence of the MP3 format, the role of piracy in distribution, or other Web retailers simply selling a wider selection of product than is possible in a physical outlet. What the authors did predict would have been enough to give any record store a look into the future and time to strategize to fight against the new trend. Thus, a complete picture isn't necessary; awareness is.

A directional sense for trends sketches a picture of the skills a company will need to compete in the future. The term "core competency" was coined by Hamel and Prahalad to describe the broad basket of skills a company needs to compete. Decisions about which core competencies to pursue dictate the markets a company can compete in, and the long-time horizon for competency development can put a company in the right (or wrong) place at the right (or wrong) time. Honda has concentrated its core competencies on engine and power-train development, and this has allowed it to enter markets ranging from motorcycles to small jet aircraft. JVC started investing in the competencies needed to build video cassette recorders twenty years before the product became a mainstream consumer device, and benefited handsomely when that time came.

"[S]eeing the future first may be more about having a wide-angle lens than a crystal ball."

Each chapter in *Competing for the Future* has the thought density of a *Harvard Business Review* article, with the tone of a Sunday fire-and-brimstone sermon. Hamel and Prahalad are preaching the same thing you might hear in the pew on Sundays: consider the choices you make today, for they are the seeds of tomorrow's success.

Competing for the Future, Harvard Business School Press, Paperback 1996, ISBN 9780875847160

WHERE TO NEXT? » Page 170 for **the ideology the authors oppose** » Page 100 for **the realities of market leadership** » Page 274 for **exercising your wide-angle lens** | EVEN MORE: *The Art of the Long View* by Peter Schwartz; *Fortune at the Bottom of the Pyramid* by C. K. Prahalad; *The Mind of the Strategist* by Kenichi Ohmae

Beyond the Core

CHRIS ZOOK
Reviewed by Todd

Market leadership feels good. The company grows. Employees are having fun. Shareholders are happy. At some point though, the growth curve flattens. The search for the next source of growth begins—and this is where the mistakes occur.

Consider the numbers. Only one in three new product introductions is successful. The odds of creating growth through acquisitions are about the same. And finding partners and forming joint ventures only succeeds 20 percent of the time.

Chris Zook, head of Bain's Global Strategy Practice, has been looking at where growth comes from for almost two decades, and he has written three books that detail his work. The first, *Profit from the Core*, cowritten with James Allen, summarizes ten years' worth of research and proves that successful growth comes from focusing, not diversifying. The third book, *Unstoppable*, explains how the need to redefine a company's core strategy might be the only option and how to make that transition successfully. The second book in the strategic trilogy, *Beyond the Core*, is the one that provides the most insights for a company focused on expanding its reach.

Zook refers to these areas of expansion as "adjacencies," a theme that appears in all three books. His thinking and the data he shares evolve with each book, but the definition never changes. Business adjacencies are growth opportunities that allow a company to extend the boundaries of its core business by drawing on skills that already exist. Amazon's acquisition of audiobook provider Audible fits as much as Starbucks' multiple attempts at entering the media business do not.

Even with the constraint of close proximity, deciding which adjacencies to pursue requires careful consideration. First, the adjacencies must build and reinforce the business core. Second, adjacencies should move the company toward markets with high potential for profit. Finally, the adjacent move should provide the same opportunity for market leadership that exists with the core business.

Each of those suggestions seems obvious, but it is the next level of detail in Zook's research that has made it one of the books I often recommend on strategy. His research identifies five dimensions to consider when planning an adjacent move.

- Customers: Are they the same as or different from those currently served?
- Competitors: Are they the same as or different from those currently encountered?
- Cost structure: Is the cost structure the same or different?
- Channels of distributions: Are these the same or different?
- Singular capability: If there is a single capability (brand, asset, technology) that gives the core business its uniqueness, then is this relevant in the new opportunity?

These questions ensure that growth comes from opportunities close to the business core.

"Strong leaders in robust markets epitomize the epithet of Sun Tzu: 'The more opportunities I seize, the more opportunities multiply before me.'"

The remainder of the book discusses orchestrating and executing adjacent moves. The chapter on orchestrating is really about honestly assessing the health of the core of the business. Zook's research shows that being the market leader improves the chances of success with adjacent moves threefold while followers face dreadful odds of gaining meaningful market share without industry consolidation or shrinking the business to focus on a smaller, more loyal segment.

When executing adjacent moves, the key decision point is the level of integration with the existing business. This is largely determined by the number of shared customers, the need for common decision making, and the recognition of similar cultural values. Zook also stresses the benefits of being able to repeat adjacent moves. Nike is the best example having moved from running to basketball to football to soccer by repeating the same set of moves: develop shoes with celebrity endorsements, develop soft goods (clothing), develop hard goods (equipment), and expand across geographies.

In a business world of infinite possibility, focus is often underrated, and *Beyond the Core* reminds us of the real power in sticking to your knitting. TS

Beyond the Core: Expand Your Market Without Abandoning Your Roots, Harvard Business School Press, Hardcover 2004, ISBN 9781578519514

WHERE TO NEXT? « Page 100 for **help on finding your core** » Page 186 for the **doing that comes after the finding** | EVEN MORE: *Profit from the Core* by Chris Zook with James Allen; *The Breakthrough Imperative* by Mark Gottfredson and Steve Schaubert

SALES AND MARKETING

Peter Drucker said the singular goal of a company is to create customers. Marketing gathers information, formulates product offerings, and develops messages to attract precious prospects. Sales translates interest and intent into dollars and cents. This section covers approaches and pitfalls in the never-ending process of creating customers.

Influence

ROBERT B. CIALDINI, PHD
Reviewed by Todd

The simple act of accepting a flower from a stranger starts a chain reaction. The recipient immediately feels compelled to reciprocate in some way. Humans are preprogrammed with a whole set of these types of innate behaviors that move us through life. If we were required to consciously consider every decision we made, we would quickly become paralyzed. As humans have evolved, we have developed a set of "mental shortcuts" that helps us deal with this onslaught of choices. Many of these mechanisms are generally positive and have served to help society function and flourish.

Social psychologist Robert Cialdini's deep understanding of human behavior is evident in the wide array of examples he uses throughout *Influence*, especially, as the subtitle tells us, in the psychology of persuasion. Here, university research is interwoven with well-known, often infamous events in U.S. history. He adds personal anecdotes from field research, ranging from busing tables at a high-end restaurant to enrolling as a sales trainee at numerous companies. His research draws together what con men and car dealers have known for a long time: unconscious reactions can also be used to exploit us. He links this phenomenon to a variety of forms of persuasion (identified here in italics).

Back to that flower. This kind of age-old compulsion for *reciprocity* allowed ancient tribes to divide tasks among members and cultures to trade goods across oceans. The Hare Krishnas maintain their sect financially by giving flowers to travelers passing through airports; most recipients automatically return the favor with a small donation. Samples at your local supermarket can create the same feeling of indebtedness; you might pick up the product just to please the salesperson who offered you the sample.

Making commitments and staying consistent with those commitments turns out to be very important to us and those around us. Once a person commits to a point of view, he often has a very hard time doing a U-turn. If you are ever elected the foreman of a jury, Cialdini recommends requiring secret ballots when voting to avoid public commitments that may later cause difficulty in reaching a unanimous verdict. Signing petitions has the same effect; people will commit to bigger and bigger supportive acts (like putting billboards for a social cause in the front yard) after agreeing to little things like a signature. To use this tendency to your advantage when setting a goal—whether quitting smoking or starting a business—the act of writing and sharing your dream activates that dual mechanism of commitment and constituency.

People are also persuaded by taking social cues from others around them. Cialdini labels this form *social proof* and says we are most susceptible under two conditions. The first is when there is uncertainty. Laugh tracks on sitcoms use this opportunity to engage viewers by giving them confirmation that the scene or line should be interpreted as funny. The second condition is when we take cues from those who are similar to us. The more similar, the more likely we are to follow. From the clothing we wear to the music we listen to, social proof is a powerful form of persuasion.

Sales professionals are specifically trained in a technique that plays on *affection.* A bag of golf clubs or baby stroller in your trunk gives the car dealer checking out your trade-in a topic of conversation in which to invoke emotion. Consultants at Tupperware understand and use this technique in a different way, organizing their parties around the host and the bond of friendship shared by the attendees. The strength of affection between attendees is a better predictor of purchase than the affection for the product itself. Our best defense, Cialdini says, is to concentrate on the transaction and not the person presenting it.

The better judgment of our conscious minds can be bypassed, prompting us to do the inexplicable, through the use of *authority.* Cialdini tells of Stanley Milgram's set of experiments conducted in response to the Nazi war crime trials, in which he attempted to determine if individuals could be put in a situation where they would willingly follow orders despite knowing those actions would cause harm to others. Test subjects were told by an authority figure, the researcher, to ask questions of an actor (collaborating with Milgram) and to press a button to send an electric shock to the actor upon each incorrect answer. The shocks increased in intensity with each incorrect answer. The final shock administered a whopping and painful 450 volts to the actor, and about two-thirds of Milgram's subjects willingly flipped all thirty switches needed to reach that point. Milgram concluded that the researcher, firmly exerting authority, created the influence necessary for the subjects to proceed.

Scarcity is probably the easiest type of persuasion to understand, and is the method of influence we are most exposed to. It is a favorite tool of marketers (e.g. "Limited time offer!!!") and salespeople ("I am not sure how much longer this car will be on the lot."), because we hate losing out on things. Lost opportunity creates a stronger desire for what can't be obtained readily. Hence, misprinted stamps and Brett Favre's rookie card carry higher value due to their limited supply.

"I can admit it freely now. All my life I've been a patsy."

There is protection against becoming a victim of manipulation, Cialdini assures readers. After explaining each type of persuasion, he offers antidotes to being fooled, tricked, and exploited. For example, if a salesman tries to employ his charms, remember to focus on the merits of the deal and not the person selling it to you. But Cialdini believes the reliability of these shortcuts must remain intact for us to function in a world that is growing ever more complicated.

After the entertaining stories and cautionary tales fade away, Cialdini leaves us with two key insights. First, our lives would be difficult without the mental shortcuts that influence our decision making, and second, those same assets leave the door open to exploitation, creating a blurry line between an innocuous recommendation and a planned deception. **TS**

Influence: The Psychology of Persuasion, Collins Business Essentials edition, Paperback 2007, ISBN 9780061241895

WHERE TO NEXT? » Page 329 for **more than you know** « Page 67 for **how stories can influence** « Page 21 for **a classic on influence** | EVEN MORE: *Nudge* by Richard H. Thaler and Cass R. Sunstein; *Sway* by Ori Brafman and Ron Brafman; *The Art of Woo* by G. Richard Shell and Mario Moussa; *Blink* by Malcolm Gladwell

Positioning: The Battle for Your Mind

AL RIES AND JACK TROUT

Reviewed by Jack

When you think of portable music, one brand rules: iPod. How Apple came to dominate this market is simply an extraordinary example of successful "positioning." Positioning is the process by which you get your product into the minds of prospective customers. In 1972, Al Ries and Jack Trout introduced their idea of positioning in a series of articles in *Advertising Age* called "The Positioning Era Cometh." In 1981, they published *Positioning: The Battle for Your Mind*. Positioning becomes necessary for a product, service, or company because overcommunication in today's world leads to what Ries and Trout call an "oversimplified mind"—a defense mechanism consumers use to deal with all the clutter companies and, subsequently, marketers throw at them. The choices available to us today can be overwhelming. For example, in the 1970s, Frito Lay offered ten chip varieties; in the 1990s, it offered seventy-eight. Running shoes? There were five choices in the 1970s, 285 varieties in the 1990s. With this kind of contemporary overload, the mind just shuts down. So, for Ries and Trout, "[p]ositioning is an organized system for finding windows in the mind."

Since advertising's effectiveness is weakened by this overload, the authors advise marketers that only a simplified message will actually make it through the clutter. One of the ways they suggest positioning a product is by "[o]wning a word in the mind. Volvo owns 'safety.' BMW owns 'driving,' FedEx owns 'overnight,' Crest owns 'cavities.' Once you own a word in the mind, you have to use it or lose it." Just how do you embed a word that symbolizes your product in a person's mind? One way is to get there first. We remember Charles Lindbergh and Roger Banister as the "first" to fly across the Atlantic Ocean and to break the four-minute mile, respectively, but we don't remember who the next person was. Another powerful way to be memorable, the authors say, is "If you can't be the first in a category, then set up a new category you can be first in." For example,

Miller Brewing certainly wasn't the first brewer, but it created Miller Lite, the first mainstream light beer.

For the twentieth anniversary of this classic, the publisher reprinted a new version in hardcover, and the authors added comments in the margins of the expanded format. What really adds value in the new edition are stories of more recent successes and failures. The authors' concise and direct writing style made this book a success when it was first published in 1981, and their clear communication of facts and opinions, continued in subsequent editions, compels readers to think about marketing in a new way.

"Positioning is an organized system for finding windows in the mind. It is based on the concept that communication can only take place at the right time and under the right circumstances"

Ries and Trout believe you can position just about anything. Their case examples range from the Catholic Church to the country of Belgium to the biotech firm Monsanto. The authors believe you can even position yourself. In each case, the end game is clarity, and the primary mission is to become the customer's first thought. **JC**

Positioning: The Battle for Your Mind, McGraw-Hill, Twentieth Anniversary Edition, Hardcover 2001, ISBN 9780071359168

WHERE TO NEXT? « Page 58 for **the power of being number 1 or number 2** » Page 253 for **the power of consistency** » Page 218 for **the power of low prices** | EVEN MORE: *Ogilvy on Advertising* by David Ogilvy; *Building Strong Brands* by David A. Aaker; *The 22 Immutable Laws of Marketing* by Al Ries and Jack Trout

A New Brand World

SCOTT BEDBURY WITH STEPHEN FENICHELL
Reviewed by Jack

Scott Bedbury was at the epicenter of the ascent of two of the most recognizable brands in the world. He was senior vice president of marketing at Starbucks from 1995 to 1998. During that period Starbucks had over 40 percent annual growth. Before Starbucks, he was head of advertising at Nike for seven years during the period in which the company changed its image radically. In *A New Brand World*, he offers insight into these classic brand creations and delivers a relevant book about brand building, brand extension, and brand loyalty. The book is heavily reliant on the Starbucks and Nike examples, but he also looks at other branding successes and failures.

Bedbury helped launch the "Bo Knows" and "Just Do It" campaigns. In rich detail, he relates stories of internal tension at Nike as it moved from its previous testosterone-heavy, "wimps need not apply" attitude to a brand with enough room for the entire family, and, ultimately, to the leading sports and fitness company. "Just Do It" became a brand that isn't about sneakers or products but about values and ethos.

Bedbury went on to help create an actual brand definition for Starbucks, which, the year after he started, opened its first outlet outside the United States, in Japan. In a role that was much different than his previous one at Nike, he worked with Howard Schultz to create a brand code that helped define who Starbucks was. To do that he needed to gather intelligence, and to procure the intelligence, he used a three-pronged approach. First, he researched the product: coffee. He found that it was "... estimated that more than 3 billion cups of coffee were brewed around the world every day. Out of this, I figured that at least 2.7 billion of those cups sucked. In short, we faced a target-rich environment." Then he learned as much as he could about the customer. Finally, he gained a clear understanding of where Starbucks stood in the marketplace by doing market research.

This rich information then allowed Starbucks to avoid brand extensions that were tempting but very wrong for the company. Bedbury explains that the "Starbucks brand's core identity was less about engineering a great cup of coffee than about providing a great coffee experience," and so they took pains to attend to that philosophy. Because Starbucks knew its brand so well, it realized that offering punch cards or volume discounts would not be in line with its commitment to the customer. "We wanted to reward our customers with consistently better service, not a sometimes cheaper cup of coffee," says Bedbury. To dismiss a strategy most coffee companies use to compel customers to come back into stores might have been a mistake for another kind of company, but Starbucks knew its brand and its customers and made a choice that was unusual.

In addition to sharing his experiences working with these powerhouse brands, Bedbury teaches that every company should have one organizing principle: brand building. As opposed to looking at the brand as a message created by your marketing department, he believes brand building is a process that every part of the company must be centered around. As part of his eight universal principles of brand building, Bedbury lays out the core values that all brands should embody: simplicity, patience, relevance, accessibility, humanity, omnipresence, and innovation. Want a quick prescription for adding some humanity to your brand? Laugh at yourself; show genuine compassion; stand for something; listen and watch; admit your mistakes; find your soul; and become a more human employer.

"Relevance, simplicity, and humanity—not technology—will distinguish brands in the future."

What I found particularly revealing about *A New Brand World* was Bedbury's championing of two important aspects of brand—love and trust. Whether of a product or service, love and trust, he says, are crucial for brand building. Since the most aggressive advertising campaign cannot make a brand when a company or product lacks a soul or heart, both are required for marketing to resonate with consumers. Bedbury makes it clear that the best brands in fact started as great products or services. They don't come out of the gate as great brands, but once a brand is chosen by the public, an opportunity exists for you to let the rest of the world know about it.

In most books written about or by entrepreneurial superstars, you can get a general feel for the leaders of world-class brands or perhaps a glimpse at an industry at one moment in time. What Scott Bedbury gives us in addition is an in-the-trenches look at brand creation. **JC**

A New Brand World: 8 Principles for Achieving Brand Leadership in the 21st Century, Penguin, Paperback 2002, ISBN 9780142001905

WHERE TO NEXT? » Page 117 for **brands in black and white** » Page 147 for **using data across the organization** » Page 221 for **the case study in brand building** | EVEN MORE: *Lovemarks* by Kevin Roberts; *The Lovemarks Effect* by Kevin Roberts; *Pour Your Heart Into It* by Howard Schultz and Dori Jones Yang

Best-selling Business Books

We publish our Inc. | 800ceoread Business Book Bestseller List each month so readers can stay current with business book trends. But for a view of the overall best sellers in the business genre, we reached out to Nielsen BookScan.

The World Is Flat
2,371,394 copies

The Tipping Point
2,257,115 copies

Blink
2,167,343 copies

Freakonomics
2,035,431 copies

Good to Great
1,766,809 copies

Strengths Finder 2.0
1,415,054 copies

Who Moved My Cheese?
1,237,518 copies

Now, Discover Your Strengths
1,068,005 copies

The Five Dysfunctions of a Team
954,606 copies

Getting Things Done
669,709 copies

Data from Nielsen BookScan 1/4/04 to 11/14/10
Written by Aaron Schleicher

Selling the Invisible

HARRY BECKWITH

Reviewed by Jack

Harry Beckwith's contention is that it takes a completely different skill set to market a service versus a physical product. In his introduction, Beckwith talks about going through the Harvard Business School's catalog of marketing case studies and finding that, in 1997 when the book was written, one out of four case studies involved a service company. Looking at the Fortune 500 that included service companies, he discovered that three out of four Americans work in service companies. "In short, America is a service economy with a product marketing model. But services are not products, and service marketing is not product marketing."

With this thesis, Beckwith explains that *Selling the Invisible* is "not a how-to book, although it contains many concrete suggestions. Instead, this is a how-to-think-about book." He asserts that the key to service marketing is the *quality* of the service being provided, despite people's wrong assumption that marketing is what is *said* about a service. In fact, Beckwith concludes that you may not have to *say* anything about your service if the quality really shines. With this focus on quality in mind, Beckwith recommends taking the following fundamental steps: "defining what business you *really* are in and what people *really* are buying, positioning your service, understanding prospects and buying behavior, and communicating."

Pretty straightforward stuff, but the delivery is refreshing. His chapters are like bright flashes, some less than a page in length. In the "Getting Started" section is a chapter called "The Lake Wobegon Effect: Overestimating Yourself." Beckwith points out that we Americans have an inflated view of ourselves and, in turn, our businesses—much like in radio-host Garrison Keillor's fictitious Lake Wobegon, "'where the women are strong, the men are good-looking, and all the children are above average.'" This type of inflated opinion does not lead to self-examination, and, as a result, the odds are that our service is, at best, average. We should assume that our service is poor, which will force us to improve.

In the "Quick Fixes" section comes the chapter "Shoot the Message, Not the Messenger: The Fastest Way to Improve Your Sales Force." Beckwith tells the story of three top-notch salespeople who are capable of selling refrigerators to Eskimos, but they are struggling at a brokerage company. Beckwith explains that the company's selling problem is in fact a marketing problem. "The company has failed to create or identify the distinction that makes a selling message powerful, and that makes the salespeople true believers." Imagine a crack sales force struggling to sell something as nebulous as "good service." This is something our book company tried to do in countering Amazon's more concrete approach of promoting their ability to discount individual books. When prospective customers would call and ask, in not so many words, "Why should we use you?" we didn't have that powerful selling message. Not until we found a distinct advantage—our ability to customize any order—did "good service" become concrete for our consumers. Only then did we have a chance to turn a consumer into a customer. To successfully market a service business, you have to clearly identify the distinction of your offering because your service isn't intuitive to the customer.

In the section entitled "Anchors, Warts, and American Express" is a chapter called "Last Impressions Last." In it is an example: Charlie Brown noticed that Linus's shoes were nicely polished on the toes but the backs were all scuffed. After Charlie told Linus about this, Linus said he cared about what people thought about him when he entered a room but didn't care what they thought when he was leaving. Beckwith says that this is wrong. Many studies have pointed out that people remember the beginning *and* the end of an encounter and often forget the middle. If you want to make an impression concentrate as always on the first impression, but don't overlook your last.

The "Marketing Is Not a Department" section contains a chapter called "What Color Is Your Company's Parachute?" From the classic career book *What Color Is Your Parachute?* by Richard Boles comes the question "What am I good at?"—a question you need to ask yourself when looking for a new career. Beckwith thinks that when businesses ask themselves that same question, however, they often paint themselves into the corner of "We are an architectural firm." That general definition statement only results in a comparison between your business and all the other similar firms, and does not allow you to look for ways to differentiate your business. Often the areas of growth are outside your current industry description. "In planning your marketing, don't just think of your business. Think of your skills."

"The central fact of service marketing is this frustrating one: It is much easier to fail in a service than to succeed."

Harry Beckwith has done what many authors have tried to do but failed. He has found a patch of blue water—a place without a lot of competing products—and he has claimed it for his own. The book explains simply and understandably what you need to do to survive and thrive when marketing a service. Whether you are a lawyer or an accountant or a dry cleaner, this book will certainly change what you think about, just as Beckwith promises. **JC**

Selling the Invisible: A Field Guide to Modern Marketing, Business Plus, Hardcover First Edition 1997, ISBN 9780446520942

WHERE TO NEXT? « Page 92 for **companies with service at their core** » Page 240 for **starting a service-based business** » Page 215 for **a story of a service-based business** | EVEN MORE: *Ted Levitt on Marketing* by Ted Levitt; *Getting Everything You Can Out of All You've Got* by Jay Abraham; *The Invisible Touch* by Harry Beckwith

Zag

MARTY NEUMEIER
Reviewed by Jack

Our first books as children are filled with pictures and very little text, allowing us to learn visually. And our ability to learn from pictures doesn't disappear after we reach a certain age. In fact, I believe the use of pictures in business books is underrated and we will see more books employing this approach in the future. Marty Neumeier's marketing books have led the way in this trend. They are short, perfect for a plane ride, but they take a subject of great importance to every business—identity—and break it down into bite-size pieces by using pictures to emphasize the key points. Neumeier knows the effectiveness of pictures in communication. He began his career as a graphic designer and, in 1996, started *Critique*, a magazine about graphic design theory. He is now the president of a firm that specializes in "brand collaboration." Each of his books is excellent, though *Zag*'s message stands out.

Neumeier's broad but clear approach is conveyed even through the cover verbiage that calls the book "A Whiteboard Overview." *Zag* is high-concept and brilliant in its economy. Take Neumeier's display of six pictures, each featuring one pair of silhouettes conversing. In each picture, Neumeier conveys the most concise and effective explanation of advertising, marketing, and branding that I have seen. For example, his depiction of "Marketing" is a man telling a woman, "I am a great lover." But "Branding" is the woman saying to the man: "I understand you are a great lover." The difference is subtle but clear: branding is all about what your customer *understands* about your product or message and has nothing to do with what you are *telling* the customer.

Neumeier believes that consumers are being hammered with noise—or, using his word, clutter—about products and services. Because of all the clutter, you must differentiate—and not only differentiate, but embrace radical differentiation. As he puts it, "When everybody zigs, *zag*" (emphasis added).

Acknowledging that zagging is not instinctual for most of us, Neumeier spends the rest of the book giving you his ideas on implementation. One of the secrets to successful implementation is looking for "white space," the place nobody currently occupies. Most businesses understand the need for differentiation but struggle with the concept of radical differentiation. When Neumeier discusses radical differentiation, he means: "[If] ANYBODY'S doing it, you'd be crazy to do it yourself. You can't be a leader by following the leader. Instead, you have to find the spaces between the fielders. You have to find a zag."

"The quickest route to a zag is to look at what competitors do, then do something different. No—REALLY different."

Neumeier presents a process for differentiation by including chapters to help you find, design, build, and renew your zag. Established companies can reposition their brand or learn where to take the brand after launching it. But, Neumeier says, to do that you need to know where your company is within the "competition cycle." He uses the child's game of Rock Paper Scissors as an analogy to show the way large, medium, and small organizations go through that cycle. Start-ups are "scissor" companies and grow because of their sharp focus. They grow by taking "white space" from larger "paper" companies because they can move more quickly to market or the large business is too busy to notice. The small business eventually morphs into a "rock" or medium-sized business. Rocks thrive by crushing scissor companies that don't have the resources to compete. Eventually, rocks become paper companies that use their network and resources to smother rock companies. The Rock Paper Scissors analogy beautifully illustrates how companies of different sizes transition between cycles and how the strengths and weaknesses of those companies change over time.

In the final chapter, called "Take-Home Lessons," Neumeier summarizes each chapter with a short paragraph, describing its key points. This approach offers a helpful summary and serves as a future refresher.

He also includes a list of recommended reading, offering concise, one-paragraph descriptions along with all the information you need to find the suggested book.

Zag is an unconventional book with an unconventional message. It is a potent and enjoyable zag for business books as well. **JC**

Zag: The #1 Strategy of High-Performance Brands, New Riders, Paperback 2007, ISBN 9780321426772

WHERE TO NEXT? ›› Page 281 for **another book with pretty pictures** ›› Page 284 for **learning to make cool stuff** ›› Page 193 for **Marty's method of client collaboration** | EVEN MORE: *The Brand Gap* by Marty Neumeier; *The 22 Immutable Laws of Branding* by Al Ries and Laura Ries; *Brand Sense* by Martin Lindstrom

Crossing the Chasm

GEOFFREY A. MOORE
Reviewed by Todd

In the late 1950s, sociologists developed a bell-shaped curve to describe how farmers adopted new varieties of potatoes. In this initial study, five distinct groups were identified, each adopting the change at different degrees of acceptance. The new techniques were first enthusiastically embraced by a small group of leading-edge innovators, followed by a larger group of early adopters. As the innovation spread, the bulk of farmers, the early majority and late majority, changed their planting practices. Laggards were the last to commit to any change, and often did only when there was no other option. In 1962, Everett Rogers popularized and expanded this framework to broader trends of consumerism and change in his landmark book *Diffusion of Innovations*, and the technology sector has long used this paradigm to describe the adoption of products and services.

Geoffrey Moore published an important caveat in 1991 with *Crossing the Chasm*. The conventional marketing wisdom instructed companies to build momentum in each segment of the adoption curve and use that to energize the next group along the curve. Moore's research confirmed small acceptance gaps between each of the groups, but his true insight was the discovery of a chasm between early adopters and the early majority.

With the discovery of this chasm, Moore was finally able to explain the difficulties many early-stage technology companies experience with this discovery. Just as start-ups feel they are gaining traction due to success in the early markets, the initial revenue growth starts to flatten and the companies start to burn through cash. Firms find themselves unable to leverage the reputation and word-of-mouth they accumulated with the early groups as they sell into the early majority because the chasm that separates the two groups is one of opposing motivations.

Customers who are early adopters approach technology as an opportunity to upstage their personal competition and bring change to the companies they work for. The early majority, in contrast, wants moderate improvements with reliable components. The early adopters want revolution; the pragmatic early majority wants evolution.

The chasm is crossed only with a D-Day–style invasion, Moore says. The potential customers in the early majority are quite satisfied with what they have. Moore implores invaders to strike at a single niche and concentrate all of their efforts on a single subset of customers. Only by creating a small beachhead in the early majority will there be the needed reference point for others in the early majority to feel comfortable in adopting a new product.

Moore is quite specific in the ways companies need to plan the attack. Niches are chosen based on the industry of an existing customer or an identifiable, inefficient operating method that can be improved. As an example of the latter case, Moore introduces Silicon Graphic, a manufacturer of high-performance computing solutions which targeted Hollywood by proposing their high-end workstations as a replacement for the physical editing of film stock.

"The chasm phenomenon . . . drives all emerging high-tech enterprises to a point of crisis where they must leave the relative safety of their established early market and go out in search of a new home in the mainstream."

Moore also believes you should build alliances and bring partners in to wage the war. Those of the early majority want compatibility with their existing purchases, plug-and-play accessories, and published how-to manuals waiting for them when they sign the check.

For those who read the original 1991 edition of *Crossing the Chasm*, the 1999 revised paperback may be worth a second read. Moore rewrote most of the anecdotes and introduced a new set of companies trying to cross the chasm. But even more interesting are his descriptions of how companies use this knowledge. Some companies now piggyback on the success of others' crossings; Moore points to Netscape's successful chasm crossing and Microsoft's follow-up in the Internet browser market. He even discusses companies that are building strategies to deter and foil chasm crossings.

Crossing the Chasm addresses major change events and references the experiences of many high-tech companies, so the book is laden with tech-speak and insider acronyms. I only mention it as fair warning, but in no way should that deter you. Moore's hypothesis is about change and the naturally varying receptivity to it. I'll bet there is some change you are trying to get adopted, and there are more than a few lessons in *Crossing the Chasm* for change agents and the challenges you face. TS

Crossing the Chasm: Marketing and Selling Disruptive Products to Mainstream Customers, Collins, Paperback Business Essentials Edition 2006, ISBN 9780060517120

WHERE TO NEXT? » Page 229 for **starting your high-tech company** « Page 9 for **how geeks manage their lives** » Page 209 for **the start of a great tech company** | EVEN MORE: *The Change Function* by Pip Coburn; *Dealing with Darwin* by Geoffrey A. Moore; *The Cluetrain Manifesto* by Christopher Locke, Rick Levine, Doc Searls, and David Weinberger; *The Long Tail* by Chris Anderson

Secrets of Closing the Sale

ZIG ZIGLAR
Reviewed by Jack

I have been a salesman all my life. I started with a newspaper route, then ran a record store, and now I've been selling books for more than twenty-five years. That said, I have always considered salespeople who talk about "closing" and "techniques" akin to the snake-oil salesmen of old. My approach has been more instinctual, perhaps even more humanistic: if people aren't interested in what I have to offer, the problem is with my offering, not my presentation or close. But even the greatest natural technicians (and I am not referring to me) can benefit from study and practice, and for that, Zig Ziglar's book, *Secrets of Closing the Sale*, is essential reading.

Ziglar tells us that selling and closing are not mysteries to be solved; instead they are as tangible as when his wife up-sold him on a new house. Even a visit to his dentist illuminated this for Ziglar: he noticed that the dentist and his staff used predominantly positive words during that visit—words like restoration instead of filling; reception room instead of waiting room; discomfort or pressure instead of pain; and confirm or verify an appointment instead of remind. Words make a difference, and spin matters—so much so that Ziglar lists the twenty-four words that "sell" (like proven, health, easy, and discovery) and the twenty-four words that "unsell" (like deal, pay, contract, and sign). Just check out any late-night infomercial to see these methods in action.

Despite its name, the book unveils truths and approaches applicable to the entire sales process, with a focus on the close. Certainly the close is the key part of a sale, but in order to close, one must understand aspects like the attitude of selling, dealing with objections, and then the psychology of the closing. *Secrets of Closing the Deal* breaks the sales process into its component parts and thus is the perfect reference guide for every new salesperson.

Guides to selling are a dime a dozen, but the heart of this book lies in a series of entertaining stories Ziglar tells to demonstrate the many aspects of selling. I found one story particularly amusing. During a rainstorm, he pulled into a gas station and learned that the owner considered rainstorms to be fortuitous. The rain washed nails and other debris onto the road, which led to flat tires—and increased business. The owner had on staff a great tire changer who actually made his customers' visit pleasant. " 'There's nothing I can do about the rain falling, but there is a lot I can do about solving people's problems when that rain does fall,' " the owner explains. Ziglar shows through this story how it pays to know your customers, treat them right, and still take advantage of opportunity.

"The prospect is persuaded more by the depth of your conviction than he is by the height of your logic."

Throughout the book, Ziglar is your personal sales instructor. He asks you to get a pen and notepad in hand as you begin to read, because he wants readers to treat his book as a manual, almost an academic text. I've certainly marked up my copy with notes over the years. Yet this book is anything but an academic read. Each page is loaded with pithy sayings that might be just the nudge you need to take that next step toward improvement. Here are a few examples:

- "The prospect is persuaded more by the depth of your conviction than he is by the height of your logic."
- "You don't sell what the product is—you sell what the product does."
- "Spectacular achievement is always preceded by unspectacular preparation."
- "Your business is never really good or bad 'out there.' Your business is either good or bad right between your own two ears."

Ziglar's goal is to inspire and instruct us on how to refine our daily sales activity. The overall message in this book encourages you to stick to the basics. We sometimes overthink what is as inherently human as the sales process, and this is the book you need to stay focused on those basics. Sometimes a book's value is in its ability to get you back on track or to show you a better way to do your daily work. Zig Ziglar's classic, practical advice from an acknowledged master fits that criteria perfectly. **JC**

Secrets of Closing the Sale, Fleming H. Revell, Paperback 2006, ISBN 9780800759759

WHERE TO NEXT? « Page 24 to **swim with a shark** » Page 243 to **swing with a guerrilla marketer** » Page 136 to **see a purple cow** | EVEN MORE: *How to Master the Art of Selling* by Tom Hopkins; *The Sales Bible* by Jeffrey Gitomer; *Cold Calling Techniques (That Really Work!)* by Stephan Schiffman

Selling

on the Silver Screen

These films capture our attention because they deal with the very real issues of honesty, competition, and self-worth prevalent in the sales profession.

The Big Kahuna [1999]

Anyone who has attended an industry convention will relate to this movie. Kevin Spacey and Danny DeVito just need to land the hot account and the company will be saved. Things become complicated when a greenhorn from HQ balks at using a personal connection to reel this one in. Some will find the movie slow (the entire film takes place in the company hospitality suite with those three characters), but the dialogue is clever and engaging. This movie shows how we are all selling something.

The Boiler Room [2000]

Proponents of cold calling are going to point to this film as proof that it works. The main character, played by Giovanni Ribisi, is pulled into a stockbroker firm that uses high-pressure sales tactics on its customers (and employees). *Wall Street*, a celebration of greed and ruthlessness, is considered a training film at this company.

Death of a Salesman [1985]

This Arthur Miller play is a classic in American theater. What we witness through this story is the destructive side of holding onto dreams—dreams for yourself and dreams for those around you. Dustin Hoffman plays the role of Willy Loman in this TV adaptation recorded after its Broadway run in 1984.

Glengarry Glen Ross [1992]

A masterpiece by David Mamet, this play is all about motivation and what happens when you take reward and punishment to the extreme. The corporate sales manager rolls into town and sets up the latest sales contest—the winner gets a Cadillac, the losers get fired. How's that for motivation? The cast is peerless—Jack Lemmon, Al Pacino, Ed Harris, Alan Arkin, Kevin Spacey, and Alec Baldwin.

Tin Men [1987]

Danny DeVito and Richard Dreyfuss play competing aluminum siding salesmen—a profession whose days are numbered—in 1960s Baltimore. Their less-than-ethical sales tactics have caught the attention of the city. Neither of these characters have the bravado or charisma of those in the other films listed; they are just regular folks who you will recognize. We think it makes this movie the most believable.

Written by Todd Sattersten

How to Become a Rainmaker

JEFFREY J. FOX
Reviewed by Jack

How to Become a Rainmaker will help you recharge your sales force, or, as the book did for me, return your focus to the people who pay the bills: the customer. That quality—the nudge this book gives me when I stray from the most essential goals—places it very near to my heart. I wrote one of my first "Jack Covert Selects" reviews on this book when it came out in 2000. It was a fortuitous match. At the time, our business was struggling in the shadow of Amazon, which was emerging as a new powerhouse in the book business. Through Fox's book, I quickly learned that I had forgotten the basic needs of my company: happy customers who wanted to buy what we could provide. Seems obvious, but this is the kind of insight Fox presents in this book: simple but always valuable. Each of the 160 pages contains easily digestible, practical advice for the sales professional who knows that life is nothing but selling—either yourself or a commodity.

A rainmaker is a person who brings the revenue into an organization. What this book offers are strategies for maximizing your success as a rainmaker. Here's an example from the chapter on "Why Breakfast Meetings Bring Rain": You do a breakfast meeting because: (1) breakfasts are the least expensive meal—the selection is simple so a minimum of thought is needed and no alcoholic beverages are a temptation; (2) breakfast saves time—try to set up the meeting on the customer's way to work; (3) breakfast meetings are canceled less because the problems of the day are out of the picture. (Often rainmakers have two breakfast meetings per day.)

This book presents some of the best act-on-it-today advice that will immediately change the way you do business. Under the heading "Don't Drink Coffee on a Sales Call," Fox explains that because the average sales call runs only eighteen to twenty minutes, you don't want to be distracted from your presentation, and, as he says, "You can't take notes with a coffee cup in your hand." In the chapter "Be the Best-Dressed Person You Will Meet Today," Fox asserts that it is important to dress better than your client (though don't overdress) to make them feel that you are professional, confident, successful. "Dressing with care flatters your customer. . . . Your respect for your customer will show, and your customer will appreciate it; your customer will reelect you, sale after sale." It is not often that we think about how our customers see us, especially if they are people we have worked with for some time. And I would take this a step further. I would add to Fox's advice that dressing with care in the workplace shows that you respect your work. And your employees or coworkers will appreciate, and maybe even be influenced by, your effort.

"[T]he paramount job of every single employee in an organization is to, directly or indirectly, get and keep customers."

I've given a copy of this book to every newbie sales associate who begins in my company; there is no limit to its practical application. And whether you are an old-line sales manager, a C-level manager, or a college graduate looking for a job, *How to Become a Rainmaker* speaks a language of sales that will turn the oft-cited cliché "when it rains, it pours" on its head. **JC**

How to Become a Rainmaker: The Rules for Getting and Keeping Customers and Clients, Hyperion, Hardcover 2000, ISBN 9780786865956

WHERE TO NEXT? « Page 15 for **how to be a star** « Page 24 for **how to compete** » Page 261 for **how corporate sales forces work** | EVEN MORE: *Hug Your Customers* by Jack Mitchell; *Secrets of Great Rainmakers* by Jeffrey J. Fox; *The Rainmaker's Toolkit* by Harry Mills

Why We Buy

PACO UNDERHILL

Reviewed by Jack

Several careers ago, I owned a record store. Often I would sit behind the counter and watch my customers, trying to decipher their buying habits. For example, did they respond to a certain color or style of album cover to make their final choice? I did not know then that there was a "science" to my customers' interests, but I sure could have used this book, *Why We Buy*.

Twenty-five years ago, self-proclaimed urban geographer and retail anthropologist Paco Underhill founded a company called Envirosell that basically observes people shopping. His company then advises organizations, from banks to The Gap, on how to best communicate with their customers and ultimately sell more "stuff," the goal for all retail organizations. Underhill's science of shopping involves "trackers," whom he calls the field researchers of the science. These trackers stealthily follow shoppers through a store, noting on a paper form everything the shopper does. With the help of video, they personally measure "close to nine hundred different aspects of shopper-store interaction." Their findings are then factored into store design, signage, and product placement. Underhill took this rich material and wrote *Why We Buy* based on the mechanics, demographics, and, finally, the dynamics of shopping.

Underhill sets the scene by detailing the current problems in retail. Many experts agree that the marketplace is "overretailed." Retailers are opening stores not to find or to service new customers, but to directly compete with their competitors. With the decline of newspapers and the increase of information via the Web, it is becoming harder and harder to convince people to buy your product from *you*. Decisions are made with much less consideration of brand. In the past, there were Buick people, but not anymore. Now, there are "best deal" or "smartest buy" people.

While the state of retail is indeed under siege, Underhill is fundamentally concerned with what takes place once a customer is in the store. He claims compellingly that the most important way to communicate with your customer and to close the sale is to have people on the floor talking to and assisting shoppers. Underhill's studies show that the longer shoppers stay in your store, the more they buy. Engaging shoppers and listening to their needs is still the age-old solution to success.

In many ways, Underhill's message is to leave nothing to chance. Make sure there is a strategy to everything you do in your store to maximize that sale. Because the trackers are on the store floors and their observations are retold here, the book is loaded with practical advice. The author shares the following story about a Bloomingdale's store in New York that evidenced the importance of flow and merchandising. There was a rack of neckties close to one of the main entrances, and as the store got busier, people looking at the ties were jostled and bumped because the aisle was narrow. Quite quickly the shoppers moved on without choosing a tie. This phenomenon became known as the "butt brush." The trackers observed that women especially didn't like to be jostled from behind, and would abandon their quest when it happened. Sales were being lost by the placement of that rack; the same effect can happen in any narrow aisle.

"Why not take the tools of the urban anthropologist and use them to study how people interact with the retail environment?"

As much as Underhill's advice can be about opportunity lost, the right location for a product can stimulate sales. At the grocery store, dog treats are bought mostly by senior citizens and kids because these people are more likely to buy a little extra for their dog. Yet the treats are often stocked at the top of the store shelves. The trackers suggested moving the treats to a lower level and sales went way up. This is a lesson that can have broader application as retailers consider, for example, how to plan for aging baby boomers. Accurate product placement makes the buying process easier for the customer. The retail environment is about physics and mechanics, and how your customers touch things can gravely impact their desire to buy.

The real strength of *Why We Buy* is the relevance of each "Why didn't I think of that?" scenario. But the book isn't simply anecdotal; Underhill's data is meticulously gathered by Envirosell experts, and will provide you with the tools to determine what your customer really wants. One intriguing point Underhill makes is that he feels the Internet can never truly replace the experience of the physical act of shopping. Retailers must, however, listen to the customer and make even the smallest change that could keep a customer either in the store or coming back. As a brick-and-mortar retailer for many years, I immerse myself in this book time and again, and am always surprised by how many stores get the simple things so wrong. **JC**

Why We Buy: The Science of Shopping, Simon & Schuster, Paperback 1999, ISBN 9780684849140

WHERE TO NEXT? » Page 218 for **where we buy** » Page 132 for **what we buy** | EVEN MORE: *Trading Up* by Michael J. Silverstein and Neil Fiske; *Being the Shopper* by Phil Lempert; *The Culture Code* by Clotaire Rapaille

The Experience Economy

B. JOSEPH PINE II AND JAMES H. GILMORE
Reviewed by Todd

The Hard Rock Cafe, Disney World, and Starbucks all deliver more than food and drink. These establishments create theatre—the script, the props, and the actors all synced to create memorable experiences. The $3 latte or $75 park admission is just a sampling of what customers will pay for help in creating memories.

Consider the evolution of the birthday party. There was a time when birthday cakes were made from scratch by mothers using flour, eggs, sugar, and milk. But I grew up in the seventies and I remember my mom making cakes from inexpensive, time-saving packaged mixes bought at the grocery store. For the couple of big gatherings in my teenage years, it was a trip to the bakery to pick up the yellow sheet cake with "Happy Birthday, Todd" in custom frosting. When my son Ethan turned four, we gathered his friends at Chuck E. Cheese's for pizza, cake, and electronic games. For the next year, whenever anyone asked him his age, he would say, "I'm four years old and I had my birthday party at Chuck E. Cheese's." Could there be a better commercial? There was no question about the dramatic effect it had on him (or the expectations it created for subsequent celebrations).

Joseph Pine and James Gilmore use the birthday party example in *The Experience Economy* to illustrate a progression of economic value from commodities to goods and services, and now to experiences. The cost of ingredients for a cake might be a few dollars, but purchase a birthday experience and the receipt will be twenty to fifty times that amount. And parents are willing to pay that premium because they receive huge perceived value in providing a fun and flawless party for their child. Companies are also able to maintain premium pricing because of the ease of creating experiences distinctive from their competitors'. The authors' analysis of gross domestic product and employment bears this out, showing experiences growing faster in both categories than goods or services in the overall economy.

Like all good consultants, Pine and Gilmore provide a 2 × 2 matrix for evaluating experiences. On one axis is the level of guest participation and on the other is the connection the guest has with the event or performance. *Entertainment* is the oldest and most familiar of the four "experience realms," where the audience is watching passively, absorbing the performance. A similar level of absorption but higher level of participation creates an *educational* experience, like one provided by the hands-on exhibits at a children's museum. An *escapist* experience describes a visit to a Las Vegas casino or an Internet chat room, where the participant is completely immersed and actively participating. The *esthetic* experience is also familiar, whether it's a visit to the Guggenheim or outdoor retailer Cabela's for high immersion and low physical involvement. The goal is to incorporate all four realms and eliminate activities that don't fit within any of them.

"Those businesses that relegate themselves to the diminishing world of goods and services will be rendered irrelevant. To avoid this fate, you must learn to stage a rich, compelling experience."

Creating experiences is not a new endeavor. The authors draw on the arts—in particular theatre—as a model for business. The performance itself is the offering, the value created. The model grows as human resources become the casting department and the director's role resembles a more dynamic version of the typical project manager. Disney has long borrowed this language to convey to its "cast" what their role is in making memorable experiences for their "guests."

Published in 1999, the book captured early on the trend of customers demanding more experiences. Consider our industry of bookselling. Barnes & Noble's CEO Leonard Riggio is quoted in *The Experience Economy* describing his superstores as theatres for social experiences. Amazon has experienced tremendous growth by creating its own unique experience, using personalized recommendations based on past purchases, customer participation in the form of reviews and wish lists, and unparalleled product selection impossible to replicate in retail. And today, digital book readers and tablets such as Apple's iPad now compete for which provides the best reading experience.

Maybe your business needs a new script; *The Experience Economy*—now in 2011 with an Updated Edition with new ideas, new frameworks, and many, many new exemplars—will show you there is a stage waiting. TS

The Experience Economy: Work Is Theatre and Every Business a Stage, Harvard Business School Press, Hardcover 1999, ISBN 9780875848198

WHERE TO NEXT? » Page 293 for **creating experiences** » Page 221 for **a company that's all about experiences** » Page 289 for **experiences we recommend** | EVEN MORE: *Improv Wisdom* by Patricia Ryan Madson; *On Caring* by Milton Mayeroff; *Performance Theory* by Richard Schechner

>1000 words

"A picture is worth a thousand words." It's a familiar adage usually trotted out in response to a piece of art or a photo of a guiltily grinning two-year-old with telltale smudges of chocolate around his mouth. But given the growing interest and overall effectiveness of visual thinking in business, it might be time to apply this truism to your next work project. Whether using pen and pencil or intricate technologies, visual thinking's worth lies in its ability to help communicate ideas.

Back of the Napkin
by Dan Roam

Roam says anyone can draw, and the simplicity and immediacy of pictures make them a powerful tool to discover and clarify ideas. Roam's Visual Thinking Codex lays out precisely what kind of pictures to use given the questions you are trying to answer.

Beyond Bullet Points
by Cliff Atkinson

Atkinson advocates using Aristotle's three-act story structure as the backbone for making better presentations in PowerPoint, advice that can also be applied when developing slide shows. He argues that we move too fast into creating the visuals before we even know what we want to tell the audience.

Resonate
by Nancy Duarte

Duarte and her company have produced presentations for renowned product launches and speaker presentations, such as Al Gore's *An Inconvenient Truth.* Anyone can tell a story, but how it's told—visually, sonically, physically, and linearly—is the key to true resonance, which in turn transforms your audience into active participants.

Wall Street Journal Guide to Information Graphics
by Dona W. Wong

This is a how-to book with a capital H. A follower of information graphics guru Edward Tufte, Wong stresses the importance of removing everything that distracts from the idea you are trying to communicate. Font, color, and chart forms are all discussed and displayed using the same simplicity she advocates.

Written by Todd Sattersten

Purple Cow

SETH GODIN
Reviewed by Todd

In 2003, *Purple Cow* changed my life.

Yes, it really was that dramatic for me. At the time, I was working with my father in his sheet metal fabrication business and trying to create awareness for the company. The subtitle of the book, *Transform Your Business by Being Remarkable*, offered the insight we needed to change our thinking. The market barely knew our little four-person shop existed and we needed a way to get some attention. We focused our marketing on a single industry segment, developed a remarkable marketing kit, and doubled our customer base in twelve months. All that from a book that came in a milk carton.

To understand *Purple Cow*, you have to start with that word: "remarkable." I am not talking about the synonym of the more commonly used "incredible" or "extraordinary." Godin meant remarkable as "worthy of remark"—an adjective to describe the ability of a product or service to inspire users to spread the word to someone else. "Wow!" is not enough. "Wow! Hey, Jack, did you see that?" is the goal—just as if you had spotted a real purple cow.

People talking to other people is more important than ever given that the "tried and true" tools marketers have been using for the last fifty years are becoming ineffective. TiVo has changed the world of television advertising: when was the last time you sat through a commercial break? The Internet has altered the effectiveness of print advertisement: readership is down for almost every print medium. Advertising imagery can be found now on every surface a person might glance at, from coffee cups to airplane tray tables to bathroom stall doors. All are desperate attempts to get our attention.

Accepting word of mouth as a legitimate marketing tool, *Purple Cow* propels the tactic one step further and inspires thinking about how to optimize this method for your business. People talking to people is essential, yes. But how do you control that medium or ignite the spreading of

the word? Godin suggests you concentrate on a small, specific set of people when developing your "purple cows." Cater to the early adopters in your market. These folks are willing to pay more than anyone else to say they were first to get it. You want the people who seek out a new restaurant every weekend because they want to be the first to tell their friends about it. You want the companies who believe in being the first to implement new technologies because they want to boast that they are on the cutting edge.

"My goal in *Purple Cow* is to make it clear that it is safer to be risky—to fortify your desire to make truly amazing things. Once you see that the old ways have nowhere to go other than down, it becomes even more imperative to create things worth talking about."

The marketing of *Purple* Cow itself is an outstanding example of theory put into practice. Godin printed 10,000 paperback versions of the book and put each copy inside a *Purple Cow*–themed milk carton. The nutritional information on the outside told you the serving size—the number of pages you would be consuming (152), the number of good examples (38), and the number of cow puns you would find in the book (14), among others. The final note on the carton told the real story: "Once opened, consume within seven days. And don't forget to share your copy with a co-worker."

Having been a columnist for *Fast Company* magazine for the previous four years, Godin had a built-in audience for his milk carton campaign. He offered his readers the milk carton for $5. The carton itself was designed to be sent in the mail and had a blank panel for the recipient's address. If readers wanted additional copies, the price was the same, but they had to buy them in quantities of twelve. The idea was that they would keep one or two and give the rest to friends. He sold out of the entire print run in nineteen days. The book has gone on to sell 250,000 copies since its 2003 publication.

Being remarkable doesn't come without problems. Word of mouth works only if customers talk to each other about what you do, but encouraging conversation invites both good and bad commentary. Or you may try many ideas that won't succeed, so you will need to overcome any sensitivity to failure (as will your bosses). But, there is no alternative. The only way you are going to grow your business, get the job you want, or see your cause get traction is to be remarkable, to stand out from the herd.

How many experiences did you have today that you are going to tell your five closest friends about? One? None? Now, think about the experiences your customers had today. Will they be raving to their friends? If your answer to the question is not a confident "yes," then it's time to do something remarkable. **TS**

Purple Cow: Transform Your Business by Being Remarkable, Portfolio, Hardcover 2002, ISBN 9781591840213

WHERE TO NEXT? » Page 326 for **making marketing stick** » Page 286 for **creating compelling ideas** | EVEN MORE: *The Big Moo* by Seth Godin and the Group of 33; *Creating Customer Evangelists* by Ben McConnell and Jackie Huba; *The Anatomy of Buzz* by Emanuel Rosen; *The Pursuit of WOW* by Tom Peters

The Tipping Point

MALCOLM GLADWELL

Reviewed by Jack

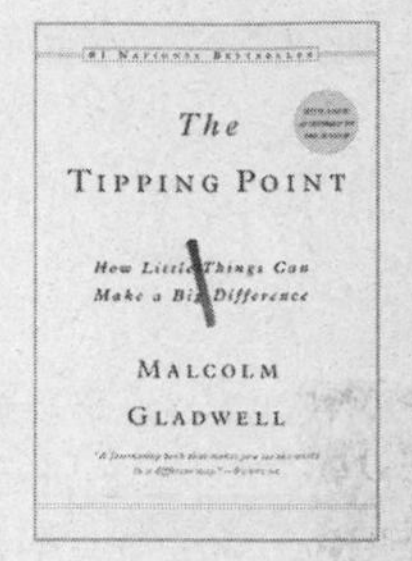

The Tipping Point begins with Gladwell's story of the resurgence of Hush Puppies' shoes as a fashionable trend. The brand's renaissance took place in the early 1990s when a small group of kids in the East Village of New York City started wearing them. By late 1994, the hip fashion designers were using them in their shows. Suddenly this somewhat tired shoe brand had become all the rage just when Wolverine, the shoe's manufacturer, was considering discontinuing the line because of weak sales. How did these nondescript oxford shoes explode onto the scene? To help the reader fully understand the phenomenon of Hush Puppies and the other examples he includes, Gladwell explains that "[i]deas and products and messages and behaviors spread just like viruses do." And once we understand the concept of viruses, we can understand just such epidemics.

In his introduction, Gladwell tells us that there are three principles of epidemics: contagiousness; little causes have big effects; and change happens not gradually but at one dramatic moment. To illustrate how epidemics grow and multiply through geometric progression, Gladwell uses a simple puzzle to help us understand exponential growth. He instructs: if you take a large sheet of paper and fold it over itself fifty times, the folded paper will reach almost to the sun. This exercise shows that while people are inherently gradualists, that is not how viruses spread. "To appreciate the power of epidemics, we have to abandon this expectation about proportionality. We need to prepare ourselves for the possibility that sometimes big changes follow from small events, and that sometimes these changes can happen very quickly."

In social epidemics, Gladwell presents three essentials to the phenomenon: the Law of the Few; the Stickiness Factor, and the Power of Context. The Law of the Few introduces us to three social groups; the Mavens, the Connectors, and the Salesmen. The Mavens are the "databank," brilliant people to whom we look for answers; Connectors are the "social

glue," those people who know people; and Salesmen are the people who have "the skills to persuade us when we are unconvinced of what we are hearing, and they are as critical to the tipping of word-of-mouth epidemics as the other two groups."

To explain the second essential, the Stickiness Factor, Gladwell offers examples that include my favorite about the television show *Blue's Clues*. To make sure the show resonates with the audience, researchers test every show three times before it goes on air, meeting with preschoolers every week to tweak the scripts. I just love the concept of going directly to your audience and using the data to create a product that is memorable, even if the changes are small.

The Broken Windows theory is an example of the third essential, the Power of Context, which argues that an epidemic does not occur in a vacuum. In the Broken Window theory, if a window of a building is broken and left unrepaired, people will conclude that nobody cares, nobody is in charge, and, as a result, more windows will be broken, leading to more crime in the vicinity. Gladwell uses David Gunn's work in overseeing a multibillion-dollar reclamation of the New York City subway system to show the reversal of just such a trend. In the 1980s, crime in NYC was at its highest level in history. The subway system was in a shambles, the cars were often covered with graffiti, and people were afraid to use the system. One of the first things David Gunn did was set up a plan to clean the graffiti off the subway cars and keep it off. The transit workers became almost obsessive about removing the graffiti: no car with graffiti would leave the yard. This cleaning of the cars showed riders that the system, the "broken window," was being fixed and the momentum of crime was interrupted.

"*The Tipping Point* is the biography of an idea, and the idea is very simple."

The Tipping Point is the type of book that helps us make sense of the world around us. It is a practical, nonacademic guide to the social epidemics going on around us, and perhaps to how we might take advantage of them. As people try to stay in step with a rapidly evolving business landscape, they are turning to journalistic books that bring the big picture into focus, like Thomas Friedman's *The World Is Flat*, Gladwell's next book, *Blink*, and Steven Levitt and Stephen Dubner's *Freakonomics*. Not

only is the context broader, but the writing is significantly better than that in traditional business books. *The Tipping Point* is the book that started this trend, perhaps its own epidemic, and continues to carry the banner as the best. **JC**

The Tipping Point: How Little Things Can Make a Big Difference, Back Bay Books, Paperback 2002, ISBN 9780316346627

WHERE TO NEXT? » Page 322 for **another *New Yorker* writer** » Page 326 for **a book inspired by this one** » Page 142 for **Gladwell's trading card** | EVEN MORE: *Blink* by Malcolm Gladwell; *Collapse* by Jared Diamond; *Freakonomics* by Steven D. Levitt and Stephen J. Dubner

FOUR {SUPER} POWERFUL WRITERS

MALCOLM GLADWELL

SUPERPOWER:

* * * **ENCHANTMENT** * * *

Writes for: *The New Yorker*

Famous for: An October 2000 *New Yorker* piece on Ron Popeil, called "The Pitchman," which won the National Magazine Award for Profiles; *The Tipping Point*, *Blink*, *What the Dog Saw*, and *Outliers*.

Flash of brilliance: "We don't know where our first impressions come from or precisely what they mean, so we don't always appreciate their fragility." (*Blink*)

* * * * * * * * *

CHARLES FISHMAN

SUPERPOWER:

* * * **INVESTIGATION** * * *

Writes for: *Fast Company*

Famous for: A December 2003 *Fast Company article* titled "The Wal-Mart You Don't Know," which won the 2004 Best Business Magazine Story award from the New York Press Club; *The Wal-Mart Effect*, and *The Big Thirst*.

Flash of brilliance: "In the end, of course, it is we as shoppers who have the power, and who have given that power to Wal-Mart. Part of Wal-Mart's dominance, part of its insight, and part of its arrogance, is that it presumes to speak for American shoppers." ("The Wal-Mart You Don't Know")

* * * * * * * * *

MICHAEL LEWIS

SUPERPOWER:

* * * **INTERPRETATION** * * *

Writes for: *New York Times Magazine*, *Vanity Fair*, and *Slate*

Famous for: A December 2005 *New York Times* article, "Coach Leach Goes Deep, Very Deep"; *Liar's Poker*, *Moneyball*, *The Blind Side*, and *The Big Short*.

Flash of brilliance: "[Coach Leach] thinks the team that wins is the team that moves fastest, and the team that moves fastest is the team that wants to. He believes that both failure and success slow players down, unless they will themselves not to slow down." ("Coach Leach Goes Deep, Very Deep")

* * * * * * * * *

DANIEL H. PINK

SUPERPOWER:

* * * **FORESIGHT** * * *

Writes for: *Wired*

Famous for: *A Whole New Mind*, *Free Agent Nation*, and *Drive*.

Flash of brilliance: "We are moving from an economy and a society built on the logical, linear, computerlike capabilities of the Information Age to an economy and a society built on the inventive, empathic, big-picture capabilities of what's rising in its place, the Conceptual Age." (*A Whole New Mind*)

* * * * * * * * *

Written by Rebecca Schlei

Little Red Book of Selling

JEFFREY GITOMER

Reviewed by Jack

At the risk of jumping feet first into an existential debate without the proper intellectual floatation device, I ask: "What can a book about selling really teach you about selling?" Selling is a pretty basic process, an elemental part of being. We have been selling to one another for as long as tribes have been bartering seeds and spices, for as long as babies have been smiling those innocent smiles that have us offering up our hearts for free. So shouldn't selling be a skill we all have programmed into our DNA? And if so, then why are there so many books and different approaches to selling? Perhaps it is because just as we are all innate salespeople, we are also skeptical buyers who don't want to be taken for a ride. So we need to continue to sharpen our skills and perfect our pitch to a public who has heard just about every proposal.

There is no better person to help us become better salespeople than Jeffrey Gitomer, who, if I'm a natural salesperson, is a sales savant. Jeffrey Gitomer is also a force of nature. His presentations are legendary. His intensity is off the chart. A syndicated columnist, he has a huge audience for his weekly e-mail newsletter, "Sales Caffeine." In *Little Red Book of Selling*, Gitomer has a book that perfectly represents his expertise and outsize personality. Printed on glossy paper, and sized nicely to fit into a pocket or carry-on bag, this book is the gold standard of how a book should look and feel. And it is a pleasure to read. Every page is stocked with advice and real-life scenarios usually summed up in a pithy and "streetwise" quote that summarizes the basics of selling. For example:

- If you can't get in front of the real decision maker, you suck.
- Kick your own ass.
- When you say it about yourself it's bragging. When someone else says it about you it's proof.

Gitomer acknowledges his aggressive and in-your-face tone by including this disclaimer: "If any of this is offensive, get out of sales as fast as you can and take a nice safe job with some big company where you can whine all day and complain about your low pay." He puts the responsibility for success or failure expressly on you, no escape, no excuses. After reading the book, you will feel profoundly empowered to make something happen, whether it is improving your voicemail message, your preparation for a presentation, or your ability to bounce back after rejection.

"People don't like to be sold, but they love to buy."

Selling for a living isn't for everyone, regardless of how often we use innate sales techniques to sell our points of view to others in our daily lives. What *Little Red Book of Selling* does for sales professionals is motivate you to get started on Monday morning or restarted after the profession wears you out. Between these two small red covers is a great sales philosophy that will improve your daily approach presented with a dash of spice and a whole lot of fun. **JC**

Little Red Book of Selling: 12.5 Principles of Sales Greatness, Bard Press, Hardcover 2004, ISBN 9781885167606

WHERE TO NEXT? » Page 261 for **seeing these principles in action** « Page 127 for **sharp sales techniques to add to your quiver** | EVEN MORE: *The Sales Bible* by Jeffrey Gitomer; *Cold Calling Techniques (That Really Work!)* by Stephan Schiffman; *SPIN Selling* by Neil Rackham

RULES AND SCOREKEEPING

How can you play the game if you don't know the rules?

Naked Economics

CHARLES WHEELAN
Reviewed by Todd

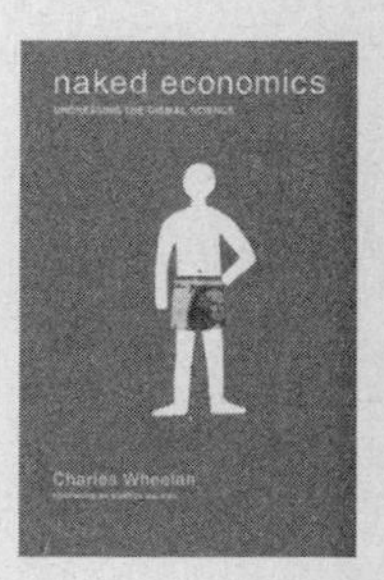

The most-often quoted sentence from Peter Drucker must be this one from his 1954 book, *The Practice of Management*: "There is only one valid definition of a business purpose: to create a customer." Here, Drucker found a simple way of saying what economists have said for a hundred years. In market-based economies, customers and firms are doing a dance. The former are looking to fulfill their own needs and desires, and the latter are trying to make a buck. So, if you find Drucker's insight illuminating, then Charles Wheelan's *Naked Economics* will provide your most refreshing economics lesson yet.

"Why did the chicken cross the road? Because it maximized his utility."

Many people have a hard time understanding economics, let alone finding a useful way to apply economics in their daily lives. Much of that has to do with Econ 101 courses gone bad—the supply and demand curves, anecdotes involving firearms and dairy products, the need to fill required courses in your university curriculum. But in his introduction Wheelan describes his intent to offer something different: "This book is not economics for dummies; it is economics for smart people who never studied economics (or have only a vague recollection of doing so)." You will not find graphs, equations, or incomprehensible terms in Wheelan's presentation of economics. Instead, you'll find him talking about how the The Gap determines what price to charge for its new wool sweaters. Or why Burger King has the nice note at the register that says you get a free meal if you don't get a receipt. Or what clean bathrooms, seven-days-a-week service, and consistently made hamburgers do for McDonald's restaurants. With each of these stories, Wheelan gets you thinking about concepts such as supply and demand, incentives, and information. The concepts become tangible and relevant to everyday life, and you find that economics can give us very useful information about how people and companies make decisions.

Wheelan starts his lesson with microeconomics, covering markets and incentives. Chapters 3 and 4 cover the role of government and how markets would have a hard time existing without government. There is a chapter on the economics of information as a transition to macroeconomics in the second half of the book. Productivity, financial markets, the Federal Reserve, and globalization round out the major topics. The epilogue takes a look ahead to 2050 and encourages readers to use some of their newly gained knowledge to think about potential problems that lie ahead.

This book delivers an entire college economics course, albeit an introductory one, in 228 pages. Wheelan moves quickly and covers an expanse of ground with the goal of exposing you to the not-so-dismal science and allowing you a look at the world around you through another lens. TS

Naked Economics: Undressing the Dismal Science, W.W. Norton & Company, Paperback 2002, ISBN 9780393324860

WHERE TO NEXT? » Page 271 for **application of economic theory** « Page 81 for **more application of economic theory** » Page 154 for **what the boss wants you to know** | EVEN MORE: *The Economic Naturalist* by Robert H. Frank; *New Ideas from Dead Economists* by Todd G. Buchholz; *The Undercover Economist* by Tim Harford

Financial Intelligence

KAREN BERMAN AND JOE KNIGHT WITH JOHN CASE

Reviewed by Todd

For as much press and as many op-ed columns as were dedicated to the collapse of Enron and WorldCom, the average American did not comprehend the magnitude nor the implications of those failures. If we are to truly understand business and the effects financial firms have on the world, we must understand the rules and the principles of accounting. What we need is *Financial Intelligence*.

Accounting is often likened to scorekeeping in the game of business, but that is a bad comparison. It perpetuates misconceptions about the role of bookkeeping. The 24/7/365 marketplace is much more complicated than a head-to-head matchup completed in 60 minutes of regulation time. A final score and the associated win or loss might be an able comparison to a company's net income, but net income is not the binary function of each goal line crossed or basket made. Instead, net income is more holistic, a mathematical function of costs subtracted from sales.

The underlying question always present in accounting is "When?" and the fundamental rule of accounting is the *matching principle*—the idea that sales and their associated costs should be reported together. This is where authors Karen Berman and Joe Knight, with their writing partner John Case, begin. The cash register ringing at your local bookstore records a sale and an associated expense for the book sold, the difference reported as profit. An equipment purchase like a new computer for the front counter is recorded as a series of monthly expenses, with the intention of accurately representing use over time. When companies get into trouble, their interpretation of the matching principle, the authors point out, is likely the source. In the case of WorldCom, everyday expenses like office *supplies* were being treated like office *buildings*, with their financial recognition delayed for decades.

As a manager looks over a set of financial statements, his understanding of the underlying assumptions for how a company has chosen to interpret the proper matching of sale to expense is essential. Knowing, for example, whether the revenue from an extended warranty is recognized in its entirety on the date of purchase or spread out over the subsequent months of the contract can affect everything from commissions for salespeople to calculation of product profitability to the decision to offer similar products in the future. These distinctions are not trivial concerns, and *Financial Intelligence* offers us the know-how with which to make educated decisions about the basics of business.

"Financial information is the nervous system of any business."

The authors use straightforward language throughout the book to explain income statements, balance sheets, and statements of cash flows. Terminology is defined, and common synonyms are provided, though the authors declare with pride that the words "debit" or "credit" do not appear anywhere within the pages of *Financial Intelligence*. They give the same plainspoken treatment to measurement ratios, such as return on assets and receivable days, that managers use routinely to assess the health of a firm.

The book's subtitle, *A Manager's Guide to Knowing What the Numbers Really Mean*, is the only misstep to be found in this well-constructed book. That positioning statement narrows too far the potential audience for *Financial Intelligence*. We wholeheartedly recommend this book for any employee, from service technician to shop floor manager, because it will allow every person to participate in a wider conversation about business. TS

Financial Intelligence: A Manager's Guide to Knowing What the Numbers Really Mean, Harvard Business School Press, Hardcover 2006, ISBN 9781591397649

WHERE TO NEXT? » Page 176 for **the power of sharing numbers** « Page 78 for **the strategy that creates great numbers** » Page 173 for **the knobs to turn** | EVEN MORE: *How to Read a Financial Report* by John A. Tracy; *Managing by the Numbers* by Chuck Kremer and Ron Rizzuto, with John Case

1982: WAKING A GIANT (GENRE)

The 1970s were a turbulent decade: Watergate, oil embargoes, the end of the Vietnam war, the beginning of the Iranian hostage crisis, staggering interest rates, the federal government "bailing out" Chrysler.

Out of the confusion left behind by the '70s came three books, each published in 1982, each directed to different audiences, each selling millions of copies, that defined the business wing of the book industry—and helped change business, for the better.

The One Minute Manager

by Kenneth H. Blanchard and Spencer Johnson

A bite-sized parable with applicable managerial techniques that spawned many sequels, including *Who Moved My Cheese?* Advice for new managers.

In Search of Excellence: Lessons from America's Best-Run Companies

by Thomas J. Peters and Robert H. Waterman Jr.

Introduced common attributes of successful organizations as defined by McKinsey research. Theory for senior-level executives.

Megatrends: Ten New Directions Transforming Our Lives

by John Naisbitt

Identified evolutionary trends such as shifts from an industrial to information society and from a national to a global economy. Inspiration for the futurist.

Less than three years later, the president, CEO, and chairman of the Chrysler Corporation, Lee Iacocca, wrote *Iacocca, An Autobiography,* a book that wove advice, theory, and inspiration into a riveting personal narrative about success. *Iacocca* became the best-selling nonfiction title for both 1984 and 1985. This sequence of releases validated business books as a genre and the industry has never looked back.

Written by Jack Covert, with Sally Haldorson

The Balanced Scorecard

ROBERT S. KAPLAN AND DAVID P. NORTON
Reviewed by Todd

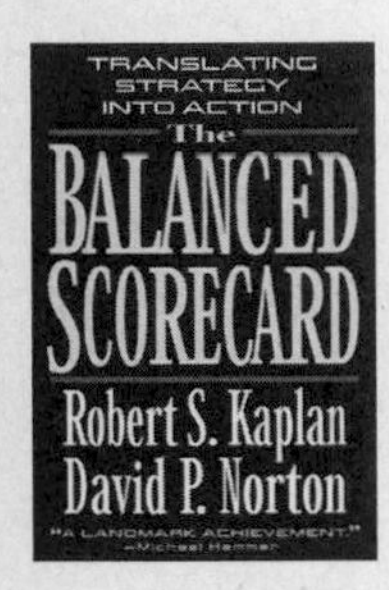

For more than a thousand years, the scientific method has served as the basis for technological advancement. Experience informs conjecture, educated guessing leads to hypothesis, and testing confirms or denies the prophecy. In business, strategy plays the part of hypothesis, as business leaders place their bets on what will work in the marketplace. Most executives fail to connect strategy and action, and when they do, they lack the measurements needed to prove success or failure. Authors Robert Kaplan and David Norton propose a more methodical metrics-based approach to link the two in their book *The Balanced Scorecard*.

The scorecard serves as a dashboard for how the company is operating, creating feedback mechanisms that align business strategy and the actions of management. First is a financial set of metrics that are common and are based on the life-cycle stage the business is in. So, growth companies focus on sales and market share while maturing firms watch unit costs and operating expenses. Customer metrics like satisfaction, retention, and share-of-wallet measure a company's value proposition. Next, a whole host of internal metrics brings focus to innovation, operations, and services—processes that provide customer and shareholder value. Finally, companies cannot deliver value without investing in the growth and development of its workers, so measurements like employee satisfaction gauge success.

"If you can't measure it, you can't manage it."

The authors report that most senior leadership teams settle on fifteen to twenty-five metrics but quickly find that 20 percent of metrics on new scorecards fail to have supporting data. "If data do not exist to support a measure, the management process for a key strategic objective is likely inadequate or nonexistent." The development process helps uncover gaps and oversights in aspects of the business that need attention.

The Balanced Scorecard is definitely the advanced class on scorekeeping. The process the authors propose must start at the top, with senior management defining an actionable strategy and vision for the company. The strategic measurements must be transferable down through the corporate hierarchy so that team goals and individual goals match the overall strategic goals. And feedback from the scorecard should provide a clear confirmation or denial of senior management's strategic hypotheses.

Poring over sales results, return-on-capital calculations, and cash flow projections is the preoccupation of almost every business leader. The appeal of *The Balanced Scorecard* is in the direct link that is created between top-level strategy and decision making at all levels of the organization. Rather than searching for unknown causes of unexpected results, executives can finally see the relationship between internal indicators, both leading and lagging, and the always-scrutinized financial results. TS

The Balanced Scorecard: Translating Strategy into Action, Harvard Business School Press, Hardcover 1996, ISBN 9780875846514

WHERE TO NEXT? « Page 149 for **the basics on financials** » Page 166 for **fourteen key management principles** » Page 286 for **using data-driven marketing**
| EVEN MORE: *The Strategy-Focused Organization* by Robert S. Kaplan and David P. Norton

What the CEO Wants You to Know

RAM CHARAN
Reviewed by Jack

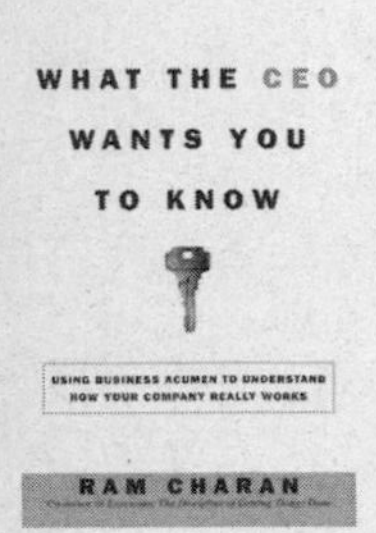

Like many American kids in the 1950s, I learned some basic business essentials via my paper route, such as having to collect payment from my customers before I could pay for the previous week's newspapers. I have carried these hard-won principles of making money with me my entire career. The growing pangs I suffered at every new business endeavor could have been lessened, however, if I'd had a copy of Ram Charan's *What the CEO Wants You to Know* in my bike basket or on the crowded counter of my record shop.

Ram Charan got his early education working in his family's shoe store in India. He moved from that shoe store to working for a gas utility in Australia, then to Harvard for an MBA and also his doctorate. The author is now an advisor to CEOs and senior employees in Fortune 500 companies. As an example of his heavyweight status, Charan was the first outsider Jeff Immelt turned to for advice when he took over GE following Jack Welch's departure. He is also the author or coauthor of many important business books including *The Leadership Pipeline* and *Every Business Is a Growth Business.*

What the CEO Wants You to Know, which runs a very readable 130 pages, offers a crash course in what Charan calls "business acumen." The first half of the book serves as a manual, explaining a set of financial metrics that managers value, such as return on assets and cash flow. Charan then includes sections on international business and getting things done, as well as an eight-page action plan geared toward project implementation.

Charan concludes his section on business acumen with a section called "Understanding Your Company's Total Business: How the Pieces Come Together." Charan reasons that it isn't enough to simply know the "elements of moneymaking" by rote. Instead, "people with business acumen don't memorize these words like terms in a textbook. They understand their real meaning, instinctively sense their relationships to one another, and use them to create a mental picture. True businesspeople combine the elements of moneymaking to get an intuitive grasp of the total business." Then a good leader can bravely face the complexities of the business world and set clear priorities for employees. Repeatedly, Charan warns, "Don't let your formal education or the size of your company obscure the simplicity of your business."

"Use this book to learn the language of business. Then put the book aside and practice until the fundamentals of business become instinctive, as they are for the street vendor."

Many people begin their business careers in one area of an organization, like accounting or marketing, and generally move up within that silo, and may believe that basic business principles aren't relevant to their specialty. Charan instead preaches that business acumen allows anyone to look at their organization holistically and make decisions for the common good of the organization. This is particularly important in a small business or in organizations that are committed to hiring within. So important, really, that new employees need only two things for their first day on the job: the company handbook and a copy of *What the CEO Wants You to Know*. JC

What the CEO Wants You to Know: How Your Company Really Works, Crown Business, Hardcover 2001, ISBN 9780609608395

WHERE TO NEXT? » Page 232 for **teaching at a small business level** « Page 149 for **how to understand financials** | EVEN MORE: *How to Read a Financial Report* by John A. Tracy; *The Personal MBA* by Josh Kaufman; *Managing by the Numbers* by Chuck Kremer and Ron Rizzuto with John Case

MANAGEMENT is the punching bag of the leadership crowd. They say the discipline is boring and uninspiring. The cool kids don't like admitting how essential it is to any organization. Management is the blocking and tackling of business, and the books that we think are the best address the interpersonal dynamics of groups both big and small. It's about time that management got a little respect.

The Essential Drucker

PETER F. DRUCKER

Reviewed by Jack

When we were choosing the books for the management section of our *100 Best* list, we both knew that Peter F. Drucker had to be represented. But which book to include? Though his name is often bandied about in business thought circles, Drucker's books are often considered too dense to tackle in order to access his invaluable ideas and observations. Since Drucker wrote thirty-nine volumes on everything from business management to entrepreneurship to nonprofits, the options can be somewhat overwhelming.

Now, as a music fan (some might say obsessed music fan), I would never recommend purchasing a "Greatest Hits" CD. The problem with these types of collections is that they miss the nuances of the complete package the artist intended when he or she created the original album. I find this to be true of iTunes and other "singles" sources too, because listeners can pick and choose the tracks they already know. Many times I have found my favorite track only after listening to an entire CD multiple times—and I highly value that opportunity for discovery. Regardless, *The Essential Drucker*, indeed a "Greatest Hits" collection of sorts, is a must-read because the entire body of Drucker's work is a tall mountain to scale. While I, as a self-described music snob, may not run out to buy *The Best of Mahler*, there is something to be said for making academic literature accessible to the common reader, and that is what *The Essential Drucker* does for this brilliant man's work.

The genesis of *The Essential Drucker* occurred when Drucker's longtime Japanese editor and good friend Atsuo Ueda, who had retired from publishing and gone into teaching, needed an abridged version for his students to read. The resulting collection was published in Japan in 2000. However, even abridged, it ran three volumes. The American edition published in 2001 was edited down to one volume. Mr. Drucker approved of the edited compilation as a good overview of his work.

The Essential Drucker is organized around the three emphases that

Drucker focused on throughout his career: Management, the Individual, and Society. He was intensely interested in the role people play in organizations. Each chapter within these sections is derived from a single Drucker book, and a curious reader will be able go back to the source book to delve more deeply into the subject. While excerpting from only ten of Drucker's thirty-nine books, the editor acknowledges that there are five other books that could have been included but which are more technical, and therefore not included in a book meant to introduce Drucker essentials.

"Business management must always, in every decision and action, put economic performance first."

Clearly, the man was prolific, but what makes the late Mr. Drucker's writings so important? I read a ton of business books, but reading Drucker is a different kind of experience. His passages require multiple readings, not because the writing is hard to understand, but because every single word is chosen with care to optimize the point he wishes to make. His sentences are sculpted, and the thoughts are read-out-loud important. If you usually read a book with a highlighter to help remember key thoughts, you might be better served to only highlight the words that you *don't* want to remember, because there are far fewer of those and you will save money on pens.

For example, Drucker says that the purpose of a business is to create a customer. Simple. He states that a business enterprise has only two basic functions: marketing and innovation. Important. In the chapter on time management, he presents a strategy I have used many times when writing reviews or other important memos, and I have found it very effective. He suggests that when you have a large writing project, you should go heads down and write a "zero draft"—which is very rough—even before the first draft. The "zero draft" will generally take much less time, and then you can edit and revise the piece in short chunks of time—which are always easier to find. Practical. Yes, these are simple concepts, but the meat is in the implementation. As managers and leaders, we realize that every business has a different way of going to market, but this little volume offers essential concepts everyone can implement in their individual organizations.

Ask those you know who have a business degree and you will be astonished by the number who say they have not read Drucker. Beginning his career as a journalist, this was a man who never stopped writing, never stopped observing, and his insights were always well-founded in industry dynamics. This is not to say his books aren't daunting, and that is why we recommend *The Essential Drucker* as an access point to a world of unparalleled reflection on this pursuit we call business. **JC**

The Essential Drucker: The Best of Sixty Years of Peter Drucker's Essential Writings on Management, Collins, Paperback Business Essentials Edition 2008, ISBN 9780061345012

WHERE TO NEXT? « Page 12 for **the other Drucker book on our list** » Page 204 for **the subject of Drucker's first case study** « Page 98 for **an irreverent look at management** | EVEN MORE: *The Daily Drucker* by Peter F. Drucker; *Adventures of a Bystander* by Peter F. Drucker (his autobiography); *The Last of All Possible Worlds* by Peter F. Drucker (one of his two works of fiction)

PETER DRUCKER SAID . . .

"There is only one valid definition of business purpose: to create a customer."

The Practice of Management (1954)

Out of the Crisis

W. EDWARDS DEMING

Reviewed by Jack

On a summer Saturday night in 1980, in the back of a motor home in the wilds of Michigan, I watched a documentary on NBC called "If Japan Can . . . Why Can't We?" The documentary was about how Japanese manufacturing was growing at an amazing rate while U.S. firms were struggling. Despite spotty ratings, this documentary has been generally credited with sparking the quality movement in the United States. It also introduced the United States to an octogenarian mathematician, statistician, and musician: Dr. William Edwards Deming. Rumor has it that Donald Petersen, president and COO of Ford Motor Company, was also watching that show (likely *not* in the North Woods) and hired Deming to help dig the giant auto company out of a severe decline. The Ford Taurus and Mercury Sable arrived in 1985, and Deming helped change the Ford culture to "Quality Is Our Number One Priority."

Deming was eighty years old when that show was aired, but he was changing the face of business long before his contribution to Ford. During the 1940 census, the government used a sampling technique that Deming developed. As a result of this experience, after World War II, the government sent Deming to Japan to help rebuild that country's industrial infrastructure. There he found a receptive audience for new tools to improve manufacturing processes as the country tried to restart its industry. In appreciation of his work there, a prize was created to commemorate Deming's contribution and to promote the continued development of quality control in Japan. The influence of Deming's philosophy in Japan was unprecedented and continues today, though he did not get this same level of appreciation in the United States.

In the States, to help spread the word and to explain the concepts of the quality movement, Deming published *Quality, Productivity, and Competitive Position* in 1982, renamed *Out of the Crisis* in 1986. This landmark book is the culmination of over fifty years of experience. The centerpiece of the book is Deming's "14 Points," which enumerate key management principles. Though Deming's background was mathematics and statistics, over time Deming came to believe that what was important were the people in the process, and that management had incredible amounts of control over the output of an organization.

"Improvement of quality transfers waste of man-hours and of machine-time into the manufacture of good product and better service."

Take, for example, Deming's classic "Red Bead" experiment. He was known to bring audience members on stage and tell them that their task was to deliver white beads, and only white beads, to a fictitious customer. Each audience member was blindfolded and instructed to draw fifty beads from a large bowl filled with both red and white beads. Each "employee's" output was then recorded, noting the number of white and red beads drawn. With each draw, Deming would use the methods that management might try to influence results: awards for those who did well, intimidation directed at those who did poorly. Clearly, anyone who witnessed this exercise would see the futility of these managerial techniques. Though the customer will not accept any red beads, it is inevitable that some percentage of red beads will be drawn. The conclusion is that one's performance is a direct result of what one is given to work with rather than of any external influence. Thus, the people who draw more red beads are not poorer employees and should not be docked pay or receive other consequences based on their performance. The job of management is to improve the process, to increase the likelihood that an employee will draw white beads.

Red beads are the result of a bad system. "The worker is not the problem," Deming is well known to have said. "The problem is at the top! Management!" He discussed his views on the role of management in a 1993 article published by the *New Economics for Industry, Government, and Education*. Deming explains his theory of the role of management as follows: "It is management's job to direct the efforts of all components toward the aim of the system. The first step is clarification: everyone in the organization must understand the aim of the system, and how to direct his efforts toward it. Everyone must understand the damage and loss to the whole organization from a team that seeks to become a selfish, independent, profit center." With these statements, Deming makes clear how connected the concept of team is to the quality movement.

Out of the Crisis walks the tightrope between the science of statistics and process and the art of management. Within its pages, the book gives testimony to the genius of Deming, whose message began to get traction in America only after his death in the early 1990s. JC

Out of the Crisis, MIT Press, Paperback 2000, ISBN 9780262541152

WHERE TO NEXT? » Page 196 for **more on teams** « Page 92 for **wiring service into your group's DNA** » Page 319 for **the dark side of quality** | EVEN MORE: *The Deming Management Method* by Mary Walton; *Juran on Quality by Design* by J. M. Juran; *Understanding Statistical Process Control* by Donald J. Wheeler and David S. Chambers

Deming's 14 Points of Management

1.
Create constancy of purpose for the improvement of product and service, with the aim to become competitive and to stay in business, and provide jobs.

2.
Adopt the new philosophy. We are in a new economic age. Western management must awaken to the challenge, must learn their responsibilities, and take on leadership for change.

3.
Cease dependence on inspection to achieve quality. Eliminate the need for inspection on a mass basis by building quality into the product in the first place.

4.
End the practice of awarding business on the basis of price tag. Instead, minimize total cost. Move toward a single supplier for any one item, on a long-term relationship of loyalty and trust.

5.
Improve constantly and forever the system of production and service, to improve quality and productivity, and thus constantly decrease costs.

6.
Institute training on the job.

7.
Institute leadership. The aim of supervision should be to help people and machines and gadgets to do a better job. Supervision of management is in need of overhaul, as well as supervision of production workers.

8.
Drive out fear, so that everyone may work effectively for the company.

9.
Break down barriers between departments. People in research, design, sales, and production must work as a team, to foresee problems of production and in use that may be encountered with the product or service.

10.
Eliminate slogans, exhortations, and targets for the work force asking for zero defects and new levels of productivity. Such exhortations only create adversarial relationships, as the bulk of the causes of low quality and low productivity belong to the system and thus lie beyond the power of the work force.

11.
a. Eliminate work standards (quotas) on the factory floor. Substitute leadership.

b. Eliminate management by objective. Eliminate management by numbers, numerical goals. Substitute leadership.

12.
a. Remove barriers that rob the hourly worker of his right to pride of workmanship. The responsibility of supervisors must be changed from sheer numbers to quality.

b. Remove barriers that rob people in management and in engineering of their right to pride of workmanship. This means *inter alia,* abolishment of the annual or merit rating of management by objective.

13.
Institute a vigorous program of education and self-improvement.

14.
Put everybody in the company to work to accomplish the transformation. The transformation is everybody's job.

Toyota Production System

TAIICHI OHNO
Reviewed by Todd

The Japanese automotive industry was in its infancy following World War II. The total market in Japan for passenger cars in 1949 was 1,008 units. Many of the industry's executives looked with envy across the Pacific. The five-million-unit U.S. market and the mass production techniques born from Henry Ford's assembly line granted their American counterparts advantageous economies of scale.

Taiichi Ohno took exception. As a machine shop supervisor at Toyota, he saw the American auto companies reducing the varieties of styles they offered and standardizing parts to gain these advantages. He saw a very different problem in his country. "Our problem was how to cut costs while producing small numbers of many types of cars," Ohno writes in *Toyota Production System*.

Toyota's rise to global automotive juggernaut came on the back of Ohno's system for shop floor coordination and was based on a deceptively simple insight: *the absolute elimination of waste.* Moving parts, waiting for parts, and even stocking parts as inventory are all forms of waste. Dealing with waste in a compartmentalized manner generates some marginal gains, but nothing compared to the quantum improvements possible when waste is dealt with on a system level.

Ohno's Toyota Production System is supported by two pillars: just-in-time and autonomation. Just-in-time is often referred to as pull production. Rather than use a centralized production schedule, each operation requests parts from upstream feeders based on their current needs, meaning engines are assembled when final production signals the need. Autonomation is the concept of giving machinery human intelligence—for example, enabling a lathe to detect faulty material or a broken tool. Smarter machinery reduces the risk of defective parts and creates a shift from craftsmen running individual machines to a team of semiskilled generalists able to handle several pieces of equipment.

The advances Ohno made were direct results of his natural curiosity and observation of the world around him. The decentralized decision making of his pull system mimicked the human body's unconscious variation of the heart and lungs based on its level of exertion. The concept of teamwork didn't really exist in Japanese culture until the import of Western sports like baseball and volleyball after World War II; traditional Japanese sports, like sumo wrestling and judo, focused on the individual. And Ohno's early years working in Toyota's textile department exposed him to operations where one worker could keep forty or fifty self-repairing looms running, leaving him shocked when he moved to the automotive individual craftsman mentality.

In the mid 1990s, I instituted a pull system for bringing raw materials into a GE plant in Columbus, Ohio, and I learned the benefits of this system firsthand. Prior to the change, purchasing and production control developed monthly schedules and ran extensive computations to determine material requirements. Purchase orders were placed and suppliers made shipments based on the initial plan. But nothing ever operated according to plan. Shifting customer demands, variable product yields, and inconsistent machine uptime all led to too much or too little of what was needed. By setting up standard ordering quantities and simple barcode tags, operators on the floor took charge of ordering the raw materials they needed. Materials were moved from a centralized warehouse to the factory floor. When completed, the project lowered the cost of purchased inventory by $2 million, or over 30 percent, but most important, the change to pull eliminated material shortages caused by the drawbacks of centralized planning.

"Industrial society must develop the courage, or rather the common sense, to procure only what is needed when it is needed and in the amount needed."

Several books have been written about Toyota and its production system, and Ohno's is the best. At 120 pages, it is a quick read, but his three decades of refining the system brings purity to the elements of his argument for a new systemic view of organizing supply chains. But there is one other advantage as well. What sounds like a completely internal effort is really about producing exactly what your customer wants when they want it. Ohno says the closer Toyota has gotten to the 100 percent elimination of waste, the "clearer [becomes] the picture of individual human beings with distinct personalities." While this conclusion is not an obvious one, it ultimately shows the elegance of the efficient system he created. **TS**

Toyota Production System: Beyond Large-Scale Production, Productivity Press, Hardcover 1988, ISBN 9780915299140

WHERE TO NEXT? » Page 306 for **more on self-sustaining systems** » Page 204 for **what Ohno was improving on** | EVEN MORE: *The Machine that Changed the World* by James P.Womack, Daniel T. Jones and Daniel Roos; *The Toyota Way* by Jeffrey K. Liker; *The Elegant Solution* by Matthew E. May

Reengineering the Corporation

MICHAEL HAMMER AND JAMES CHAMPY

Reviewed by Todd

Reengineering became the magic managerial term of the 1990s. Cover stories in business magazines touted Michael Hammer and Jim Champy as the strategic gurus of the moment. Companies like Deere, Ford, and Duke Power all found huge success using the concepts. Even Lou Gerstner, in his autobiography *Who Says Elephants Can't Dance?*, calls out reengineering as having played a role in his turnaround of IBM. The trouble with every fad is the ridicule that follows.

In the 1990s, the term "reengineering" became an easy substitute for the prior decade's "reorganizing," "restructuring," "delayering," "downsizing." The popularity of the term gave embattled executives needed cover when faced with media scrutiny and stock market pressure. The mere mention of a new reengineering initiative acknowledged the severity of a problem and indicated to shareholders that proper steps were being taken. But the actual results varied widely, and business leaders and journalists were quickly off to find and report on the next silver bullet. What's left is general ambivalence for one of the most important business concepts in the second half of the twentieth century.

In *Reengineering the Corporation*, Hammer and Champy center their argument on Adam Smith and his theory of the division of labor. Smith believed that the shift from a craftsman mentality—when all tasks were done by a single person—to a separation of simple, repeatable tasks among specialists was the key to economic growth. Henry Ford's assembly line and Alfred Sloan's introduction of managerial specialists are the modern embodiment of Smith's thinking.

Many organizations still model their operations on the division of labor used by their automotive forebearers. But inherent in Smith's theory are productivity issues. Handoffs between specialists create queues and introduce the opportunity for errors; ninety minutes of actual work is drawn out over several days as the work snakes its way through the organizational labyrinth. And when someone raises a hand to suggest a better way, multidepartmental finger-pointing delays any real progress in determining where the problem really lies.

Reengineering the Corporation turns that theorizing on its ear. Hammer and Champy believe it is the whole process, not the individual steps that make up the process, that should be simple. Generalists take on the responsibilities of several specialists, making the decisions about what will be done and when. Multiple processes replace standardization, and with individuals or small teams responsible, quality control checks and oversight controls are reduced or eliminated. The measurement of success in the new work flow is the satisfaction of the end customer.

COMMON ERRORS DURING REENGINEERING

- **Trying to fix a process instead of changing it**
- **Trying to make reengineering happen from the bottom up**
- **Skimping on assigned resources**
- **Trying to make reengineering happen without making anybody unhappy**
- **Neglecting people's values and beliefs**
- **Being willing to settle for minor results**

(Full list in *Reengineering the Corporation*, chapter 13)

More important, the nature of work itself changes. Workers hired as automatons become case managers, empowered to deal with situations as they see fit. Their managers shed responsibility and become coaches, monitoring performance based on how *well* something is done, rather than how *many* units are completed.

"'Reengineering,' properly, is the fundamental rethinking and radical redesign of business processes to achieve dramatic improvements in critical, contemporary measures of performance . . ."

Hammer and Champy recommend bold moves, suggesting "starting over" as a synonym for reengineering. The blank sheet of paper may be daunting, but broken processes that directly affect the customer are the place to start. The visual evidence, whether an unaccounted-for pallet of boxes or notorious piles of paperwork, is an indicator of systemic uncertainty. E-mail trails or full voicemail boxes show overcommunication among individuals, a prime spot for process redesign. The natural evolution of a company creates these complexities as products and customers evolve. Reengineering gives leaders the opportunity to untangle these webs and simplify overgrown business processes.

Jack Welch said he always needed to be on the "lunatic fringe" to get his company to move just a little, and reengineering's extreme form of process redesign has a similar effect. *Reengineering the Corporation* has permanently added process analysis to the toolbox of every business leader, whether they know it or not. TS

Reengineering the Corporation: A Manifesto for Business Revolution, Collins Paperback Business Essentials Edition, Revised and Updated 2003, ISBN 9780060559533

WHERE TO NEXT? » Page 208 for **a primer on Adam Smith** « Page 89 for **an ex-CEO's endorsement of reengineering** « Page 61 for **how to implement change** | EVEN MORE: *Lean Thinking* by James P. Womack and Daniel T. Jones; *The Discipline of Market Leaders* by Michael Treacy and Fred Wiersema; *Business Process Improvement* by H. James Harrington

The Goal

ELIYAHU M. GOLDRATT AND JEFF COX
Reviewed by Jack

Eliyahu Goldratt and Jeff Cox published *The Goal* in 1984, and shortly after, a company in Milwaukee placed an order with us for ten copies of the book. I had not heard of the book before, and I was surprised to discover when I received the shipment and perused a copy that *The Goal* was a novel. While common today, writing about business in story form was striking and original at the time. What caught my eye was how the authors brought to life, using realistic, flesh-and-blood characters and fast-paced storytelling, the story of one company's struggle to turn around a failing division.

The story features Alex Rogo, a new plant manager who is leading six hundred employees in a division of UniCo. The parent company is unhappy with the UniWare division's productivity and Alex is given three months to turn the plant around. Alex must solve myriad problems, such as late shipments, soaring inventory, and unacceptable quality levels, to reverse the trend.

Flummoxed by where to start the transformation, Alex recalls a chance encounter he had with a physicist named Jonah. The two had struck up a conversation during an airport layover when Alex proudly told Jonah about his company having just installed state-of-the-art robots. Alex told Jonah the robots had increased productivity 36 percent in some departments. Jonah asked Alex a series of questions about the resultant effects of the robots: Is your company making more products? Was manpower decreased? Or did you reduce inventory? When Alex answered no to all, Jonah explained to him how his perception of success was incorrect. Alex did not internalize the advice at the time, but with a deadline looming, he reconnects with Jonah.

Through a series of short meetings and phone calls, Jonah teaches Alex the metrics he *should* be looking at to match the outcomes, rather than just the output of the robots that Alex had celebrated in their earlier conversation. What should Alex track to know whether the changes he implements will help in the turnaround? First Jonah explains to Alex the results that Alex's bosses at UniCo really care about. These financial measurements are indicators of how a business is doing on the top level: net profit, ROI, and cash flow. Jonah then explains that the best internal metrics that Alex can control in the turnaround—i.e. to make factory floor decisions that will ultimately inform those top level metrics—are throughput, inventory, and operational expense. Jonah reminds Alex that "'the goal is not to improve one measurement in isolation. The goal is to reduce operational expense and reduce inventory while simultaneously increasing throughput.'"

Alex has trouble visualizing how Jonah's ideas will work on his factory floor until he takes his son's Boy Scout troop on a long hike. He has a hard time keeping the boys together because some are faster than others. He begins to see the variations or deviations in real time. One of the really slow boys is Herbie, and Alex realizes that Herbie was being slowed up by carrying too much in his backpack. Alex removes and redistributes the heavy items, Herbie catches up, and the boys make great time. Here is where Goldratt and Cox introduce one of the most popular takeaways from *The Goal*: the Theory of Constraints. TOC is a metaphor for looking at a process—be it an assembly line or any kind of repetitive process—as a living entity and finding the bottleneck that is preventing its maximum output. By studying the actual flow of the parts through the factory and looking for and dealing with "Herbies" immediately, the plant is able to show the corporate headquarters success. Ultimately, Alex is promoted and the conglomerate incorporates the TOC into the other divisions.

"Why can't we consistently get a quality product out the door on time at the cost that can beat the competition?"

In the past twenty-plus years, *The Goal* has sold over three million copies, been translated into twenty-one languages, been taught in over two hundred colleges and universities, and was made into a movie. Goldratt, an Israeli physicist, is, of course, present in the character of Jonah and advocates that in teaching there should be more question marks and fewer exclamation points. Jonah embodies this Socratic approach, and through Jonah's questions, we are afforded the chance to learn along with Alex. *The Goal* does, however, provide plenty of answers relating to viewing a process as a whole and the need to continuously improve that process. **JC**

The Goal: A Process of Ongoing Improvement, North River Press, Paperback Third Revised Edition 2004, ISBN 9780884271789

WHERE TO NEXT? » Page 189 for **a story about teams** « Page 56 for **a story about leadership** « Page 67 for **how you can use stories** | EVEN MORE: *The Toyota Way* by Jeffrey Liker; *Deming and Goldratt* by Domenico Lepore and Oded Cohen; *We All Fall Down* by Julie Wright and Russ King; *The Machine That Changed the World* by James P. Womack, Daniel T. Jones, and Daniel Roos

The Great Game of Business

JACK STACK WITH BO BURLINGHAM
Reviewed by Jack

Jack Stack is credited as the first person to have written about Open-Book Management (OBM) when he penned *The Great Game of Business* about his company, Springfield Remanufacturing Corporation (SRC), a division of International Harvester. OBM is a management policy based on sharing all of a company's financial data with employees. The theory is that if employees understand how they affect the company's health as a whole, they will work harder and more efficiently. There are, however, a few codicils that can affect the success of this approach: management has to have credibility—this cannot be another "theory/flavor of the month"—and the employees have to have some fire in their eyes.

I began sharing numbers, or using OBM, years ago, because I felt that my employees, as a group, were way smarter than I could be working alone. I have always believed that transparency is the best and most honest way to work, and, as such, allows me to sleep better at night. When times were hard (we had several lean years), the employees knew why we needed to tighten our belts and why certain perhaps unpopular decisions were made. And when the company became more prosperous, the employees understood what it took to climb the mountain and were able to genuinely celebrate their contribution to our successes. But in order for this type of management to work, education—providing employees with an understanding of the basics of business finance—is key. OBM remains an uncommon management approach because it requires constant engagement with everyone on every level of the organization. I happen to believe, and I suspect Stack would agree, that it is this engagement that makes the workday worthwhile.

Stack and a group of managers bought a division of IH that refurbished diesel truck engines; then called Springfield Renew Center, the division was in sad shape. Introducing OBM meant first committing to employee engagement. In the early days, Stack knew that you couldn't engage people unless they had pride in what they did and where they did it. He held an open house and provided employees with the equipment to paint and spruce up their work areas, and brought in finished company products to display. On the weekends, families were invited to see where their family member spent the day.

"The best, most efficient, most profitable way to operate a business is to give everybody in the company a voice in saying how the company is run *and* a stake in the financial outcome, good or bad."

Then for OBM to work, management needs to present the big picture to every member of the organization. This runs counterintuitive to old-style management practices, but as the Springfield division has proven and I have observed, it works. Employees also have to step up and speak up, become motivated by the information that has been shared, and make everyday decisions based on this knowledge. An analogy that best sums up the power behind OBM is that of "everybody pulling on the same oar." Teams and team building play a large role in the success of OBM. Stack provides a list of some of the goals that worked best for SRC:

1. Business is a team sport—choose games that build a team.
2. Be positive, build confidence.
3. Celebrate every win.
4. It's got to be a game.
5. Give everyone the same set of goals.
6. Don't use goals to tell people everything you want them to do.

This approach may seem quaint since the book was written in 1992, but currently SRC Holdings has fifteen separate companies with overall sales of $300 million. A $1 investment in SRC stock in 1983 is now worth $800. The people who work at SRC own this stock, and the company has never laid off an employee.

I firmly believe that OBM played a significant role in my company's growth and is the reason we have extremely low employee turnover. But the OBM approach Stack advocates requires a constant commitment from managers to completely share information with employees. It is a one-way trip: giving people more means that you can never take a step back, withhold information, or deny participation. **JC**

The Great Game of Business: Unlocking the Power and Profitability of Open-Book Management, Currency/Doubleday, Paperback 1994, ISBN 9780385475259

WHERE TO NEXT? « Page 149 for **more about accounting** » Page 240 for **how to grow a business** » Page 256 for **a narrative of heavy industry** | EVEN MORE: *Open-Book Management* by John Case; *Managing by the Numbers* by Chuck Kremer and Ron Rizzuto, with John Case; *Maverick* by Ricardo Semler

First, Break All the Rules

MARCUS BUCKINGHAM AND CURT COFFMAN

Reviewed by Todd

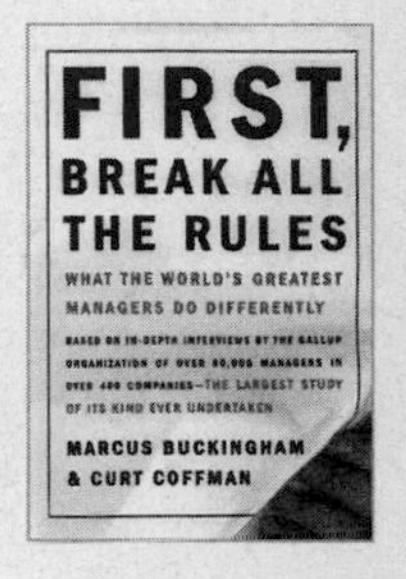

Caricatures that appear on the big (and small) screen portray managers as either tyrants or buffoons. In Pixar's *The Incredibles*, Bob Parr's manager, Gilbert Huph, exemplifies all of the prescribed attributes of a tyrant, right down to his pivotal demand, "Stop right now or you're fired!" Organizational vocabulary still draws strongly from its militaristic roots, but the "manager as major" fades as a new generation fills middle management. The business media reports on fallen leaders and inevitably points to the desire for power as their downfall when the real fall was a company's market valuation.

For a fresh idea of what a manager *should* be, *First, Break All the Rules* by Marcus Buckingham and Curt Coffman is your guide. Both authors worked for Gallup Inc., and the book was the result of a massive project to determine what good management looks like. The research starts at the logical beginning: "Do managers matter?" Managers have incredible influence over the success of a company, but Gallup wanted to prove this common wisdom analytically. And it did. When Gallup looked at individual business units within larger companies, great managers delivered greater sales, greater profitability, and lower turnover than poor managers.

Separating good management from bad came in the form of Gallup's keystone Q12 survey. Gallup's history as a polling company came in handy; it had over one million workplace interviews to draw from for this survey. The researchers looked for a set of applicable questions and found twelve that "capture the *most* information and the most *important* information." The queries linked directly to business outcomes like productivity, profitability, retention, and customer satisfaction:

1. Do I know what is expected of me at work?
2. Do I have the materials and equipment I need to do my work right?

3. At work, do I have the opportunity to do what I do best every day?
4. In the last seven days, have I received recognition or praise for doing good work?
5. Does my supervisor, or someone at work, seem to care about me as a person?
6. Is there someone at work who encourages my development?
7. At work, do my opinions seem to count?
8. Does the mission/purpose of my company make me feel my job is important?
9. Are my co-workers committed to doing quality work?
10. Do I have a best friend at work?
11. In the last six months, has someone at work talked to me about my progress?
12. This last year, have I had opportunities at work to learn and grow?

These twelve questions were given to over 105,000 employees at 2,500 business units in 24 separate companies. Employees who gave more favorable responses to the questions worked in higher-performing business units. The correlation gave Gallup the methodology to identify good managers. Gallup went ahead and interviewed 80,000 highly rated managers, generating over 120,000 hours of tape.

Over and over, in one form or another, researchers heard: "[Great managers] help each person become *more* and *more* of who he [or she] already is." The managers Gallup interviewed consistently recognized that the development of their employees came through focusing on their natural strengths as opposed to shoring up their weaknesses. This insight runs completely counter to conventional wisdom. Their research points to a change in managerial focus from making an employee fit into a position to finding the right position for the employee. Three words, "manager as coach," best describe Buckingham and Coffman's findings.

The process starts with hiring, where talent becomes the primary criterion in the selection of a new employee. Take the seven men chosen for NASA's Mercury space program, and consider how the most important human endeavor of the twentieth century missed the mark. All the candidates had the most applicable experience possible as military test pilots. The initial cadre spent two years acquiring the skills necessary for space flight. But when those astronauts were put into the capsule and shot into orbit, each performed very differently, despite the common experience. Their performances in the new environment ranged from problematic to flawless. What the hiring manager didn't consider were the individual abilities of each astronaut. Everyone has natural tendencies and reacts differently to the same stimuli. During liftoff, for example, the pulse of one topped out at 150, whereas Neil Armstrong's never got above 80, an indictor of how much each astronaut would struggle later in the mission.

Behavior-based questions ("Tell me about a time when . . . ?") during an interview can provide insight into a person's talents. Listen for quick responses that indicate the recurring use of a talent. Asking a candidate what he or she finds satisfying also can lead an interviewer toward where the person projects strength and finds fulfillment. For example, the best truck drivers will describe the constant assessment of surrounding traffic and the natural enjoyment they feel from anticipating potential problems.

"The energy for a healthy career is generated from discovering the talents that are already there, not from filling oneself up with marketable experiences."

Matching an employee's natural talents with the right job can produce remarkable results. Consider Jean P., a character in one of the authors' scenarios. This data entry clerk was averaging 560,000 keypunches a month, over 50 percent higher than the national average of 380,000. Recognizing her innate talent, the manager sat down with Jean and created a series of goals and rewards. Over the next several months, Jean improved her performance to 3.5 million keypunches, ten times the industry standard. Equally important, her manager created a talent profile for hiring, and now has Jean surrounded by people who average over a million keypunches a month. By spending time with the best people, managers learn what makes them different and how their strengths can be applied to the whole team.

Talent is not distributed equally, but everyone possesses unique skills and abilities. *First, Break All the Rules* shows the changes managers need to make in their approach to draw the greatest potential from the people who work for them. **TS**

First, Break All the Rules: What the World's Greatest Managers Do Differently, Simon & Schuster, Hardcover 1999, ISBN 9780684852867

WHERE TO NEXT? » Page 313 for **how management is about more than IQ** « Page 51 for **a research-based approach to leadership** « Page 152 for **how metrics meet management** | EVEN MORE: *12* by Rodd Wagner and James K. Harter; *Vital Friends* by Tom Rath

Now, Discover Your Strengths

MARCUS BUCKINGHAM AND DONALD O. CLIFTON, PHD

Reviewed by Jack

We are taught at an early age to improve on our weaknesses in order to become a well-rounded person. During our school years, few of our parents and teachers celebrated our A's, and instead asked, "What is this C in math all about?" In business, these expectations continue, but Marcus Buckingham and Donald O. Clifton, along with Gallup Inc., argue that this is an ineffective approach. They assert that we can grow more quickly and get the most satisfaction in our work life when we utilize our strengths, which the authors define as a "consistent near-perfect performance in an activity." In preparing the book, Gallup asked a sampling of 1.7 million employees whether they were given an opportunity to do what they do best and found that globally only 20 percent said yes. *Now, Discover Your Strengths* aims to change this depressing reality for an entire generation of workers.

Just as the research in *First, Break All the Rules* showed that changes in a manager's approach can encourage an employee's best performance, *Now, Discover Your Strengths* resets the parameters for that employee's improvement. The previously held assumptions were that any employee could learn to be competent in almost anything, finding their "greatest room for growth is in his or her areas of greatest weakness." Instead, *Now, Discover Your Strengths* teaches managers and employees how to build on one's strengths to maximize performance. There is simply no upside to trying to fit a square peg into a round hole.

The obvious next question is, after years of worrying about our weaknesses, how do we determine our strengths? Gallup conducted over two million interviews to determine patterns of behavior and skills among successful people. Thirty-four patterns or themes prevalent in human talent consistently appeared. Now, Gallup has created an online assessment tool called StrengthsFinder to help individuals discover their strengths. When you buy the book *StrengthsFinder 2.0*, a code on the back cover allows you online access to the 180-question timed examination.

After you finish the test, you are presented with a list of five signature themes within which you have the greatest potential for strength. The book offers a one-page analysis of each theme. There are 16.7 million possible combinations, so the results are tailor-made for you.

When I took the test, I found that my first strength is harmony, which is "looking for areas of agreement," and I quickly realized that harmony may not be the best strength for a guy leading a group into the twenty-first century. While this strength *has* garnered me a fair amount of loyalty among my employees, sometimes strategic decisions must be made regardless of harmony. My coauthor's main strength is in his ability to "peer over the horizon" and ask "wouldn't it be great if . . ."—the Strengths-Finder label for this is "futuristic"—and we succeeded as a team because our strengths struck a good balance. I firmly believe that our company's four years of double-digit growth in a flat industry was due to this effective partnering.

"We want to help you . . . *to capitalize on your strengths,* whatever they may be, *and manage around your weaknesses,* whatever they may be."

One of my shortfalls in improving the performance of my employees was indeed in trying to fit square pegs into round holes. For example, trying to get a quiet, task-oriented person to be a better salesperson when really he is an excellent support person, is a waste of his talents and my energy. Buckingham and Clifton discovered that the best managers understood two things: each employee has unique and enduring talents, and each employee's greatest room for growth is in the areas of his or her greatest strengths. They give examples of successful managers who deliver on these ideas. Phil Jackson, the famous NBA basketball coach (some would say guru), gave hand-selected personal development books to his players in order to further an inherent ability. Sam Mendes, a successful movie director, manages his movie sets through respecting the strengths of his actors, and, as a result, gets the best possible performances from them. The authors provide another treasure: a one-page bulleted list of ways to manage each of the thirty-four strength types. This online assessment is a valuable resource and well worth the price of admission.

Most of us pick up this book expecting to find answers to questions such as: "Can my themes reveal whether I am in the right career?" Certainly there are commonalities to be found among people in some careers. For example, journalists may share "adaptability" because their profession changes daily depending on the stories they are assigned that day. But generally, the authors believe that your signature themes have little to say about the field you are in and instead offer some direction for the role you play in any given field. In fact, Gallup discovered some surprising data in the number of people with similar themes who excel in very different fields. The distinction that StrengthsFinder is not a career guidance test but a performance enhancer is an important one.

Despite our tendency to focus on our shortcomings, there is great advantage in switching to a StrengthsFinder mentality. Warren Buffett is the poster child for knowing one's own strengths and staying the course. He knew he was a patient, practical man whom people trusted. The authors tell us that Buffett refrained from investing in technology because he didn't understand it, but "[h]e identified its strongest threads, wove in education and experience, and built them into the dominating strengths we see today." We might not all achieve Buffett's level of success, but if *Now, Discover Your Strengths* succeeds in making us more satisfied and confident on the job, then that will indeed be a success. **JC**

Now, Discover Your Strengths, Free Press, Hardcover 2001, ISBN 9780743201148

WHERE TO NEXT? « Page 12 for **what Drucker says on strengths** » Page 232 for **the strengths an entrepreneur needs** » Page 271 for **how understanding strengths helped a baseball GM** | EVEN MORE: *StrengthsFinder 2.0* by Tom Rath; *Discover Your Sales Strengths* by Benson Smith and Tony Rutigliano; *What Got You Here Won't Get You There* by Marshall Goldsmith with Mark Reiter

The Knowing-Doing Gap

JEFFREY PFEFFER AND ROBERT I. SUTTON

Reviewed by Todd

"Hear one, see one, do one."

That's how surgical residents learn new procedures. The final step of performing the operation proves that knowledge has been acquired and transferred. This training construct matches one used by the U.S. military during simulated drills and live-fire exercises to prepare soldiers for combat. Airline pilots, ocean freighter captains, and professional athletes follow the same strategy, but business practitioners seem to favor theory over practice.

Knowing what to do is not the problem. Over 11,000 business books, 80,000 MBAs, and $60 billion worth of corporate training each year show the wide avenues by which knowledge is dispensed and acquired. But Jeff Pfeffer and Bob Sutton, authors of *The Knowing-Doing Gap*, describe an intellectual divide, saying, "[T]here are fewer and smaller differences in *what firms know* than in their *ability to act* on that knowledge." They call that divide the "Knowing-Doing Gap."

With knowledge widely accessible, the authors' next query was "Does a Knowing-Doing gap really exist?" They cite numerous academic and industry studies to show substantial performance differences within and between companies because of the failure to adopt superior business practices within an industry, or due to the lack of sharing of best practices among plants within a single company. Rather than putting these strategies into action, organizations and their leaders choose from an array of hollow alternatives.

Pointless communication leads the list, say Pfeffer and Sutton. Talking about innovative strategy and organizational realignments with PowerPoint decks and spiral-bound planning documents resembles action in effort alone. Mission-statement development retreats consume equivalent brainpower but generate little more than frequent flier miles for the participants. Another barrier between knowing and doing are naysayers.

These individuals sound smart to their coworkers and are quick to dismiss anything new as "been done before," killing action before any momentum is reached. Naysayers are not the only impediment; strong culture, a quality of success held up by Jim Collins in *Good to Great*, can also stop action and smother needed change. History and tradition act as decision-making shorthand and can either keep the ship on course or lead it astray.

The authors further suggest that the "Knowing-Doing Gap" originates from fear. A primary by-product of action is failure, and mavericks willing to take chances fear losing their jobs, or, worse, suffering the humiliation of their peers' reactions. As Deming has famously advised, drive out fear. Pfeffer and Sutton agree. Surgeons have done this by building a culture where mistakes are shared with colleagues. Business leaders should follow the example, sharing their failures and what they learned, and bring that habit to employees. Reward the risk takers with second and third chances.

"[T]here are fewer and smaller differences in *what firms know* than in their *ability to act* on that knowledge."

The authors end the book by recounting the story of a workshop given for retail executives. A manager from Macy's came up afterward to offer thanks and to describe how none of this would work at her company. In the parking lot was a small group from Trader Joe's who also approached with thanks for the talk. They said that many of the lessons offered were already in place at their company, but there were some things they could do better. One of them was already on the phone with corporate headquarters sharing what was learned and was assured that those changes would "be implemented by Monday." The group was inspired to take action rather than consider the authors' advice as only theory. At the very least, they were willing to give it a try. As Pfeffer and Sutton say, "If you know by doing, there is no gap between what you know and what you do." TS

The Knowing-Doing Gap: How Smart Companies Turn Knowledge into Action, Harvard Business School Press, Hardcover 2000, ISBN 9781578511242

WHERE TO NEXT? « Page 9 for **doing more personally** « Page 95 for **doing more organizationally** « Page 123 for **more sales** | EVEN MORE: *Hard Facts, Dangerous Half-Truths, and Total Nonsense* by Jeffrey Pfeffer and Robert I. Sutton; *The No-Asshole Rule* by Robert I. Sutton

The Five Dysfunctions of a Team

PATRICK LENCIONI

Reviewed by Jack

Teams are a tremendously important part of modern management. But this has not always been the case. Previously a worker was given a job, shown how to do it, and then expected to do the same job over and over again until the supervisor dictated changes. Organizing individuals into a team with a common goal often results in better decision making and task completion due to diverse perspectives. However, the maintenance of a team is loaded with pitfalls because its success is dependent on the idiosyncratic nature of the people within the team—people with conflicting goals or dissimilar work habits. It can be a serious challenge to get disparate people to work together and pull on the oars at the same time and in the same direction. Herding cats comes to mind.

There have been many books written about teams: the theory of teams, managing teams, creating teams, and motivating teams. But in *The Five Dysfunctions of a Team*, Pat Lencioni has taken the subject and created a novel centered around this prevalent management approach. Lencioni's success as a storyteller lies in his ability to create believable characters and put them to work in believable companies, dealing with believable situations. Doesn't sound like much, but in the same way that some novels work and others don't—depending on how grounded they are in reality—many business novels often come off as being too pat, like a sitcom or soap opera that might reflect life in hyperbole. Lencioni's novels don't always conclude with a completely happy ending, but they are reality-based and therefore more applicable to the people who need it, the people you are training.

In *The Five Dysfunctions of a Team*, Lencioni creates a fictitious company of 150 employees located in Silicon Valley during the Internet bubble. Only two years earlier, the company was considered one of the hot new technology start-ups. But from the start, its executive team suffered from backstabbing and a lack of unity. The board asks the current CEO and cofounder to step down and hires a new CEO from outside the

THE FIVE DYSFUNCTIONS OF A TEAM

- **Absence of trust**
- **Fear of conflict**
- **Lack of commitment**
- **Avoidance of accountability**
- **Inattention to results**

industry. After she observes her new company for a couple of weeks, she hosts an off-site meeting with her direct reports, saying, "We have a more experienced and talented executive team than any of our competitors. We have more cash than they do. . . . We have better core technology. And we have a powerful board of directors. Yet in spite of all that, we are behind two of our competitors in terms of both revenue and customer growth. Can anyone here tell me why that is?" In each subsequent off-site session, as the executive team struggles with turning around the company, she starts the meeting with this exact statement until the team is able to answer the question.

"Not finance. Not strategy. Not technology. It is teamwork that remains the ultimate competitive advantage, both because it is so powerful and so rare."

As the company and its new CEO deal with both internal and external issues, the different personalities of the executive team come to light and are used by the author to illustrate five common dysfunctions: absence of trust, fear of conflict, lack of commitment, avoidance of accountability, and inattention to results. The five dysfunctions are interconnected: You can't have spirited discussion without trust between team members. You can't have commitment to decisions unless you have open discussion without the fear of expressing your honest opinion. Consensus won't be reached without a little or maybe a lot of conflict. As my company has grown and we have added people with differing points of view, I have found that conflict can be positive, and is essential for a total buy-in on a new program or plan. And as Lencioni states: "All great relationships, the ones that last over time, require productive conflict in order to grow. This is true in marriage, parenthood, friendship, and certainly business."

In this case, Lencioni concludes his story with a happy ending. With a revitalized executive team, the company grows to over 200 employees and is able to draw even with the leader in its field. With a team that is working together efficiently, both morale and quality improve. But *The Five Dys-*

functions of a Team offers more than a well-told tale from which to intuit a new approach for your team or business. The fable is an effective vehicle for Lencioni's lessons, but also included are forty pages of worksheets and assessments to begin your own new team-building program or redesign of an existing team. **JC**

The Five Dysfunctions of a Team: A Leadership Fable, Jossey-Bass, Hardcover 2002, ISBN 9780787960759

WHERE TO NEXT? « Page 51 for **stories of leadership** » Page 234 for **a story on starting a business** » Page 196 for **a practical guide to teams** | EVEN MORE: *The Five Dysfunctions of a Team: Participant Workbook* by Patrick Lencioni; *Leading Teams* by J. Richard Hackman; *Peak Performance* by Jon R. Katzenbach

Choose Your Approach

Every person learns differently; the challenge is finding the right medium for the message. Here are three ways we classify books and a few examples to show there is something for everyone.

1. Fables
Short fictional scenarios packing a punch with symbolism and analogies.

2. Modern
Less than ten years old with contemporary perspectives and anecdotes.

3. Classics
Business ideas that have survived the test of time.

on Change

Who Moved My Cheese?
by Spencer Johnson, M.D.
A popular parable about adapting when circumstances change.

Switch
by Chip Heath & Dan Heath
Learn to send your Elephant and Rider down the right path to lasting change.

Leading Change
by John P. Kotter
The famous Harvard professor shares eight steps for leading and guiding change.

on Motivation

Fish
by Stephen C. Lundin, Ph.D., Harry Paul & John Christensen
One manager rises to the challenge of infusing motivation at Pike Place Fish Market in Seattle.

How Full Is Your Bucket?
by Tom Rath & Donald O. Clifton
Shows how to fill, with positive experiences, the metaphorical "bucket" inside each of us.

The Power of Positive Thinking
by Norman Vincent Peale
This classic book teaches how to overcome obstacles by thinking positively.

on Leadership

The Radical Leap
by Steve Farber
The guru Edg shows that love, energy, audacity, and proof are the key traits of extreme leaders.

The Leadership Challenge
by James M. Kouzes & Barry Z. Posner
Equips leaders with five usable practices to apply at every level of the company.

Leadership
by James MacGregor Burns
The original, definitive leadership text.

Written by Roy Normington and Sally Haldorson

Six Thinking Hats

EDWARD DE BONO

Reviewed by Todd

Imagine your company is facing a big problem. And I mean a your-biggest-client-has-left-for-your-competitor kind of problem.

The president calls a meeting to figure out what happened and each attendee enters the conference room with something different on his or her mind. The folks from research arrive with binders of pie charts detailing how well the campaign is (rather, *was*) going. The creative team has half a dozen ideas for how to improve the messaging. The account manager is wondering if he'll still be employed when the meeting is over. And the office manager walks in shaking her head, remembering how she told everyone that taking on this client was a bad idea.

The discussion becomes an argument about whose perspective has more merit. Each member's verbal commitment to his position makes considering other options difficult; however, considering a wide range of thought is the key to moving through these organizational impasses.

To move just such a discussion forward, Edward De Bono, in *Six Thinking Hats*, delineates six clear directions, or hats, that represent a particular line of human thought. To each hat he assigns a color. The metaphor of a hat is effective here because it implies that the kind of thinking one is doing can be donned, changed, or removed according to a situation. Let me use De Bono's descriptions to quickly introduce each hat:

White is neutral and objective. The white hat is concerned with objective facts and figures.

Red suggests anger (seeing red), rage, and emotions. The red hat gives the emotional view.

Black is somber and serious. The black hat is cautious and careful. It points out the weaknesses in an idea.

Yellow is sunny and positive. The yellow hat is optimistic and covers hope and positive thinking.

Green is grass, vegetation, and abundant, fertile growth. The green hat indicates creativity and new ideas.

Blue is cool, and it is also the color of the sky, which is above everything else. The blue hat is concerned with control, the organization of the thinking process, and the use of other hats.

In the scenario described here, each meeting attendee is coming at the problem wearing a different hat . . . without being aware of it. Six Hats thinking allows participants to focus their energy in a specific direction by getting everyone to "wear" one hat at a time. During a meeting, the hats can also be used in the order that is most appropriate to the discussion. For example, the president may start with a red hat to gather the feelings his employees have about the loss of this client. He may follow with a white hat to then gather the facts about the client's defection. An intriguing conclusion to the meeting would be to have the group use some yellow-hat thinking to consider the upside of the newly available resources.

A variety of practical benefits arise from the *Six Thinking Hats* approach. Discussions take less time because the group focuses on a particular line of thought at a given moment. Whether fear or fact, a hat exists for those thoughts to be shared. Arguments do not dominate the meeting. Individuals who tend toward a certain line of thought are given freedom to think more broadly under other hats. The language of colored hats itself removes ego and allows the exploration of a topic in a natural and objective manner.

"The biggest enemy of thinking is complexity, for that leads to confusion."

De Bono's writing style is worthy of note. He frequently references thoughts the reader would expect to hear from a group during Six Hats thinking. A black-hat statement might sound like "I see a danger that the competition will match our lower prices," or a red-hat confession might be "I have the feeling that he will back down when it comes to the crunch." This conversational treatment makes the material easier to internalize and apply. Even when you introduce this form of thinking to a group for the first time, the process seems familiar and you can easily anticipate questions and concerns with the group.

De Bono is serious about thinking, as his many more academic books indicate, but *Six Thinking Hats* is the most accessible and easily applicable. Businesspeople spend a lot of time in conversation—often confrontational conversation—and this method is an effective way to organize your meetings so that they actually initiate progress. **TS**

Six Thinking Hats, Back Bay Books, Paperback Revised and Updated 1999, ISBN 9780316178310

WHERE TO NEXT? » Page 284 for **a company that uses brainstorming** » Page 286 for **brainstorming your marketing** » Page 299 for **becoming a better brainstormer** | EVEN MORE: *Lateral Thinking* by Edward De Bono; *Tactics* by Edward De Bono; *Teach Yourself to Think* by Edward De Bono

The Team Handbook

PETER R. SCHOLTES, BRIAN L. JOINER, AND BARBARA J. STREIBEL
Reviewed by Jack

Brian Joiner and Peter Scholtes were early teachers of the quality movement during the 1980s and '90s. Much of their work advocated Deming's management philosophy, which, in part, touted teams as being integral to improving quality. "Once people recognize that systems create the majority of problems, they stop blaming individual employees. They instead ask which system needs improvement, and are more likely to seek out and find the true source of improvement." Joiner and Scholtes's still relevant *The Team Handbook* shows how to distribute responsibility and maximize creativity in order for companies to respond more adeptly to the growing complexity of business.

The Team Handbook sets the standard for a functional workbook that can be easily employed in the workplace, and the book has owned this category since the first edition was published in 1988. This is not a book to help you decide whether you want to start a team; instead, this is the book you need to make your next team project a success. Spiral-bound and graphic-packed, there is ample white space on each page for notes and many worksheets—also available for download online—to help your team flourish. For people who think that business books are all theory and little application, *The Team Handbook* defies such deductions. This is simply the most *usable* book included here in *The 100 Best*.

The first distinction the authors make clear is that there are different types of teams: project teams, which are temporary; functional work teams, which are permanent; and virtual teams, which use technology. Knowing which kind of team to implement is critical to the success of the team and fulfillment of the project. According to the authors, a team should have no more than five to seven members in addition to the Team Leader and the Coach. All teams need a Sponsor whose responsibilities change as the team project progresses. He or she has a large role early on and that role changes down the path. The teams need clearly defined purposes, goals, and boundaries, as well as access to resources and people in the know.

The Team Handbook also tackles the human side of the team equation. Teams are only efficient and productive when the people in them can work together effectively. The chapter on dealing with conflict is priceless. The ten common problems and solution strategies alone are worth the price of the book. These ten issues include Floundering; Overbearing Participants; Rush to Accomplishment; Wanderlust: Digression and Tangents; and Feuding Team Members. *The Team Handbook* provides solutions for each problem. The authors also go into detail on leading change and the resistance to change that often appears during a given change process the team was designed to implement.

"To succeed, organizations must rely on the knowledge, skills, experience, and perspective of a wide range of people to solve multifaceted problems, make good decisions, and deliver effective solutions. This is where dynamic, productive teams can make the difference."

Beyond the practical aspects of putting a team together, Joiner and Scholtes include sections on Decision Making, Charting, Agendas, Checklists, Process Maps, Storyboards, Methods, Collecting Data, Improvement Plans, Communication, and Advanced Tools. A true bounty of information in a comprehensive workbook with step-by-step guidelines to making your next team initiative a success, *The Team Handbook* is *the* guidebook to lead you through the minefield (and toward mastery) of team building, selling well over one million copies since its release. I guarantee you that your copy of this book will be as tattered and marked-up as mine. JC

The Team Handbook, Third Edition, Öriel Incorporated, Spiral Bound 2003, ISBN 9781884731266

WHERE TO NEXT? « Page 75 for **great historical examples of good teamwork** « Page 189 for **fictitious but fatal pitfalls of teams** | EVEN MORE: *The Wisdom of Teams* by Jon R. Katzenbach and Douglas K. Smith; *Lean Thinking* by James P. Womack and Daniel T. Jones; *The Lean Six Sigma Pocket Toolkit* by Michael L. George, et al.

BIOGRAPHIES

How did they do it? That is the question we all want to ask when we meet someone famous or wealthy. We want to mimic them, thinking that if we just follow their footsteps we'll arrive at the same place. But, as Mark Twain said, "History rhymes; it does not repeat." Biographies provide a direction and a context so we can better plot our own course.

Titan

RON CHERNOW

Reviewed by Jack

The metal titanium was named after the Titans, a mythological race of powerful Greek men. If we gave crude oil such a namesake today, we would call it Rockefeller, after the first man to transform this natural resource's power into a worldwide commodity and wealth-amassing enterprise. John D. Rockefeller set the standard (no pun intended) for big business, and it is his story that esteemed biographer Ron Chernow tells in *Titan*.

Rockefeller was in the right place at the right time to make history: Cleveland, Ohio, in 1853. Cleveland was home to one of five major refinery areas in America, and the young Rockefeller, having moved to Cleveland with his family during his teenage years, became an expert in converting petroleum into kerosene to be used for lighting. His career grew spectacularly in the early days because of hard work and his ability to cut costs and understand the big picture. Petroleum traveled on the railroads in barrels, and Rockefeller discovered he could make his own barrels cheaper than outsourcing them, thereby saving $150 per barrel: just one small example of his thrift. He also had the unusual advantage of being able to secure loans from local bankers because of his trustworthy Puritan upbringing and his smart business sense. By 1868—just five years after he began—his plants' refining capacity was greater than the next three largest refineries combined. In 1870, Standard Oil was born.

Chernow makes it clear in his retelling that Rockefeller was aggressive in his desire to maximize profits and change the industry. In 1871, the head of the Pennsylvania Railroad proposed a consolidation of the fragmented refining industry that would have benefitted Rockefeller greatly. The plan was never implemented because when word leaked out about the estimated 100 percent increase in shipping charges—the profits from which would be shared by Standard Oil and the railroads—some refiners in the East protested. Things got violent in a Pennsylvania oil field, and after the upheaval, the railroads backed off and lowered their rates. Still,

Rockefeller tried another approach and started to buy oil refineries and strengthen his hold on refining. He used aggressive tactics like selling below cost to show the other owners that they needed to sell before he put them out of business. In 1872, he bought up twenty-two of the twenty-six Cleveland competitors in a mere six weeks.

Ten years later, Rockefeller had multiple businesses in multiple states, which proved unwieldy to manage, and so the Standard Oil Trust was created to bring control to the diverse businesses. Despite the fact that the price of kerosene—the major commodity—dropped by 80 percent over the life of the company, the Trust had severe public relations issues because of Rockefeller's aggressive business practices. These business practices were not illegal since there were no laws in place to rein in this kind of big business. As a result, less than a decade later, the government ordered the breakup of Standard Oil. Very few organizations have been combated by acts of Congress, but the Sherman Antitrust legislation was created in response to the Standard Oil Trust. Today, you need only to look at the growth of Wal-Mart and Microsoft as contemporary examples of companies struggling against bad public relations and accusations of acting as a monopoly.

"He embodied all [of American life's] virtues of thrift, self-reliance, hard work, and unflagging enterprise. Yet as someone who flouted government and rode roughshod over competitors, he also personified many of its most egregious vices."

Chernow emphasizes that Rockefeller's questionable tactics and towering successes were tempered by many years of philanthropy. This dichotomy makes for an intriguing biography, and the author's passion for his subject is recognizable throughout. Chernow writes: "By the time Rockefeller died, in fact, so much good had unexpectedly flowered from so much evil that God might even have greeted him on the other side, as the titan had so confidently expected all along."

Rockefeller was a deeply religious man who believed that he was put on the earth to make money, with which he was to make others' lives better. He insisted that his greatest humanitarian accomplishment was not the philanthropic work he did in his later life, but the jobs he provided and the cheap kerosene he produced to light homes while he was making his money. But Rockefeller lived for ninety-eight years and spent more of his life giving money away than he did amassing it. While he didn't participate in philanthropy in predictable ways—building libraries or music halls as Andrew Carnegie did—he gave money to promote research that would yield widespread results. He also gave large amounts of money to schools, including Spelman College for African American women in Atlanta, the University of Chicago, and what became Rockefeller University in New York City.

This titan of oil saw opportunity and went after his vision with everything he had. Today, we have seen the same titanic ambition in revolutionaries like Bill Gates and Sam Walton. When it comes to understanding how something as innovative as the personal computer or "big box" retailing came to exist, and how their success pushed the boundaries of what we know about business, it is always informative to look to the predecessors. Ron Chernow gives readers a complete picture of this forefather of big business. **JC**

Titan: The Life of John D. Rockefeller Sr., Vintage Books, Paperback Second Edition 2004, ISBN 9781400077304

WHERE TO NEXT? » Page 256 for **the rebirth of an American industry** « Page 147 for **an understanding of the rules Rockefeller was leveraging** « Page 24 for **advice on competing with sharks like Rockefeller** | EVEN MORE: *The Prize* by Daniel Yergin; *Andrew Carnegie* by David Nasaw; *The People's Tycoon* by Steven Watts

My Years with General Motors

ALFRED P. SLOAN JR.

Reviewed by Jack

When Alfred Sloan, the longtime chairman of General Motors, contributed a management article to *Fortune* magazine in the spring of 1953, it was so comprehensive that one of the magazine's writers, John McDonald, suggested he craft it into a book. Sloan and McDonald (who would act as ghostwriter), along with a young researcher, Alfred D. Chandler Jr. (the now distinguished business historian), and Sloan's longtime assistant, pored over GM's archives to create the masterpiece *My Years with General Motors*. Because McDonald had extensive access to Sloan's files, the book is stocked with reprints of memos, detailed letters, and minutes of meetings, which, while cumbersome at times, help retell Sloan's years at GM in a uniquely comprehensive manner. In 1946, Peter Drucker published *Concept of the Corporation*, a detailed study of General Motors, a result of Sloan's invitation to Drucker to observe (while being paid) the company. Their philosophies matched well; both knew that corporations could not continue to grow unless a theory about how they should be constructed evolved.

In 1899, when GM was still headed by W. A. Durant, Sloan was the president of Hyatt Roller Bearing Company, a supplier to the nascent automobile industry. GM bought Hyatt in 1916, along with many of its other suppliers, and created a group called United Motors. Sloan was made a vice president and given some significant duties. He was also promoted to GM's board. After World War I, the auto industry faced a significant downturn, and shareholders became concerned. While Durant was regarded as a great visionary when it came to acquisitions and the automotive industry, he was not considered an effective manager. Around this same time, Sloan became head of United Motors and wrote an organization study "as a possible solution for the specific problems created by the expansion of the corporation after World War I" and submitted it to the executive committee. This study is one of the most important business documents ever written, primarily because, in those pages, Sloan revealed an organization that was so efficient, employing such processes as centralized buying and using interchangeable parts to build different GM cars, that they would ensure critical savings for GM at that time of struggle. Sloan succeeded Durant as president in 1922 and later became chairman of the board in 1937. He proved during his time at GM to be one of the management masters of the twentieth century.

During the 1920s, Ford, featuring its Model T, had captured well over 50 percent of the automobile market. Under Durant, GM had lost focus on the business at hand to pursue other sideline challenges, like the creation of a copper-cooled engine. In addition, GM had too many car brands that often cannibalized the other brands' customers. The new GM, using Sloan's organizational plan to consolidate car brands, created a concept of providing a customer with cars for a lifetime, as the slogan promoted. The first-time automotive buyer would start with the low-priced Chevrolet while the senior driver would settle back into a Cadillac. At the same time, Ford was slow to update the Model T, so when Sloan's management practices took hold, GM became the largest manufacturer of cars and trucks and remained so for decades.

"Confidence and caution formed my attitude in 1920. We could not control the environment, or predict its changes precisely, but we could seek the flexibility to survive fluctuations in business."

It would be an understatement to say that Sloan's successes were impressive during his forty-five years at GM. In 1922, Sloan captained a company of 25,000 employees; by 1962, Sloan's final year at GM, that number had grown to 600,000. During that same time, car and truck sales went from 205,000 units to 4,491,000, and total assets grew from $134 million to $9.2 billion. He accomplished this growth, in part, by being the first company to introduce new car models each year. He understood that people wanted a car that didn't reflect where they were currently, but where they wanted to be. Buyers were inclined to stretch their financial limits, so to expedite the process, he developed the General

Motors Acceptance Corporation to finance the new cars.

Sloan's management style allowed committees to make decisions, while he orchestrated debates within these committees to propel the future plans for the organization. This approach helped Sloan and GM to lead the industry for decades and with it give birth to the concept of "the professional manager," as Drucker describes Sloan in the book's introduction.

Full of lengthy excerpts from Sloan's correspondence and business documents, *My Life with General Motors* deviates from the usual biography format. The book is ideal for the student of business who wants to learn about managing both large and small groups, as Sloan offers long discourses on decision making and other key organizational issues. This book is a glimpse into the mind and actions of one of the twenty-first century's masters of business. **JC**

A GHOST MEMOIR

In 2003, John McDonald wrote a book for MIT Press called *A Ghost Memoir: The Making of Alfred P. Sloan's* My Years with General Motors. Read as a follow-up to this biography, McDonald's own book provides a revealing look at the creation of this exemplary account by one of the management masters of the twentieth century. His discussion about some of the more sensitive material included in the book is fascinating. For example, Sloan's disclosure of his cornering of the market struck fear in the hearts of GM's lawyers. McDonald details how the lawyers, after they read the manuscript, wanted to stop publication of the book over concerns about antitrust issues. McDonald took the unprecedented step of suing GM so the book could be published in 1964—two years before Sloan's death.

My Years with General Motors, Currency/Doubleday, Paperback 1990, ISBN 9780385042352

WHERE TO NEXT? « Page 159 **for more on Sloan's consultant** « Page 170 for **the revolt against Sloan's view** « Page 167 for **the evolution in auto production** |
EVEN MORE: *Concept of the Corporation* by Peter F. Drucker; *Guts* by Robert A. Lutz; *A Ghost's Memoir* by John McDonald

Classics

Wealth of Nations

Adam Smith's *magnum opus* of economics may not be suitable for light lunchtime reading, but its epic heft belies its accessibility. In fact, Smith, one of the greatest thinkers of his time or any other, somehow manages everyday parallels, many of which, despite an eighteenth-century viewpoint, still apply today.

Exhaustive in scope, he goes from micro to macro, globalization to taxes, never losing focus or steam. Actually, the true bulk here comes from the blow-by-blow bombardment of facts—seemingly anytime, anywhere that money has changed hands in modern capitalistic society, Smith has it in perspective.

No matter the industry, or level on the corporate totem pole, there is something here for any reader who thinks about why and where they go to work each day. Now-commonplace phrases like "invisible hand" and "self-interest" may echo from a distant high school history class, but the relevance of these, and others, is still unquestionable in everyone's nine-to-five world.

The Origin of Species

Few books throughout history continue to prove such an intellectual nuisance as *The Origin of Species*. Once highly controversial in terms of scientific thought and human nature, Darwin's masterpiece now finds its way into a discussion of business classics. In fact, much can be made of the change in the way the book has been received over time: it's almost as if the conclusions of natural selection—less complexity ceding to more—are demonstrated in the public's perception of the work.

Offering sweeping conclusions on humankind's interaction with the environment, this seminal work, when whittled down, can also act as a playbook of business push-and-pulls: "Struggle for Existence" is every start-up business; "Instinct" embodies every consumer.

Give Darwin a pass for his non-PC portions and ignore the historical baggage attached. At its core, *The Origin of Species* is a surprisingly readable, singularly keen observation of human nature.

The Prince

A classic study of power and control, this treatise by Machiavelli was written with little thought of business, or even politics. Rather, and quite ironically, his goal was to impress Lorenzo de' Medici, and, essentially, to gain back a cushy job. Somehow, within his most base and self-serving aspirations of comfort, the man crafted a pinnacle of business virtue that advocates manipulation, authority, and force, but also resiliency and the steadfast commitment to a purpose. The ends justify the means, etc., have become clichéd as terms, but in theory and practice they are still astounding in their economy and precision. Citing or abiding his work won't make you popular, and his name has become eponymous with the most feared and hated type of boss, but *The Prince* underscores a fundamental tenet: it's not personal, it's business.

The Art of War

By far the most "classic" of the classics, Sun Tzu's masterpiece is also the most concise and universally indispensable. No estimate could do justice to the role played in world history by this little "how to": memorized by Chinese fighters, revered by Napoleon, it was even studied by American forces during World War II.

Lately, though, this first of all military treatises has begun breaching the business battlefield in a big way. Spying, scheming, snaking, staying ahead by any means necessary is Sun Tzu's game. Upon reading descriptions of maintaining the offensive, the use of energy, and exploitative strategy, one gets the feeling that this is *not* the guy you'd want to have to scrapple with for the last cookie.

And this may be how competitors will feel about any who put his theories into practice.

While the book's popularity continues to mount, Tzu's delivery—simplistic, arcane, poetic—ensures every reader takes away something different and is entertained along the way.

Written in 500 BC, *The Art of War* is still the final word on all things competitive. While the weapons have changed with time, the immutable laws of human conflict never will.

Written by Todd Lazarski

The HP Way

DAVID PACKARD

Reviewed by Jack

Hewlett-Packard may be notable to you for a variety of reasons. You might have an HP printer on your desk. Maybe you're an avid fan of the history of the Silicon Valley and journeyed to the infamous garage where HP began. Perhaps you are intrigued by the rise and fall of Carly Fiorina, or maybe you watched the 2006 imbroglio involving leaks and finger-pointing in HP's boardroom. But maybe you also have heard of "the HP Way," the management approach about which Jim Collins writes, "The point is not that every company should necessarily adopt the specifics of the HP Way, but that Hewlett and Packard exemplify the power of building a company based on a framework of principles." Hewlett-Packard is an American success story, and *The HP Way* tells the story of how the company came to be and why its singular approach led to singular success.

Hewlett and Packard were unlikely partners. David Packard was born in 1912 and became an all-star basketball and track athlete. As a child he was very much interested in radio and electrical devices and later was accepted to Stanford to study electrical engineering. During his first fall at Stanford in 1930, he met Bill Hewlett, in many ways his opposite. Hewlett was dyslexic and struggled early in school. He was accepted to Stanford only because his father taught there. He joked that he chose electrical engineering because he liked electric trains.

While at Stanford, Hewlett and Packard became close friends. In 1937, they had their first "business" meeting to discuss starting a company together. Packard would manage the manufacturing tasks for the company while Hewlett would focus on the circuit technology and engineering. Their partnership was formed in 1939 (the sequence of the surnames for the company name came from a coin flip). Their first product was an audio oscillator used to create steady audio frequencies. (They called it Model 200A because that number made it seem like they had been in business awhile.) Meanwhile Hewlett, a bachelor, moved into the one-car garage behind the house Packard rented with his wife. That garage, now a landmark considered "the birthplace of Silicon Valley," became their first workshop.

By 1964, Hewlett-Packard had come a long way from its first product. The company's total sales were $125 million, and all revenue came from scientific instruments. The two innovated further, developing an automatic controller that quickly found more sales as a minicomputer, not as an accessory, and that set the trajectory for their future business. The company continued to evolve, diversifying its products. Consider that in 1994, HP's sales from computer products, service, and support were almost $20 billion, or about 78 percent of the total business.

"We thought that if we could get everybody to agree on what our objectives were and to understand what we were trying to do, then we could turn them loose and they would move in a common direction."

And while the products were enough to make HP successful and well-known, it was the management philosophy that gained the company another kind of respect. At the first off-site meeting in 1957, the company put into words what it believed was "The HP Way" of doing business. In five principles, it created a company philosophy to retain the small-business quality in a now very large company. Revolutionary management practices were enacted like "flextime" and creating small teams and letting the teams develop on their own. In 1966, the list of company objectives was expanded to seven. The seven objectives are, to this day: profit, customers, field of interest, growth, employees, organization, and citizenship. Packard explains that each can be summed up in one sentence. For example, *field of interest* is explained as: "To concentrate our efforts, continually seeking new opportunities for growth but limiting our involvement to fields in which we have capability and can make a contribution." These common objectives help set boundaries for all employees, yet allow for a certain freedom to play within those boundaries.

Hewlett and Packard were brilliant thinkers and perhaps even more effective in executing their vision, but they also seemed to do the right thing for their customers and employees when they came to a crossroads. The greatest lesson to be divined from this book isn't so much how to create a similar company but how creating a company based on a strong and clear set of values can lead to outstanding success. **JC**

The HP Way: How Bill Hewlett and I Built Our Company, Collins, Paperback Business Essentials Edition, 2005, ISBN 9780060845797

WHERE TO NEXT? « Page 75 for **other firms like HP** « Page 89 for **a tech turnaround** » Page 212 for **a big leader with big ideals** | EVEN MORE: *Bill and Dave* by Michael S. Malone; *Tough Choices: A Memoir* by Carly Fiorina

Personal History

KATHARINE GRAHAM
Reviewed by Jack

It is unusual in contemporary business for one person to run a major business for almost thirty years. It is even more unusual if that person is a woman. Katharine Graham ran the Washington Post Company, originally her father's company, after the death of her husband in 1963, until 1991. When she took control of the company there were no women running an organization the size of the *Post*. Katharine Graham not only succeeded, but excelled, and, in *Personal History*, she tells her life story so exceptionally well that she would go on to win a Pulitzer Prize for it in 1998. But her success was not without struggle. Throughout her tenure as publisher, she had problems garnering the respect of peers and subordinates, and, in this book, she discusses her struggle to trust her own instincts. But it is indeed her obvious success as a leader and her status as a moral icon that makes this book essential reading.

Graham was born into wealth. Her father was a financier and later a public servant. Her mother was an intellectual and involved with the Republican Party. Graham acknowledges that her childhood was sheltered. Her inherent self-awareness is evidenced in this story: every other year, the family would go on a camping trip out west to see, as her mother said, that not everybody lived in large houses. Graham reflects on the lesson with wit and wisdom: "I suppose it did, but the lesson had its limits. There were five ranch hands on the trip to California, eleven saddle horses, and seventeen packhorses—not exacting roughing it." This observation is a telling example of what makes this personal history so compelling: Graham led an extraordinary life but could recognize that her experience was the exception.

Graham wasn't afraid of hard work, though, and wasn't a slave to wealth and opportunity. After a freshman year at Vassar, she transferred to the University of Chicago and got involved in labor politics during the Depression. Certainly she had a leg up through her family connections—after graduation she got a job at a San Francisco paper with help from her father—but she still got her hands dirty while covering the labor unrest at the docks and becoming close to the union leaders.

When Graham took over the Washington Post Company after her husband died, it consisted of the daily newspaper, *Newsweek* magazine, and a few TV and radio stations. As president, she oversaw all three divisions. Both fortuitously and with a number of inherent challenges, her reign began at the start of some of the major events of the century. The assassinations of John F. Kennedy, Martin Luther King Jr., and Robert F. Kennedy, and racial unrest, made the daily newspaper even more important in American everyday life. As luck would have it, just as the *Washington Post* started to expand its influence, New York City dailies were hurt by labor troubles and three papers had to close. The writers were forced out of their jobs at the weeklies, which allowed the *Post* to gain some quality writers—especially in editorial and national and international news— and elevate the standard while other dailies were reduced.

Lack of competition and an extended editorial budget allowed Graham to undertake some unconventional risks. For example, she allowed the *Post* correspondent in Vietnam to point out that the emperor in fact had no clothes even when the U.S. government had been saying otherwise. Graham also seized opportunities to develop relationships with important figures. Included in the book is her correspondence about the Vietnam War with President Johnson as the *Post* swung to an antiwar stance, especially provocative considering her husband is credited with getting Johnson on the national ticket as VP in 1960.

Surprisingly, and somewhat refreshingly, Graham's book also reveals her insecurities with the business side of the newspaper world. She acknowledges that she was way more interested in the editorial side of the *Post*, and because of that she ran afoul of the publisher. For example, when Bobby Kennedy was assassinated, she got a call in the early morning from the circulation manager asking her what to do. It was decided that they would deliver the paper that was already planned and then do a special edition and deliver it again. She made that decision on the loading dock. Her publisher was angry with her for not consulting him first.

But it should not be assumed that she wielded her power with no interest in improving her handle on the business side. She spent time at companies such as Texas Instruments, Xerox, and NCR trying to understand the basics of good management. She spent a week at an IBM course for senior executives to learn about computers. Petrified and annoyed that she was the only woman present, she discovered that the men attending the course were as apprehensive as she was to learn about technology. She was admirably willing to put herself in situations of learning, again getting dirt under her fingernails.

"I told [Phil Geyelin, a diplomatic reporter for the *Wall Street Journal*] something I have said to every editor I've worked with—that I didn't want to read anything in the paper of great importance or that represented an abrupt change which we haven't discussed; that I wanted to be in on the takeoffs as well as the landings."

Katharine Graham believed she could make a difference. She succeeded in her business by maintaining a strict moral code while being open to change and not succumbing to her insecurities. It is impossible not to be charmed by her stories, such as her account of sitting on a boat with Truman Capote, reading and critiquing the advance review copy of *In Cold Blood*. When I read *Personal History*, I am grateful for the chance to take a peek into her amazing life and to learn about one of the most prominent female figures in modern business. JC

Personal History, Vintage Books, Paperback 1998, ISBN 9780375701047

WHERE TO NEXT? « Page 32 for **coping with an unexpected career change** « Page 47 for **memorable moments of leadership** « Page 64 for **the one periodical we recommend** | EVEN MORE: *A Good Life* by Ben Bradlee; *Power, Privilege and the Post* by Carol Felsenthal; *All the President's Men* by Carl Bernstein and Bob Woodward

Moments of Truth

JAN CARLZON

Reviewed by Jack

In the 1970s, Sweden was known for ABBA, Saab, cold weather, blonds, and socialism, but not for cutting-edge leadership. That all changed when Jan Carlzon, at the age of thirty-two, was hired to run Vingresor (a vacation packager for Scandinavian Airlines—SAS). Carlzon's success with Vingresor landed him the presidency of the parent company, SAS, which was at that time in the midst of a severe loss after seventeen consecutive profitable years. During his tenure at SAS, Carlzon turned a stodgy state-run airline into a world-class airline that has become one of Europe's biggest, operating over 1,000 flights a day to 103 destinations in 34 countries. *Moments of Truth* is Carlzon's 135-page autobiography chronicling his time at the airline in a series of stories that are relevant to anyone in business.

When Carlzon became president at Vingresor (the company at which he'd been hired right out of college), he was known around the office as "Ego Boy." The promotion had caused him to act out a role of superiority he thought appropriate for a president, providing a solution for everybody's problem. An associate took him aside and pointed out to him that he had been promoted not to have all the answers, but to be a supportive presence. He reflects on that moment as a turning point of his career.

> The company was not asking me to make all the decisions on my own, only to create the right atmosphere, the right conditions for others to do their jobs better. I began to understand the difference between a traditional corporate executive, who issues instruction after instruction from the top, and the new corporate leader, who must set the tone and keep the big picture in mind.

Six years later, when he took over as COO of SAS, he used this enlightened approach to turn around the suffering airline by giving frontline employees the power to make decisions.

Carlzon determined that every customer interacts with an employee of SAS for an average of fifteen seconds. He calls these interactions "moments of truth," because whether that brief exchange is with a ticket agent or baggage handler, it is during that time that a customer makes their judgment about his organization. All the marketing and clever slogans don't mean a thing if that moment is an unsatisfactory one for the customer. So Carlzon created an organization that gave the training and the power to each of his twenty thousand employees to fix every problem. As a result, the customer is left with a positive feeling of efficacy and efficiency after every interaction.

With this change, Carlzon successfully took SAS from the traditional "production-oriented" philosophy to a "customer-driven" philosophy. But the initial challenge, before perfecting customer service, was to determine just who SAS's customer was. Carlzon decided to focus on business travelers because they are the most profitable. They shop price less often, but are also the most fickle because they want to get where they need to be with the least difficulty. In the case of business travelers, brand is seldom favored over convenience.

"An individual without information cannot take responsibility; an individual who is given information cannot help but take responsibility."

This focus on a specific customer informed each successive decision. For example, a purchase of new Airbuses to replace the older DC-9s was already in the works when Carlzon took over. The Airbuses would operate 6 percent cheaper than the DC-9s, but the planes needed to be full to realize the savings; because the Airbus had 240 seats compared to the DC-9's 110 seats, this was a considerably greater challenge. Carlzon quickly realized that his passenger base was too small to support the bigger plane; SAS would have needed to increase passengers to reduce the number of flights. But this ran counter to the needs of the business traveler, who wants and needs many flights leaving and arriving at all hours. In an unconventional decision, SAS mothballed the Airbuses. As Carlzon writes: "Our new customer-oriented perspective starts with the market instead of the product." That decision was revolutionary then, and would still be today.

The changes Carlzon brought to SAS were not made without difficulty. As he drove to reduce the management pyramid that was the existing management style, the middle managers were feeling the pinch from both ends. Upper management wanted the frontline folks to have the freedom to do extraordinary things for the customers. This decentralizing was obviously a big hit with everyone but those in the middle. After telling some amusing stories about middle managers pushing back, Carlzon clarifies to any organization that is in this flattened world that the middle needs to realize that "[t]heir authority applies to translating the overall strategies into practical guidelines that the front line can follow and then mobilizing the necessary resources for the front line to achieve its objectives."

Most business books need 250 to 300 pages to give you what this little treasure offers up in 135. Carlzon's reorganization of a European airline during the 1980s may seem distant from our current challenges, but it succinctly teaches us about great leadership and management. That, of course, is particularly relevant, considering the current expansion of resources available at consumers' fingertips when they make their purchasing decisions. Moments of truth happen to us every day as we travel and shop, but many businesses still don't get what Carlzon was talking about over twenty years ago. Reading this book will change how you make decisions as a consumer and how you do business as a service provider. **JC**

Moments of Truth: New Strategies for Today's Consumer-Driven Economy, HarperCollins, Paperback 1989, ISBN 9780060915803

WHERE TO NEXT? « Page 154 for **what the CEO wants you to know** « Page 54 for **humanistic leadership** « Page 92 for **the power of listening to your customers** | EVEN MORE: *Service America in the New Economy* by Karl Albrecht and Ron Zemke; *Customers for Life* by Carl Sewell and Paul B. Brown; *The Customer Comes Second* by Hal F. Rosenbluth and Diane McFerrin Peters

Sam Walton: Made in America—My Story

SAM WALTON WITH JOHN HUEY

Reviewed by Jack

Sam Walton is the greatest merchant of the twentieth century. His legacy grew from a single five-and-dime in Newport, Arkansas, into a retail behemoth that earned $380 billion in revenue in 2007. Despite his unparalleled success, Walton couldn't understand what salacious news *Fortune* hoped to uncover when the magazine named him the richest man in America in 1985. Walton recounts in his memoir, *Sam Walton: Made in America:* "I drove an old pickup truck with cages in the back for my bird dogs, or I wore a Wal-Mart baseball cap, or I got my hair cut at the barbershop just off the town square. . . ." The book tells the tale of this self-made man in his own down-home words. Added quotes from those who knew him best give us a real sense of knowing the man personally. While the aw-shucks tone may be a little over the top, it does not diminish the story: Sam Walton was an extraordinary man and had an extraordinary tale to tell.

Walton was a very smart and ambitious guy beneath his seemingly ordinary outer façade. One needs only to look at his childhood to realize he was a leader early on. He was the youngest Eagle Scout in the history of Missouri at the time he was awarded the recognition. He was the quarterback of his high school football team when his team went undefeated. And as a basketball player (leading the team as a guard at only five feet nine), his team went undefeated as well. Walton was a young man with a serious competitive streak that served him well all through his life.

The stories about his early years could belong to many people in this country. He lived in a small town, graduated from college while working at a JC Penney, fell in love, and got married. He did his duty as an ROTC soldier during World War II and, after the war, moved to a small town in Arkansas because his wife, Helen, refused to live in a town larger than 10,000 people. In 1945, he used $5,000 of his money and $20,000 of his father-in-law's money to buy that five-and-dime in Newport.

Over the next fifteen years, Walton expanded his company to sixteen stores. He stayed under the radar in the early years by opening stores in smaller towns. Those towns were chosen because Walton would only open a new store within one day's delivery from the closest distribution center. By keeping its corporate headquarters in Arkansas, the company retained its small-town roots.

Walton was not the only entrepreneur, though, who saw potential in discount retail. In 1962, S.S. Kresge started Kmart, Dayton Hudson opened Target, and Woolworth launched Woolco. Walton's answer was Wal-Mart number 1, which he opened in Rogers, Arkansas, the same year. Within five years, Kmart had 250 stores with revenues of $800 million to Wal-Mart's 19 stores and $9 million in revenues because Walton stuck to his original plan of focusing on smaller markets. The other discounters beat each other up over the big markets. In the early years of Wal-Mart, Walton continued to run eighteen variety stores and a handful of Wal-Marts. The stories of his early accounting and distribution are amusing . . . and scary. For example, he continued using a pigeonhole method for receipts and paperwork until his responsibilities grew with over twenty stores.

"A lot of what goes on these days with high-flying companies and these overpaid CEO's [sic], who're really looting from the top and aren't watching out for anyone but themselves, really upsets me."

But it is the culture Walton created that was most notable. His early managers actually invested money in the stores they managed. Walton visited the stores continually and studied his competitors. As he traveled on business or even with his family on vacation, he would stop at any kind of retailer to study its tactics. Then he refined and improved these pilfered ideas and tried them out in his stores so that the company would be constantly innovating.

Occasionally in your life you meet someone who is so dynamic and full of boundless energy that there is no wondering how he excelled. I imagine this is what meeting Sam Walton would have been like. His communication skills and style played a significant role in how he convinced his employees to get (and stay) onboard his tight ship. There are many books written about his company, but if you want to know the origins of Wal-Mart, nothing is better than hearing from the man himself. The passion Sam Walton brought to his work is admirable, and he shares that passion in this memoir. In fact, he even advises the reader to "borrow/steal" from his successes. **JC**

Sam Walton: Made in America—My Story, Bantam Books, Paperback 1993, ISBN 9780553562835

WHERE TO NEXT? » Page 274 for **globalization** » Page 284 for **innovation** « Page 95 for **execution** | EVEN MORE: *The Wal-Mart Effect* by Charles Fishman; *Direct from Dell* by Michael Dell with Catherine Fredman; *Wal-Smart* by William H. Marquardt

Losing My Virginity

RICHARD BRANSON

Reviewed by Jack

Richard Branson is arguably the most successful entrepreneur of the past half-century, creating 360 different companies and brands, from Virgin Cola to Virgin Music to Virgin Atlantic. Some failed, like Virgin Cola, and some set the industry standard, like Virgin Atlantic. But don't think that Branson is done: he calls this book Volume One of his autobiographies. It covers the first forty-three years of his life, though the first chapter begins with one of his around-the-world balloon flights that failed in 1997. The book ends in 1993, when he was forced to sell Virgin Music to save Virgin Atlantic—a move he refers to as the low point of his business life. The overall theme of the book is survival, and this book is chock full of survival stories about his life, his remarkable entrepreneurial spirit, and his successes and his failures, which offer both inspiration and caution to those who would like to follow in his footsteps.

As with most autobiographies, we begin at the beginning, and Branson recounts his childhood, telling tales about family and school. Faced with the challenges of dyslexia and a rebellious spirit, Branson had an extremely hard time with authority at school. He had ideas about reforming some of the more arcane rules, and out of this desire came the student/youth newspaper called the *Student* that he started with his friend, Nik Powell (who would be a cohort of Branson's throughout, enabling Branson to explore new ideas while Nik made them work on the front lines). The first issue was published in January 1968 when Branson was seventeen. Branson retells stories about how he and Nik called banks and large companies to get advertisers, and his methods reveal his ingeniousness. The pair called Coca-Cola, saying Pepsi was in the paper, and then reversed the tactic when calling Pepsi. Also he was fearless in pursuing the big story, and his interviews included subjects like Mick Jagger and John Lennon. Lennon almost put Branson out of business when he promised him an unreleased song to be put in the paper as a flexi-disc. Branson ramped up the print run, expecting a land rush of sales, but Lennon didn't deliver. That story reflects just one of the misfortunes that Branson did not let push him offtrack.

In 1970, the *Student* employed almost twenty people—all earning £20 per week. But by that time, Branson had identified another avenue to explore. He knew how important music was to the readers of the *Student*. He also saw that regular record shops didn't discount music, so he ran an ad in the *Student* offering cheaper mail-order records. The response was huge and a business was born. Of course, he knew they needed a clever name, and Virgin was suggested because they were all novices at business. Virgin Mail-Order Records took in bags and bags of mail orders, but the boom didn't last. In January 1971, the Union of Post Office Workers went on strike for six months.

That obstacle put Branson once again in survival mode . . . a state which seemed to stimulate his creativity. He saw an opportunity to sell music in an actual retail store. At that time, record stores were dull, formal areas owned by people who knew little about what was new or exciting. The first Virgin record shop, located on Oxford Street in London, created an environment where customers could hang out, talk, and hear new music. While Nik was running the record store on a daily basis, Branson discovered that he could save some money by selling records that were for export and therefore cheaper. The decision to sell those records caused him to spend a night in jail, and his mother had to bail him out of the pokey. He ended up having to pay a fine of £60,000. Branson had always been a worker of the angles—looking for shortcuts—but that night he vowed he would never do anything that would cause him to be jailed or embarrassed again.

"But, unlike losing your virginity, in whatever world you make for yourself, you can keep embracing the new and the different over and over again."

Branson soon realized that the margin at the retail level was small and that the real money was made behind the scenes. He found a run-down manor outside London in which to set up recording studios, and bought it for £30,000, borrowing £20,000 from a bank and the remainder from friends and family. Since mainstream recording studios were not very friendly to young bands, Branson was determined that the manor would be different. It had rooms for musicians to stay in while they recorded in the state-of-the-art studio constructed in an outbuilding. Eventually the studio would be world-famous for its state-of-the-art production facilities and ambiance. In 1992, Branson regretfully sold the Virgin label to EMI for a $1 billion to help subsidize Virgin Atlantic Airways, which he launched in 1984.

These are just a few of the stories that keep you turning the pages in *Losing My Virginity*. Branson's every decision is an example of his continual search for the next big thing. And his ability to recognize it and learn from his failures or stumbles can be a model for all readers. He tells people, when asked to describe his personal business philosophy, "It's not that simple: to be successful, you have to be out there, you have to hit the ground running, and if you have a good team around you and more than a fair share of luck, you might make something happen." **JC**

Losing My Virginity: How I've Survived, Had Fun, and Made a Fortune Doing Business My Way, Three Rivers Press, Paperback 2004, 9780812932294

WHERE TO NEXT? ⏩ Page 248 for **building a compelling business** ⏩ Page 295 for **envisioning a compelling life** ⏪ Page 117 for **building compelling brands** | EVEN MORE: *The Rebel Rules* by Chip Conley; *Buffett* by Roger Lowenstein; *Giants of Enterprise* by Richard S. Tedlow

A Business and Its Beliefs

THOMAS J. WATSON JR.

Reviewed by Jack

Thomas J. Watson Jr. took the helm at IBM from his father in 1952. During his twenty-year tenure at IBM, he moved the company forward on several fronts, including the transition from mechanical to electronic computation. In 1962, Watson was asked to give a number of lectures at Columbia Graduate School of Business as part of a series that featured speakers presenting on the management of large organizations. *A Business and Its Beliefs* grew out of Watson's presentation. In it, Watson discusses the humanistic philosophy of management that has defined IBM and revolves around three tenets: respect for the individual, giving the best customer service in the world, and the responsibility to "*pursue all tasks with the idea that they can be accomplished in a superior fashion*."

Watson believes that a thriving organization needs the people within to embrace these basic tenets of the organization, that they should not be simple hollow sentiments in the form of a mission statement. His conviction is strong.

> I firmly believe that any organization, in order to survive and achieve success, must have a sound set of beliefs on which it premises all its policies and actions.
>
> Next, I believe that the most important single factor in corporate success is faithful adherence to those beliefs.
>
> And finally, I believe that if an organization is to meet the challenges of a changing world, it must be prepared to change everything about itself except those beliefs as it moves through corporate life.

The policies set the style and substance of the organization, and, in turn, the way the organization interacts with its clients and society.

As you would expect, throughout *A Business and Its Beliefs*, Watson uses IBM as a case study. He explains that his father learned humanistic management as a young salesperson at the National Cash Register Company, one of the first sales-driven companies to focus on the employees, under the leadership of John Patterson. For example, Watson Sr. instituted an open door policy that offered the individual employee recourse if his manager was being unfair. Hundreds of employees would come to the corporate headquarters on their day off to talk with the senior Watson about workplace issues. This helped connect the senior management to the shop floor. As a result, Watson Jr. was made aware of the discrepancy between hourly and salaried employees' pay, and, in 1958, IBM put everybody on salary to eliminate that unfair practice. In the book, Watson Jr. likens employees to Kierkegaard's wild ducks, each free and individual, flying as individuals, but in a group to one destination.

From 1914 to the end of World War II, IBM experienced accelerated growth and the leadership at IBM had to make decisions based on instinct rather than patient, scientific study. The success of these quick decisions was a direct result of the guiding hand offered by the organization's strong belief system. As the company continued to grow, IBM's middle managers were, quite necessarily, new to the company, so IBM created two management schools, one for junior executives and one for line managers, to teach IBM's outlook and beliefs to new employees.

"It is better to aim at perfection and miss it than it is to aim at imperfection and hit it."

This slim, concise volume shows why IBM has thrived for almost a century and how the Watson family created a modern, humanistic organization in which shared core beliefs allowed the company to expand and adapt to change. It's a model for every company, large or small. **JC**

A Business and Its Beliefs: The Ideas that Helped Build IBM, McGraw-Hill, Hardcover 2003, ISBN 9780071418591

WHERE TO NEXT? « Page 89 for **the company's turnaround story** « Page 209 for **another example of a values-based organization** | EVEN MORE: *Father, Son & Co.* by Thomas J. Watson Jr.; *Built to Last* by Jim Collins and Jerry I. Porras; *The Wizard of Menlo Park* by Randall Stross

ENTREPRENEURSHIP

The word didn't even exist until 1950. However, blacksmiths, bakers, and candlestick makers faced the same challenges as today's organic farmers and database designers. These businesses are born out of passion but often fail in practicality. Entrepreneurship is hip, treacherous, and vital—all of which served as inspiration for our selections.

The Art of the Start

GUY KAWASAKI

Reviewed by Jack

If you peruse the business shelves of the library or your local book emporium, you'll find a lot of books about starting a new business. So, how do you find the one that will make your idea into a reality without buying the entire shelf? Well, the author's credibility is crucial in this case. You want to learn from someone who has "been there, done that," certainly, but you also want someone who can translate what he or she knows into inspiring and applicable advice.

Guy Kawasaki is your trustworthy guide with *The Art of the Start*. In 1984, he was hired by Apple as a software evangelist to convince software manufacturers to develop programs for the yet-to-be-finished Macintosh computer, an undertaking chronicled in his first book, *Selling the Dream*. He is now a founder and managing director of garage.com, an early-stage investor in technology start-ups; he also sits on a number of boards and acts as an advisor to tech businesses. From this vast experience, Kawasaki is convinced that starting a business (or hiring the right person or building a brand—starting anything) is an art, not a science, and with this book he'll help you start your own endeavor with style.

If you have ever seen Kawasaki speak—and if you haven't, you must—you know he has a distinctive style. *The Art of the Start* is infused with this unique sensibility. For example, his use of Top Ten lists is famous, and he employs them here to great effect. But don't think you will be bullet-pointed to boredom. Kawasaki writes with a light tone, and maintains a sense of humor throughout. For example, in a list of ways to avoid hiring mistakes, he gives us the Top Ten lies job candidates use, including:

Lie: "I've never been with a company for more than a year because I get bored easily."
Truth: "It takes people about a year to figure out that I'm a bozo."

Lie: "I am a vice president, but no one reports to me."
Truth: "Any bozo can become a vice president at my company."

Kawasaki uses many of these unique devices in presenting the material. Frequently Asked Questions become Frequently Avoided Questions. Charts serve to contrast common wisdom with Guy's real-world advice. Each chapter begins with a GIST (Great Ideas for Starting Things) and often includes a "minichapter" covering everything from designing T-shirts to "The Art of Schmoozing." The final element of each chapter is a list of recommended reading.

"Working in a start-up isn't easy. . . . Therefore, belief in what you're doing is as important as competence and experience."

Clever organization gives way to actionable advice. In the "Pitching" chapter, he introduces the "10/20/30" rule of presentations, which states that a presentation should have only ten slides, last twenty minutes, and use a thirty-point font. Sure, most pitch meetings are scheduled to last an hour, but Kawasaki suggests twenty minutes for two reasons: one, the previous meeting may have gone long and your time will be cut; and two, you will want ample time for discussion at the end. Also in the pitch section, he tells you to set the stage for your presentation by asking the attendees three questions: "How much of your time may I have?" "What are the three most important things I can communicate to you?" and "May I quickly go through my PowerPoint presentation and handle questions at the end?" This approach may challenge you to think on your feet if their questions differ from the material you prepared, but it is worth the risk. These recommendations can change the dynamic of a presentation because it will be more transparent and considerate of the audience, which is unusual and appreciated.

When you buy *The Art of the Start*, you are investing in Kawasaki's twenty-five years of experience in Silicon Valley, his tenure at Apple, and his time as a venture capitalist. When you read *The Art of the Start*, you are experiencing his signature style. This is one of those books that is important as much for *how* he says things as for *what* he says. Starting is always the hardest part, and Kawasaki focuses on the points that need attention when you begin any kind of endeavor, business or otherwise. JC

The Art of the Start, Portfolio, Hardcover 2004, ISBN 9781591840565

WHERE TO NEXT? « Page 143 for **bytes on sales** « Page 98 for **bytes on management** « Page 136 for **bytes on marketing** | EVEN MORE: *Selling the Dream* by Guy Kawasaki; *E-Boys* by Randall E. Stross; *High-Tech Start-Up* by John L. Nesheim

The E-Myth Revisited

MICHAEL E. GERBER
Reviewed by Jack

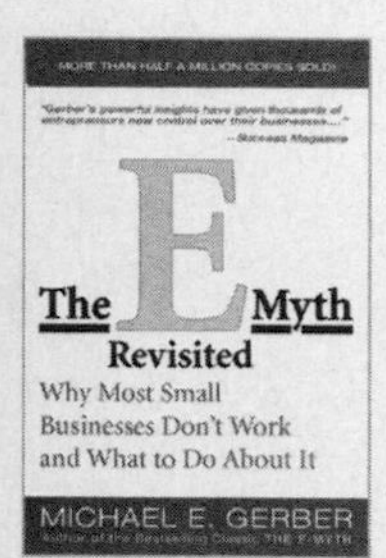

You make the best cannoli in North Boston or the best bratwurst in Sheboygan and you are thinking about going into business for yourself. Your friends and family, even strangers, assure you that your creation is so good it'll be a sure-fire hit. The first step toward your new venture is to take out a second mortgage on the house. Second step, leave your crappy day job.

Think I've just described the recipe for starting your own successful business? Think again! You're in danger of falling for the E-Myth, the entrepreneur's oft-made mistake of putting the cart before the horse, thinking he can succeed with simply a good idea and hard work. Before Gerber's first book on this subject, *The E-Myth*, was published, most small-business books were about honing an idea and then bootstrapping it. While he covered the nuts and bolts of running a new small business, his primary goal was to introduce some key business concepts by telling a story that every reader can relate to.

In *The E-Myth Revisited*, you'll meet Sarah. Sarah is a baker who makes the best pies in the county. She wants to open her own business, but wonders how to make the jump from expert baker to successful small-business owner. Initially she has some success because she hires a smart manager to run the business while she concentrates on what she does best—baking pies. Unfortunately, the manager leaves for a better job and Sarah has a meltdown. Through her story Gerber presents the lessons on making a new business successful without requiring the reader to decipher the abstract rules or hypothetical advice often included in other small-business books.

Gerber believes that a common cause of small-business failure lies within "The Fatal Assumption": if you understand the technical work of a business, you understand a business that does technical work. In other words, baking pies is *not* the same as running a bakery. Gerber instead shows that to be a successful small-business owner, you need three separate skills: the technical, the managerial, and the entrepreneurial. He considers a lack of understanding in one or more of these areas to be the cause of most small-business failures. The reassuring news is that Gerber believes these skills can be learned.

Gerber contends that the true product of a business is not *what* it sells but *how* it sells it. Gerber formalizes this belief in a system he calls the "Business Format Franchise." The key is to create a systems-dependent business, not a people-dependent business. To do this, you need to view your business as a potential franchise and construct your internal systems that way. Look at the way McDonald's, Disney, and FedEx do business. Their products are consistent. The model is systems-based so anybody hired can be put inside that Mickey Mouse costume or behind the counter asking, "Would you like fries with that?" The result is a business that is completely scalable and not dependant on a single person.

To take advantage of this scalability, a business needs to be able to grow. Gerber presents three distinct activities: innovation, quantification, and orchestration. He suggests changing something as simple as your in-store greeting as innovation. Instead of "Can I help you find anything?" why not try "Have you ever been here before?" You can then measure whether this new greeting increases sales, and using those results, you can then refine your presentation going forward.

"[Y]our business is a means rather than an end, a vehicle to enrich your life rather than one that drains the life you have."

Gerber ends the book with a letter to Sarah. He speaks with passion about the importance of caring, which is at the heart of entrepreneurship at its most pure form. But baking perfect pies is not enough. That same caring must infuse the entire business enterprise. *The E-Myth Revisited* takes the hope of a hobby and provides the skills to create a livelihood. **JC**

The E-Myth Revisited: Why Most Small Businesses Don't Work and What to Do About It, HarperCollins, Paperback 1995, ISBN 9780887307287

WHERE TO NEXT? « Page 221 for **lessons from the entrepreneur** « Page 173 for **lessons from the technician** « Page 179 for **lessons from the manager** | EVEN MORE: *You Need to Be a Little Crazy* by Barry Moltz; *No Man's Land* by Doug Tatum

The Republic of Tea

MEL ZIEGLER, PATRICIA ZIEGLER, AND BILL ROSENZWEIG

Reviewed by Todd

I love it when Jack tells stories about the beginnings of 800-CEO-READ. I always listen, rapt—wondering how three shelves in the back of a bookstore could have turned into a fifteen-person, multimillion-dollar operation, wondering what it was that Jack did that allowed us to survive as we have against big-box retailing and Internet commerce, wondering how the dynamic culture formed. I search for some meaning in our past to understand the company we have become. No definitive written history exists for the conception of 800-CEO-READ, or for most companies, for that matter. I think that is why I enjoyed *The Republic of Tea* so much. It is the genesis story of a company and its quest to change the world with tea.

Mel Ziegler, the entrepreneur behind Banana Republic, found his clothing company had over time developed "its own mind" and he was becoming increasingly at odds with his progeny. After deciding to sell the clothing retailer, and still recovering from the painful separation, the disillusioned entrepreneur serendipitously found himself on an airplane sitting next to Bill Rosenzwieg. Bill was on a search to find a living he could love. The two shared one of those life-changing conversations, and *The Republic of Tea* is a record of their correspondence over twenty months. These reproductions of faxes and letters between Mel, Bill, and Mel's wife Patricia that make up *The Republic of Tea* chronicle the evolution of an idea into a business.

Rosenzweig was immediately swept up by Ziegler's zen-inspired descriptions for how tea can create a different state of mind. They both imagined the Republic as a place, physical and psychological. Patricia's illustrations, sprinkled throughout the book, bring a visual sense to the ideas brewing among the three. Stores, serving sets, tea blends for children, and water for tea bottled at the source of the Yangtze River all burst forth as potential paths of creativity in the initial weeks of their conversation.

The shared euphoria propelled both men forward, then gave way to practicality. Rosenzweig shifted his focus to understanding the mechanics of the tea market. Trips to the supermarket, conversations with tea brokers, and Lexus-Nexus searches provided a rough sketch of the world they were moving into. Imagined organizational charts and an evolving product portfolio added more concreteness. The would-be entrepreneur will appreciate Rosenzweig's thoroughness and preparation, but some of the details conveyed in his communiqués with Ziegler foreshadow problems ahead.

"As for my role, I got him pregnant."

Tension grew between the two partners. Ziegler felt that Rosenzweig was more interested in talking about the business than in starting the business. Rosenzweig was uncertain, acknowledging in added notes to the book that he needed Ziegler for direction and support. Ziegler, sensing that uncertainty, made his role clear: he was happy to mentor and possibly invest in the unformed company, but would contribute no further. Confidence wavering, Rosenzweig abandoned the Republic and took a job at a friend's design firm, vowing to bootstrap the tea business.

Rosenzweig returned to the idea with a new energy after a year had passed with no real progress. This time he would stand on his own. He needed to become an expert in tea. He spent an intense month in London at the center of the world tea trade, learning such particulars as how to identify a first-flush from a second-flush Darjeeling. He also resumed talks with Ziegler, this time with new expectations: "I stopped waiting for him to lead the way into the tea business because it was finally clear that if I didn't start it, no one else would." The Republic of Tea was incorporated by the three authors in 1992. Their idea had finally blossomed into a business.

Insights abound in *The Republic of Tea*, conveying the yin and yang of entrepreneurship. The book captures the rush of a new entrepreneurial idea, the unforgiving practicality of the marketplace, and how, in the end, the only indicator you can trust is your heart. Shortly after Rosenzweig rediscovered his passion for the project, he asked Ziegler when the right time to start a business is. Ziegler answered, in his usual thoughtful manner, "Never and always." **TS**

The Republic of Tea: The Story of the Creation of a Business, as Told Through the Personal Letters of Its Founders, Currency/Doubleday, Paperback 1994, ISBN 9780385420570

WHERE TO NEXT? « Page 129 for **why we buy** « Page 34 for **the magic of journeys** « Page 132 for **the power of experiences** | EVEN MORE: *Brewing Up a Business* by Sam Calagione; *Pour Your Heart into It* by Howard Schultz and Dori Jones Yang; *Typo* by David Silverman; *The Dip* by Seth Godin

The Partnership Charter

DAVID GAGE

Reviewed by Todd

The Partnership Charter
How to Start Out Right With Your New Business Partnership
{or Fix the One You're In}
DAVID GAGE

Researchers at Marquette University studied over two thousand companies and found that 94 percent of "hypergrowth" companies were started by two or more people. Individual owners made up only 6 percent of the hypergrowth segment and almost one-half of the slow-growth companies.

Despite this evidence that a partnership can lead to success, the thought of taking on a partner makes most budding entrepreneurs cringe. *Inc.* magazine polled its readers on this very subject and two out of every three respondents felt partnerships were a bad idea. When asked why, the majority said "inevitable conflicts" and "unmet expectations" would lead to problems.

Since the data show that partnerships are either necessary or unavoidable, there is an opportunity for educators to address the unique relationships between partners, but instead business schools spend vast amounts of classroom time discussing the intricacies of manager/employee relationships. Medical professionals and lawyers, for example, after years in school, commonly join practices despite never being educated on the form of business in which most will spend their entire careers. There is also a void in the business-book canon regarding the management of partnerships, and *The Partnership Charter* is an excellent resource to bridge this oversight.

When running a business with one or two partners, any of the following scenarios may present themselves:

- One partner insists on hiring a key employee whom another partner dislikes.
- A partner is sued for sexual harassment.
- The company receives an unsolicited buyout offer from a competitor.
- The company runs out of money.

- An ongoing personal or family crisis interferes with the ability of one partner to perform.
- One partner suddenly loses interest in the business.
- A partner is caught stealing from the company.

(Full list is on page 196 of *The Partnership Charter*.)

David Gage lays out these possible trials and tribulations in *The Partnership Charter*, examining the unique relationship between partners. Business relationships generally lack the emotional ties found in personal relationships, and boundaries are drawn based on ownership stakes, salaries, and titles. But changes in the external lives of the partners or the health of the business inevitably impact the partnership. While some conditions may be governed by the legal documents that established the company, Gage suggests a written charter that addresses a broader set of needs partners have over time.

"A charter is a necessary tool because few people have been taught how to be partners."

The chartering process establishes the ground rules for how the partnership will operate. A common vision for the company is created and agreed upon. The ownership stakes are determined based on factors ranging from the amount of capital invested to the amount of control each partner assumes. Assigning roles and titles are a natural subsequent step as partners decide how active they want to be in the new firm and how decision making will take place. Most important, a plan is drawn up to allocate how money will be distributed. This process compares and contrasts the partners' values systems and expectations for how the partnership will operate. Making all of this apparent at the start, says Gage, reduces the potential for disconnects later in the life of the partnership.

Entrepreneurs are not wary of partnerships for the wrong reasons; business partnerships are complex, dynamic relationships. But it is those nuances and synergies that bring a greater chance of success to any entrepreneurial adventure. TS

The Partnership Charter: How to Start Out Right with Your New Business Partnership (or Fix the One You're In), Basic Books, Paperback 2004, ISBN 9780738208985

WHERE TO NEXT? » Page 316 for **understanding our basic motives** » Page 313 for **understanding emotions** « Page 209 for **the Silicon Valley's most famous partnership** | EVEN MORE: *Start-ups That Work* by Joel Kurtzman and Glenn Rifkin; *Riding Shotgun* by Nathan Bennett and Stephen A. Miles; *Team of Rivals* by Doris Kearns Goodwin

Growing a Business

PAUL HAWKEN
Reviewed by Jack

Over twenty years ago, Paul Hawken, the cofounder of Smith & Hawken, a mail-order supplier of high-end quality gardening tools, wrote this then-unusual book. Most books about creating a business were books about raising capital, hiring the best employees, or writing a business plan. *Growing a Business* is a book about creating a good business that is sustainable and that brings you, the entrepreneur, satisfaction. It will help you become a better businessperson by showing you how to focus on the *why* of business instead of on the *how.* Hawken states his goal for his book early on: "I want to demystify, not with a set of dictums and executive summaries, but with a book that illustrates how the successful business is an extension of a person."

In 1965, there were 200,000 start-ups in the United States. In 1986, a year before this book was published, that number had swelled to over one million. This proliferation informs Hawken's belief that the future of commerce will be determined on the street by the small-business owner, not in the boardroom by corporate moguls.

Hawken also believes that business is about practice, not just about theory—no different from riding a surfboard or playing a piano. To stay grounded in practice, he suggests, "Be the customer. Go outside and look back through the window of your small business. Be a child trying to figure out how the world works. Go to a crowded park on a sunny day. Don't go into the back room to read another book about business (even this one)." No newcomer is expected to be good from the get-go, so Hawken advises, "Relax. Take your time. Work and practice and learn."

Hawken spends time discussing "tradeskill," a term coined by Michael Phillips and Salli Rasberry in their 1986 book called *Honest Business*, which he believes can make the difference between success and failure. Tradeskill is the knack for understanding what people want, how much they will pay, and how they make their decisions. The smaller the business, the more important it is to learn tradeskill. Phillips and Rasberry "break tradeskill down into four specific attributes: persistence, the ability to face facts, the ability to minimize risk, and the ability to be a hands-on learner." Hawken adds to these attributes the ability to grasp numbers.

Hawken strongly suggests that you finance a new business with your own money. You can avoid interest payments and there will be no temptation to spend money foolishly, because you know how hard it was to earn. Perhaps even more important, avoiding the temptation to borrow money from friends or family will keep you from complicating those relationships. Hawken also answers the question of how much money you will need: enough to go to market. This self-sufficiency ensures a sense of urgency and quality of product that will make you learn the business fast.

"To see the reward of commerce as money and the risk of commerce as failure is to see nothing at all."

I have discovered through writing my reviews for our book that one type of successful business book is the kind that you can pick up, open to any page, and immediately find a valuable nugget of information offering a supporting fact, an inspirational story, or a profound quotation, to get you instantly looking at your world differently. This book contains page after page of read-out-loud treasures you will want to share. For example, when Hawken discusses how one should view risk, he writes: "If you persist in seeing a situation in the terms of risk, look again. If you still see risk instead of opportunity, walk away, because you just might be right." His passion for business infuses every page, and as you read, you may just find your own passion stoked by his words. JC

Growing a Business, Simon & Schuster, Paperback 1987, ISBN 9780671671648

WHERE TO NEXT? « Page 143 for **the importance of growing a business** » Page 245 for **growing a business with a soul** « Page 54 for **growing as a leader** | EVEN MORE: *Small Giants* by Bo Burlingham; *Let My People Go Surfing* by Yvon Chouinard; *Raising the Bar* by Gary Erickson and Lois Lorentzen; *Setting the Table* by Danny Meyer

MAKING CHOICES

"There are elements of chance, choice, and certainty in every aspect of our lives."
— Persian prophet Zoroaster

Remove the unpredictable and inevitable and you are left with just one aspect of your life within your control: choice. But if choice is so desirable, so controllable, why do people back away from making choices, or make decisions that are illogical? These books explain why.

Malcolm Gladwell followed up his best seller *The Tipping Point* with *Blink*, focusing on the split second decisions we continuously make, synthesizing material from sources like John Gottman's "Love Lab" at the University of Washington, Gary Klein's intuition research, and Sheena Iyengar's insights into how too much choice hinders decision making, which she would investigate further in her *The Art of Choosing*.

Barry Schwartz's *The Paradox of Choice* asserts that abundant choice reduces quality of life: more does not mean better. Dan Ariely's book *Predictably Irrational* is full of these similar "bugs" in our baffling brains.

To better avoid the pitfalls of our own hardwiring, also read: *Nudge* by Richard Thaler and Cass Sunstein, *Sway* by Ori Brafman and Rom Brafman, *Priceless* by William Poundstone, and the granddaddy of them all — *Choices, Values, and Frames* by Dan Kahneman and Amos Tversky.

Written by Todd Sattersten

Guerrilla Marketing

JAY CONRAD LEVINSON

Reviewed by Jack

Small businesses have a fundamental conflict: big marketing ideas, small marketing dollars. *Guerrilla Marketing* provides the resolution. Former advertising executive Jay Conrad Levinson created the approach over twenty years ago; now, a series of books with over fifty titles bears the *Guerrilla Marketing* moniker. In my opinion, this is the ultimate rubber-meets-the-road, take-it-to-the-bank resource for anyone in small business.

I used the first edition of this book to grow my business in the early 1980s; we were called Schwartz Business Books then, and had an employee roster of fewer than ten names. My original copy has chapters on direct marketing and catalog sales and Yellow Pages advertising. The newest edition, published in 2007, omits those aged-out approaches and includes several sections on current issues, like "new-media marketing," which addresses such new-century approaches as "e-media marketing," and "nonmedia marketing," including trade shows, PR, and community involvement. But the new edition of *Guerrilla Marketing* still retains much of what was effective in the first: the basics. For example, Levinson offers a page on how to say hello and goodbye. He suggests that customers will be more inclined to like you and continue to do business with you if you use their names in conversation. This is the kind of advice that will build your fundamental people skills.

But before you can start any kind of a marketing campaign, your business needs a predetermined, long-term goal that will get everybody within your organization on the same page. To do that, you must have a core concept of what your business is. Levinson believes that the concept needs to be expressed in a maximum of seven words. He gives the example of an entrepreneur whose business offers computer classes. Following Levinson's lead, his core concept went from almost thirty words to three words: "Computers for Beginners." That new clarity led to an increase in attendance as people readily understood the service the company offered.

Guerrilla marketers excel in using "minimedia," which includes such things as "canvassing, writing personal letters, sending postcards, marketing by telephone, distributing circulars . . . and making business cards do double duty." At one point early on in my efforts to grow my business, I made flyers and gave them to friends to put on their companies' bulletin boards. Simple, direct, and timeless. Just look at the bulletin boards of your local coffeehouse to see this approach at work.

"*Marketing is every bit of contact your company has with anyone in the outside world.* Every bit of contact."

Small-business marketing strategy isn't limited to minimedia. Levinson believes that guerrilla marketers can also use mass media outlets like TV, newspapers, magazines, and radio to promote and sell their products and services. The book provides pages of suggestions on how to use "maximedia" and get the most success for your dollar spent.

Levinson concludes with a section titled, "The Nature of the Guerrilla." Here he writes about the attributes a good guerrilla marketing company needs. In particular, he describes a meme: "The instantly recognizable transmission of an idea, simple and clear, no explanation necessary" "Green Giant" and "the Michelin Man" are classic examples.

When the original edition was published in 1983, *Guerrilla Marketing* was an instant hit. The newest edition of this perennial best seller is updated for the twenty-first-century entrepreneur. Levinson shows that small businesses can use the same methods as their bigger brethren and also have a whole host of weapons that large companies could never use. This is the book that helped me build my business and it can also help you grow yours. **JC**

Guerrilla Marketing: Easy and Inexpensive Strategies for Making Big Profits from Your Small Business, Houghton Mifflin, Completely Updated and Expanded Paperback Edition 2007, ISBN 9780618785919

WHERE TO NEXT? « Read the **sales and marketing section of this book.** It starts on page 103. | EVEN MORE: *How to Make Big Money in Your Own Small Business* by Jeffrey J. Fox; *Permission Marketing* by Seth Godin; *Getting Everything You Can Out of All You've Got* by Jay Abraham

The Monk and the Riddle

RANDY KOMISAR WITH KENT LINEBACK

Reviewed by Jack

Randy Komisar graduated from Harvard Law School, then went into private practice in Boston. After pursuing a career at Apple as in-house counsel, he cofounded Claris Corporation, a spin-off of Apple, and then held a number of top roles at game development companies. In addition, Komisar helped build WebTV, TiVo, and Mondo Media. With this overflowing resume, Komisar could be considered a sage for would-be entrepreneurs.

The unconventional nature of Komisar's career is mimicked in his pseudomemoir. Most books are either fiction or nonfiction, though a handful, like *Ragtime* by E.L. Doctorow, successfully mix the two genres. In business books, it's even harder to pull off this form. But in *The Monk and the Riddle*, Randy Komisar does it beautifully. While he shares his own quest to discover the real meaning of work, he asks the readers this question: "What would you be willing to do for the rest of your life?"

Komisar opens the book with a story. During a motorcycle trip in Myanmar, Komisar gives a young monk a ride to his temple hours away; directions are given with simple gestures and shoulder taps. Upon arriving, the author meets the English-speaking abbot of the temple. After a short visit, the monk indicates he wants to return to where the author picked him up. Frustrated and tired, the author asks the abbot why the monk wants to go back. The abbot has no answer, but does offer a riddle: "Imagine I have an egg . . . and I want to drop this egg three feet without breaking it. How do I do that?" As Komisar drives through the countryside, caught up in the beautiful scenery and suddenly not so tired despite the long ride, the answer to the riddle comes to him. And the author leaves us with that provocative teaser.

We next find ourselves in a Silicon Valley office, where Komisar is speaking to a fictional entrepreneur, Lenny, who is shopping his business plan. Lenny is outrageous. He believes his payday will come selling caskets online: "We're going to put the fun back into funerals," he says. But despite this intensity and enthusiasm, Komisar is not impressed with Lenny's pitch. He helps Lenny refine his idea by advising him to shift his focus from the huge payday to what actually motivates him. "What," he asks Lenny, "would it take for you to be willing to spend the rest of your life on Funerals.com?"

Komisar points out that once you answer your own version of that question, everything changes. The excitement and passion you find allows others to become excited about your idea. "[I]t's the romance, not the finance that makes business worth pursuing," advises Komisar.

"No matter how hard we work or how smart we are, our financial success is ultimately dependent on circumstances outside our control."

The Monk and the Riddle was written during the bubble of the Internet boom. The rules were different then. Komisar rightfully points out in the "postmortem" that fronts the new paperback edition that, despite Lenny's business idea, the lessons are not bound to Internet businesses and the "better, faster, cheaper" world that Internet start-ups strived for. Instead, he explains, "In truth, *The Monk* is not primarily a business book; that is, it is not about buying low and selling high, but rather about creating a life while making a living. It is about the need to fashion a meaningful existence that engages you in the time and place in which you find yourself. It is about the purpose of work and the integration of what one does with what one believes. *The Monk* is not about *how*, but about *why*."

What appeals to me about this book is the combination of Komisar's fascinating life and the contemplative lessons he extends through Lenny's story. It is so seldom that entrepreneurial books look to the human side of enterprise. In his search to find the answer to the monk's riddle, Komisar realizes that, as it is often said, it truly is the journey, not the destination, that makes our efforts worthwhile, and we need to focus on each step and not the finish line. This simple message can wring a huge amount of stress out of our lives, even as we try to change that life with a new business endeavor or other sea change. It is a rare opportunity indeed to learn at the feet of such a master. **JC**

The Monk and the Riddle: The Art of Creating a Life While Making a Living, Harvard Business School Press, Paperback 2001, ISBN 9781578516445

WHERE TO NEXT? « Page 7 for **how to achieve another zenlike buzz** « Page 9 for **more zen vibe** « Page 234 for **the zen of start-ups** | EVEN MORE: *The Magic of Thinking Big* by David Schwartz; *Founders at Work* by Jessica Livingston

Lucky or Smart

BO PEABODY
Reviewed by Todd

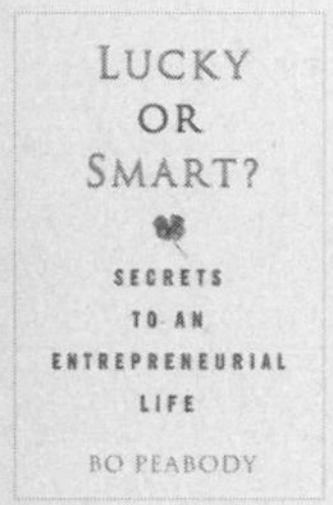

Over the course of four short years, Bo Peabody went from college dropout to Internet millionaire. Tripod, the company he started, fundamentally changed how individuals interacted with the Web by providing them, for the first time, with a set of tools simple enough to use that anyone could build their own Web site. By the time Lycos bought Tripod, more then one million people were publishing home pages with Tripod tools.

Peabody walked away from the dot-com bubble with six hundred million dollars. And while many entrepreneurs make the mistake of buying into the attention fawned on them by investors, reporters, and employees and discount the role that luck plays in their success, Peabody is particular about how he answers when asked, "Were you lucky or smart?" He says, "I was smart enough to realize I was getting lucky." This book is Peabody's fifty-eight-page manifesto on how entrepreneurs can and should position themselves to get lucky.

Peabody believes business luck can be created when entrepreneurs "start fundamentally innovative, morally compelling, and philosophically positive companies." And in return, this mission attracts the best people—the smart, inspired, and hardworking ones. However, Peabody warns us in a later chapter, these same smart people ("sociopaths" is the term Peabody uses) who are naturally attracted to start-ups will also have difficulty dealing with you, each other, and everyone else in the office.

"Entrepreneurs are B-students. There is no one thing they do well. But there are many things they do well enough."

As a result, Peabody also suggests that building and, more important, maintaining successful businesses requires skill sets that entrepreneurs often lack. His solution: hire the A-students. "A-students want to do things perfectly all of the time. This is a very bad trait for an entrepreneur, but a very good trait for a manager." On the flip side, entrepreneurs need to learn to love the word "no," because it is the one-syllable word you are going to hear most when pitching potential investors and customers.

The essay-length chapters remind me of the online writings of Union Square Ventures managing partner Fred Wilson (avc.com) and Y Combinator cofounder Paul Graham (paulgraham.com/articles.html). I wonder: if Peabody had published material like this on the Internet, would he have had a similar influence in the start-up community? Regardless, *Lucky or Smart* provides an essential set of lessons for entrepreneurs navigating their way through the challenges of starting a business. **TS**

Lucky or Smart? Secrets to an Entrepreneurial Life, Random House, Hardcover 2005, ISBN 9781400062904

WHERE TO NEXT? « Page 58 for **why this CEO never thought luck had much to do with it** » Page 306 **for what happens as we make machines smart** | EVEN MORE: *The Lean Start-Up* by Eric Ries; *The Four Steps to the Epiphany* by Steven Gary Blank; *Street Smarts* by Norm Brodsky and Bo Burlingham

NARRATIVES

When writers visit offices and factory floors, their reporting captures the romance of what many find so compelling about the pursuit of business. They also see the organizational dysfunction, and its roots in our personal flaws. The books in this chapter capture the tales of both fortune and failure at their capitalist extremes.

McDonald's

JOHN F. LOVE
Reviewed by Jack

There are areas in most towns across America in which every brand of fast-food restaurant is located seemingly one on top of the other. The most pervasive of those brands has to be McDonald's, and in *McDonald's: Behind the Arches*, John Love tells the story of this company's remarkable rise to mega-chain status. Usually industry books are either "authorized" and vetted by legal (and therefore unrevealing) staffs, or are negative, "behind the scenes" exposés. Love is careful to tell readers his position: "This is not a corporate book, not the type of history that companies commission to commemorate some milestone. I am an independent journalist, and McDonald's Corporation had no editorial control over this work." And yet *McDonald's* is written with an even hand, succeeding in giving readers a complete picture of this omnipresent brand. Love tells the story of the fast-food industry, the changing postwar society, the visionary McDonald brothers, the strategist Ray Kroc, the decision to franchise, and other facts (and fiction) about the McDonald's Corporation as we know it.

The rise of the fast-food industry was a monumental lifestyle change for our society. As usually happens when a quantum change occurs, many factors came into play. After World War II, families had more expendable money, the automobile was available to a wider consumer base and became a preferred form of family transportation, and the baby boom had begun. Entrepreneurs all over the country were exploring the opportunities made ripe by these phenomena, but few succeeded like McDonald's. Love tells readers how Bob's Big Boy, Burger King, Tastee Freeze, Dairy Queen, and Kentucky Fried Chicken got started, and shows how McDonald's broke from the pack to become the force it is today.

Despite his prominent role in the chain's success, Ray Kroc did not dream up the concept of McDonald's. It was the McDonald brothers—Richard and Maurice—who created a tiny drive-in in San Bernardino, California, in 1937 and continued to improve the business over time.

When visiting the brothers to see why these guys were buying so many of the mixers his company sold, Ray Kroc saw the potential in the brothers' simplified diner menu, speedy process of getting food to the customer, and more family-friendly restaurant atmosphere that stood in contrast to the teen-oriented, carhop-serviced hamburger joints popular at the time. The brothers' restaurant sold a ton of product; lines would form before it opened, and it would stay busy all day. On March 2, 1955, Ray Kroc became the franchiser for the McDonald brothers and their brand.

Love tells an ample number of stories to illustrate the surprisingly common struggles that new companies, even those we know now to be dominant brands, face in their early entrepreneurial days. Readers will be fascinated by how Kroc came up with the $2.7 million in cash he needed to buy the chain from the brothers, and how angry he was when he found out that the brothers hadn't included the original restaurant in the deal (he opened a new restaurant down the block and put the old place out of business). The author also tells how most of the unique McDonald's offerings—like the Egg McMuffin and the Big Mac—came from experiments the franchisees crafted and then presented to the corporate staff.

"[Ray A. Kroc] was immortalized as the founder of a major new industry. His accomplishments in food service were likened to those of John D. Rockefeller in oil refining, Andrew Carnegie in steel manufacturing, and Henry Ford in automotive assembly."

It has been said that no matter where you buy your McDonald's french fries, they will taste the same. And certainly this was Kroc's goal. The strength of the brand depended on it, because the strong psychological appeal of fast food lies in its reliability. He believed in uniformity in every restaurant. If the owner didn't follow the rules, he would not be granted a license to operate a second store. For example, there was only one

McDonald's restaurant in the area near corporate headquarters in Oak Brook, Illinois. "It was one of [the company's] most underdeveloped markets. The reason: Joseph Sweeney, who had gotten the territory in a deal he made with Kroc in 1957, ran a store that did not live up to [the company's] tough standards. Sweeney never got a license for a second store. The company bought back his franchise in 1968, and now Sweeney's old territory boasts fifteen McDonald's [restaurants]." Kroc's strict management strategy insured the uniformity of the restaurants.

This 470-page book is loaded with insightful stories told in the straightforward style of a journalist. Readers will absorb the accidental lessons surrounding developing suppliers and new products, creating franchising, and designing specific equipment. The commitment to training at all levels of the organization, and the standardization of its product offering are ideas that are still underutilized in many businesses and industries. This is not a handbook on how to make a million dollars, but it is a revealing look at one of the most successful corporations of the twentieth century. **JC**

McDonald's: Behind the Arches, Revised Edition, Bantam, Paperback 1995, ISBN 9780553347593

WHERE TO NEXT? « Page 218 for **another entreprenuer who created a global powerhouse** « Page 129 for **more on understanding the retail experience** « Page 98 for **more unexpected places to find ideas** | EVEN MORE: *The Emperors of Chocolate* by Joël Glenn Brenner; *For God, Country and Coca-Cola* by Mark Pendergrast; *The Wal-Mart Effect* by Charles Fishman; *Fast Food Nation* by Eric Schlosser

American Steel

RICHARD PRESTON
Reviewed by Jack

American Steel is a startlingly well-written story by Richard Preston about a maverick who took an age-old, declining industry—U.S. steel manufacturing—and showed that it could not only compete, but win, by employing innovative manufacturing methods and a conscientious way of treating workers. But this book's appeal goes beyond that of a conventional business book or history lesson. It reads like a romantic thriller, with Preston painting eloquent word pictures about a dangerous and desperate time in the life of the U.S. steel industry. "Long blue arcs snaked through the mountain of busted cars and smashed industry machinery. . . . The steelworkers couldn't hear their own voices screaming in terror over the noise of melting steel. The noise seemed to open sutures in their skulls, and a musky odor filled the building, the reek of a long-arc meltdown."

Since the mid-1800s and the development of the Carnegie Steel Company, the United States historically ruled the steel industry and reaped huge profits. With its comfy positioning, U.S. steel did not look for new methods to make steel more efficiently or more economically, adopting the classic "If it ain't broke, don't fix it" modus operandi. When money *was* invested, it was used to replace aged equipment, not to explore new ways to do business. Other monies went to the workforce as the unions were able to get superb contracts for their workers.

The standard production method involved using a blast furnace to turn iron into steel, but the manufacturing process was a space hog, with manufacturers such as the Gary Works in Gary, Indiana, occupying six miles of the Lake Michigan shore with a plant running a mile and a half deep. Clearly there was much wrong with Big Steel, and a perfect storm was developing—of high manufacturing costs, hubris, and growing competition from Asia and Europe.

European manufacturers developed an alternative method for creating steel. Electric arc furnaces, known as "minimills," used scrap metal as opposed to iron ore to produce steel. This manufacturing method was also beneficial because it allowed the mill to diversify its output, and it could be easily started and stopped depending on demand. In 1969, Ken Iverson, president of the Nulcraft Corporation—a steel manufacturer that would later be renamed Nucor Corporation—and the hero of Preston's *American Steel*, opened a minimill in the United States, specifically in Darlington, South Carolina, and this bold move set Big Steel back on its heels.

"[A] good businessman is hard to bruise and quick to heal."

And for years, due to this pioneering, Nucor succeeded in an industry that was failing. Iverson was innovative not only in his production methods but also in his management approach. Iverson created a company with a small hierarchy of (currently) only five levels: from janitor to CEO required only four promotions. As Nucor grew from earnings of $1.1 million in 1970 to $42 million in the late 1970s, the corporate staff was contained to under twenty people. This lean staffing allowed for quick decision making and a more autonomous work environment for the steel mills. Success did not come without some troubles, however. Attempts to unionize Nucor have failed. Though steelworkers at Nucor earn far less than their unionized compatriots, Nucor offers a bonus program that can allow workers to potentially double their earnings with success.

In 1986, Iverson saw his company's growth slowing and found new opportunity in the making of sheet steel that was in high demand in the automotive industry. He took the unprecedented step of investing in a new machine, enormous and untested, which would take the molten steel and, in one process, create rolled steel. With this new machine, Iverson believed that he could manufacture one million tons of steel with only five hundred steelworkers. In Japan—one of the most advanced steel industries in the world—2,500 steelworkers were required to do the same. The option to reduce the workforce completely changed the playing field, and Nucor significantly exceeded Iverson's original goal.

Richard Preston's tale recounts the riveting story of the building of this anomalous mill, located somewhat ironically in Crawfordsville, Indiana. But it makes sense when you consider that the mill needed scrap metal, a workforce, and good access to utilities, and these were all in plentiful supply in the Rust Belt. The cast of characters includes Iverson; the mill's colorful general manager, Keith Earl Busse; and the committed workers who manipulated the molten steel in the name of Nucor. Preston imbues the story with all the romance and thrill of a fictional drama. His retelling of an explosion as workers were using an experimental process had me reading while walking, unable to put down the book, to find out the conclusion to the accident. Here is just a taste:

> Five seconds after the ladle cleared the casting tower, there was a whining sound from the crane. Millett, standing near the control deck inside the pulpit, heard the sound and looked up. He saw that the crane cables had broken and unraveled. The ladle was falling to the ground. It was a huge object, fifteen feet high, filled nearly to the brim with liquid steel, and the bottom of it was forty feet off the floor. It seemed to pass the deck slowly as it fell, the crane cables singing in the winch. . . . There was a big, bright, yellow flash, and the lights went out.

I would be hard-pressed to find a book that I've quoted aloud to coworkers as much as *American Steel*. Richard Preston is simply a great writer of nonfiction, and I would rank him with contemporary storytellers like Malcolm Gladwell and Michael Lewis. Here he brings his talent to a tale of creativity and resurrection. The story of Ken Iverson and his success with Nucor is inspirational and educational, and demonstrates that an adoption of a new technology as well as an innovative organization that retains its humanity can succeed in business. **JC**

American Steel: Hot Metal Men and the Resurrection of the Rust Belt, Prentice-Hall Press, Hardcover First Edition 1991, ISBN 9780130296047

WHERE TO NEXT? « Page 82 for **how disruptive Nucor really was** » Page 319 for **how engineering is an art** » Page 284 for **how innovation is an art** | EVEN MORE: *Plain Talk* by Ken Iverson; *And the Wolf Finally Came* by John Hoerr; *Making Steel* by Mark Reutter; *Andrew Carnegie* by David Nasaw

Found in Fiction

From Theodore Dreiser's 1912 *The Financier* and Sloan Wilson's *The Man in the Gray Flannel Suit* in 1955 to, more recently, *Then We Came to the End* by Joshua Ferris, the business novel is slippery to define and has had a tumultuous and confounding life cycle. Classic themes of the American work ethic and pursuit of happiness, parables of self-destructive pride, and tales of the remade man make this form useful to many types of people, from high school students to high-level executives. Many business novels address business issues directly while others are infused with subtle lessons, but only a few have stood the test of time and remain poignant reminders of the need for all readers to step outside themselves and learn from others' experiences.

The Great Gatsby
by F. Scott Fitzgerald

Largely considered the greatest American novel, *The Great Gatsby* is also perhaps the best encapsulation of the American dream: Jay Gatsby, self-made, young, and rich, gazes longingly at the more exclusive lights of East Egg from his lofty new mansion. He wants more, he wants to belong, and the book is as much a testament to this rags-to-riches possibility of American life as it is a condemnation of such self-serving morals. Gatsby doesn't contain as much Rockefeller in him as his business associates might think, but rather has a bleeding, bursting heart. Fitzgerald succeeds best at demonstrating how over-ambition robs Gatsby of this one thing that made him "Great" compared to his peers.

A Confederacy of Dunces
by John Kennedy Toole

Destined to be remembered for its tragedy of the posthumous publication, and the humor and zany embodiment of New Orleans's otherworldliness, *Dunces* also demonstrates the every-man aversion to labor and toil—that is, aside from the perks and moments of self-discovery. Flatulent, obese Ignatius Reilly finds himself at a turning point while strolling the French Quarter slinging hot dogs—more going down the hatch than to customers. In fact, everyone here seems to be in a job for a reason other than making money, from the Holiday Ham-aspiring Miss Trixie to the police-dodging Burma Jones. Even Ignatius wants little more than to keep an overbearing mother at bay. Throughout, Toole captures the lonely ridiculousness of pounding the pavement, and maintains a sharp eye for the absurdity of the people, places, hungers, and tasks that make up a working day.

American Pastoral
by Philip Roth

Seymour Levov, aka "The Swede," is Roth's 1960s Gatsby, displaced by the social upheaval of the day. Pain-stakingly detailed about the Newark-area glove-manufacturing legacy that Seymour is born into, the novel explores the tender devotion requisite of a lasting family business. Lyrical and funny at once, Roth's story sweeps generations, offering a slice of Americana both specific and general that in the end proves that being righteous, steadfast, decent, and honest can't always prevent society from tumbling the walls around everything you've built.

A Man in Full
by Tom Wolfe

In Wolfe's epic, sprawling account of intersecting business, political, and social spheres in modern-day Atlanta, the focus varies but remains sharpest on disillusioned corporate magnate Charlie Croker. His plunge from grace, paralleled with the recently laid-off warehouse employee Conrad Hensley 3,000 miles away, grants empathy to the faceless, slaving masses and emphasizes the vast distance between the have-nots and the gates of their employers' mansions. Wolfe maintains a keen eye throughout, trained sharpest on the business ego's battle between self-preserving pride, and looming, devastating debt.

Then We Came to the End
by Joshua Ferris

The next generation of the business novel, Ferris's hilarious critique of modern office life and the world of marketing acts almost as the written-word companion to the movie *Office Space* or the show *The Office*. Addictively funny, it also belongs in the same vein of rumbling satire as that employed by Toole. Ferris sheds light on all of our oft-overlooked interoffice mannerisms, inanities, and silly drama. Throughout, the prose paints a portrait that, while obviously entertaining, is also sharply revealing about that forty-hour-a-week alternative universe known as "work."

Written by Todd Lazarski
with Rebecca Schlei

The Force

DAVID DORSEY
Reviewed by Jack

The Force is a nonfiction narrative about sales and very different from the other practical sales books we chose to feature. This book is, at its core, a glimpse into the dynamics of a master sales team. But the book reveals a seedy underside of selling, and, as an extension, the aggressive business practices necessary when the goal is always driven by short-term results. The book reads like a novel and reminds me of *The Office* crossed with *Glengarry Glen Ross*. Yet, through *The Force*, we get an insider's view of the personalities and perseverance it takes to excel in the highly competitive arena of sales.

David Dorsey, a former journalist, begins his story long after the glory years of Xerox, during a time when it took a lot of work to sell their expensive copiers. Given unprecedented access to a successful Xerox sales team in Cleveland, Ohio, Dorsey spends a year following Fred Thomas, the sales manager, and his group at a time when they are significantly behind their yearly goals. Thomas, a longtime high performer for the company, is doing all he can to help himself and his team succeed while questioning his commitment to the effort it requires. *The Force* goes beyond being simply an industry book to reveal the constant personal strain that each team member, as well as his family, is under when the future relies so heavily on pulling the right strings to close an all-important sale.

Dorsey excels at drawing candid portraits of the characters, allowing us to see all the facets of these relentless achievers. Frank Pacetta, a star salesperson at Xerox and one of the most intriguing subjects in Dorsey's book, embodies both the heroic and the distasteful in the sales profession. His drive and success in taking the district from the rank of 57 out of 67 Xerox sales districts to number 1 in the country is legendary. His people would walk through walls for him. And understandably so, given his power to motivate the sales force with speeches like this: "You can have fun and call it work, gang. You can escape the dull reality of work that most human beings face, because here, with me, you can be as wild as you were in college and still earn six figures a year." The reality was that while they were having fun, they were always selling. When they succeeded at making their sales numbers, Pacetta staged celebrations that were without restriction—think renting the classic Firestone Country Club for a day. Yet he drove his people mercilessly, requiring uniformity and expecting outstanding results. Of course, the people he led were required to view the world in black and white. They were out to win. If they didn't win, they lost. There was no in-between. Over and over again, Pacetta used sports or war analogies to motivate his people. Despite Dorsey's intense portrayal of Pacetta, despite the bravado and rah-rah, I found a real sadness running through the story.

"When you sold, you took control of other people, you motivated them to do things they wouldn't otherwise have done—all the while making them feel as if *they* were in control."

The mantra of this dark side of sales—where each day revolves around the thirty-day goal, and where salespeople live and breathe the end result—is epitomized in Frank's words to Fred: "'Put your helmet on, Freddie. It's a war out there.'" The fly-on-the-wall perspective of *The Force* also allows readers to bear witness as a new salesperson, a miserable cold caller, is groomed into a successful closer. Learning ways to sweeten a deal, like baking faux charges into a deal at the start so they could be taken away during negotiations, was part of his training. These kinds of manipulations let the customer feel he was gaining the upper hand when all along the salesmen "were giving away money you never expected to get in the first place," writes Dorsey. *The Force* reveals it all, and we are privileged for—and maybe a little shocked by—the view.

I appreciate that *The Force* reveals the less-than-favorable underside of the sales profession, a reality I have battled through the years of building up my business. But the book's value is as a narrative of an industry that was in a severe transition and the struggles many salespeople faced each month to make their numbers when they had previously been very successful. Perhaps you will find *The Force* a cautionary tale about life in sales or perhaps you will read the book for inspiration, desiring to succeed in a competitive profession. Either way, *The Force* is an unparalleled look at the day-to-day reality of the fuel that powers business: sales. **JC**

The Force, Ballantine Books, Paperback 1995, ISBN 9780345376251

WHERE TO NEXT? « Page 126 for **selling in films** « Page 143 **for a starter book on sales** « Page 127 for **great tips on being a better salesperson** | EVEN MORE: *Xerox: American Samurai* **by Suzanne Snyder Jacobson;** *SPIN Selling* **by Neil Rackham;** *Selling to VITO* **by Anthony Parinello;** *Hope Is Not a Strategy* **by Rick Page**

The Smartest Guys in the Room

BETHANY MCLEAN AND PETER ELKIND

Reviewed by Jack

I read crime fiction, watch English police procedurals on PBS, and wait hungrily for new books from my favorite mystery authors James Lee Burke and James W. Hall. Perhaps my natural appreciation for a good mystery story is one of the reasons the story of Enron intrigues me. If you can wipe away the haunting images of the crying employees, the victims in this story, sitting outside the headquarters on the base of the company's big "E," their careers packed away with their possessions in the banker's boxes balanced on their laps, the story of Enron's deceit and demise has the makings of the most engrossing mystery. And as with all good whodunits or whydunits, the story is populated with rich characters with questionable (or admirable) motives and all the ingredients for a perfect storm.

First, let's set the scene. Originating in Omaha, Nebraska, Enron became a holding company in 1979. The company moved to Houston and made its money in the transmission and distribution of gas and electricity. Previously the energy industry was regulated by the government, and costs and profits were controlled. During deregulation in the 1980s, opportunities to experiment and make piles of money arose. The company's CEO, Ken Lay, knew that deregulation was a good thing, but didn't have a plan to take full advantage of it going forward. Enter Jeffrey Skilling: he sure knew how, and Enron took off like a shot. In 2000, Enron became a Fortune 500 company with $60 billion in market capitalization. The time between Skilling's arrival and the day Enron declared bankruptcy comprised some of the most compelling moments in corporate history.

Now let's get to know the essential characters in this drama. First, there's the inspector who unearthed the clues and narrates our story, Bethany McLean. Two traders who got an initial whiff of Enron's decay while looking for a short position went to Ms. McLean. One of the traders told her, "'Read the 10-K and see if you can figure out how they're making money.'" The traders went to the right person. McLean had become a writer at *Fortune* after being an investment banker/analyst for Goldman Sachs. So, when she talked with the Enron people, she was able to ask the right questions. What McLean then did was write an article in the March 5, 2001 issue of *Fortune* called "Is Enron Overpriced?" which asked, essentially, where is the money coming from?

"The tale of Enron is a story of human weakness, of hubris and greed and rampant self-delusion; of ambition run amok; of a grand experiment in the deregulated world; of a business model that didn't work; and of smart people who believed their next gamble would cover their last disaster—and who couldn't admit they were wrong."

Next, let's look at the antagonists, Jeff Skilling and Ken Lay, and the murder weapon, a form of accounting called "mark-to-market." Both Lay and Skilling were born to lower-middle-class families. Both men were smart and driven. Lay had a doctorate in economics and Skilling was a Baker Scholar—meaning one of the top 10 percent—from Harvard Business School's MBA program. Lay started at the soon-to-be called Enron in 1984 as chairman and chief executive officer. Within a year, he had merged with an Omaha company called InterNorth, and to help with that purchase, the company retained the consulting firm of McKinsey & Company. One of the consultants there was a young Jeffrey Skilling. In 1990, Skilling was hired as chairman and CEO of a new division of Enron called Enron Finance.

Despite the similarities in accomplishments and ambition, the differences between Lay and Skilling couldn't be more pronounced. Lay really wanted to be liked. He loved to socialize and was really more of a politician (he thought he had a shot at being U.S. treasury secretary in 2000) who disliked making hard business decisions. He loved the frills of being a high roller; the corporate jets were well used by Lay and his family. In the executive dining room for lunch, an assistant would take Lay's sandwich and put it on fine china while his top executives ate the sandwiches wrapped in paper.

Jeff Skilling was a brilliant man who could conceptualize new ideas very quickly and simplify complex issues, but he had poor people skills. He didn't care what people thought of him; instead, he focused on the stock price and satisfying Wall Street's next quarterly conference call. He came up with great ideas but had difficulty putting them into action. An Enron executive later explained this chasm well: "Jeff Skilling is a designer of ditches, not a digger of ditches." He also had a very hard time knowing when to pull the plug on an obviously unsuccessful idea, and as time went on this problem would lead to disaster.

Because Enron dealt in long-term contracts to supply energy to large consumers like cities and utilities, customers would often sign ten-year contracts. Normal accounting practices would have you "book" the assets and liabilities on your balance sheet over the entire period of the contract. Mark-to-market accounting allows you to book the entire estimated value of the contract on the day it is signed. In 1992, Skilling and Enron got SEC approval to use this system. The problems with this form of accounting are twofold: One, when you book the sale is not when you get the cash. This results in huge sales and often serious cash issues. And two, with this type of accounting you can show the investors huge growth well before you see revenue. What ultimately brought Enron to its knees was a lack of cash caused by the constant drive for growth at all costs in an effort to keep the stock price growing—along with all those glorious stock options. Debt is what did them in. When all was said and done, Enron was rumored to have $38 billion in debt with no cash flow.

Smart, rich, influential men do not deliberately destroy the source of their wealth and influence. In this case, they got trapped in a nightmare of their own creation, or perhaps their own egos. Enron's failure was not deliberate; it was the result of a series of interconnected events. Can this happen again? Sure, particularly, when you have hubris at the CEO level, salespeoples' compensation based on short-term success, upper-level people totally focused on growth to satisfy short-term Wall Street success, an accounting system that supports this concept, and, finally, an accounting firm that doesn't do a good job of oversight. Add to this a deregulated industry and watch what happens.

When this story first broke I devoured any information on the subject. I read the *Wall Street Journal* every day to keep up with the latest news.

And I read several of the books that came out right after the decline. However, this book came out later, intentionally, because the authors wanted to have the full story and all the facts before they published the definitive title on the subject . . . which is exactly what *The Smartest Guys in the Room* is. **JC**

The Smartest Guys in the Room: The Amazing Rise and Scandalous Fall of Enron, Portfolio, Paperback 2004, ISBN 9781591840534

WHERE TO NEXT? » Page 268 for **Hubris: The Sequel** « Page 201 for **Hubris: The Prequel** « Page 65 for **stories of hubris** « Page 149 for **all the rules they broke** | EVEN MORE: *Den of Thieves* by James B. Stewart; *The Predators' Ball* by Connie Bruck; *Barbarians at the Gate* by Bryan Burrough and John Helyar

When Genius Failed

ROGER LOWENSTEIN
Reviewed by Todd

Throughout *When Genius Failed*, financial journalist Roger Lowenstein foreshadows the coming doom, and so there is no surprise in how the story of the Long-Term Capital Management fund ends. But what Lowenstein does best is show how blind arrogance brought down the company and almost the entire financial system. Building on the work of two Nobel laureates and the growing capabilities of computer technology, Long-Term Capital Management pushed academic theory further into real-world practice than had ever been done before, and it became a case study for how markets defy formulaic explanation. Lowenstein's narrative, while set in the complicated financial market of today, tells an age-old story many will recognize.

The story begins with a Midwestern kid named John Meriwether, whose penchant for gambling and stocks eventually led him from teaching math in a high school classroom to trading bonds at Salomon Brothers. In the 1970s, the bond market was being revolutionized by the instant access to pricing that new computer technology brought, and Meriwether saw favorable odds everywhere. His earliest trading concentrated on spreads between various bond interest rates. These bonds were easy to value, and Meriwether found that the market often oversold the debt instruments in reaction to unfavorable news. As the spread widened, arbitrage opportunities were created, allowing him to place bets that spreads would contract after the emotion dissipated. His calculated gambles paid off handsomely for his employer, and he was quickly given more latitude in trading, but Meriwether believed he needed an edge in this new game.

His answer was to hire the best and brightest from academia. His growing Arbitrage Group was made up of students and professors with degrees from MIT, Harvard, and the London School of Economics. These data jockeys were quick to take to Wall Street. Their models suddenly meant something more than simply accolades in obscure journals; they were playing with real money now. Meriwether managed them, encouraged them, and protected them from the fraternity of Salomon's trading floor. He also encouraged their interest in gambling, with internal wagering on everything from elections to frequent games of liar's poker.

As his career at Salomon reached an apex, Meriwether was forced to leave after a trader under his watch was found to have committed several securities violations. Meriwether wanted to quickly regain his stature on Wall Street and formed a hedge fund under the name Long-Term Capital Management (LTCM). He sought to replicate the size and scope of the operation he had at Salomon. Meriwether easily recruited most of his intensely loyal team and added to the roster Robert Merton and Byron Scholes, superstars in academic finance and who, as the story of LTCM unfolds, both win the Nobel Prize in Economics for their overall work. And for his team he provided the means: one-and-a-quarter billion dollars to work with.

The traders picked up where they left off and started placing trades on bond interest spreads. Scholes had described the small amounts of money made on each trade to investors during the fund-raising as "vacuuming up nickels that others couldn't see." The only way to make large sums of money was through leverage, through taking on incredible amounts of debt to make the thousands of trades needed to earn substantial profits. This was both the genius and, as it turned out, the flaw of the strategy.

"'You're picking up nickels in front of bulldozers,' a friendly money manager warned."

The modeling that had been tested at Salomon and polished at the new company was working perfectly. Meriwether and his dream team had delivered a panacea: guaranteed results with little risk. In the first year, LTCM returned twenty-eight cents for every dollar their investors put in. The formulas told traders exactly what and when to buy. But as time went on, LTCM started to believe their modeling could work for other wagers. They were becoming victims of their own success: the money they were making needed someplace to go and opportunities in bonds were becoming harder to come by. It was relatively simple to predict a value of a bond; other instruments, like stocks, currencies, and interest rate swaps, carried higher risks, many of which required judgments on the part of the traders. This moved the firm dangerously further from the strategy of their success; regardless, in four years, LTCM quadrupled their capital and investors were ecstatic.

But in August 1998 everything came apart, and in a matter of five weeks, LTCM lost everything. Many of the bets they made were going the wrong way; rather than returning to historical norms, the bond spreads were widening. Meriwether's traders watched in disbelief. The incredible amount of leverage that LTCM was using exacerbated the problem. Almost every firm on Wall Street was involved somehow, most having lent huge sums to LTCM. These firms had also built similar internal operations, making similar trades and competing with LTCM in many ways. In the end, the Federal Reserve pulled together a coalition of fourteen banks, which provided $3.65 billion to keep LTCM solvent. The bailout calmed markets, money was returned to investors two years later, and a chapter closed with real-world proof that markets are more than random movements.

We read narratives on history or industry for the lessons, and Lowenstein has many to share. He argues that the Fed's intervention stopped the market from correcting itself, providing tinder for other financial recklessness. And while the fall of Enron was brought on by greed, the collapse of Long-Term Capital Management was a function of hubris: the traders believed they could predict the future. The book ends with a short note about Meriwether and his traders. They moved on two years after the collapse and formed JWM Partners with $250 million dollars of seed capital from the same people who helped start LTCM. With no consequences, was there ever a lesson learned? TS

When Genius Failed: The Rise and Fall of Long-Term Capital Management, Random House, Paperback 2001, ISBN 9780375758256

WHERE TO NEXT? » Page 271 for **a book by Meriwether's former trading colleague** « Page 264 for **another corporate failure that still reverberates** » Page 319 for **how to learn from failure** | EVEN MORE: *The Bonfire of the Vanities* by Tom Wolfe; *Liar's Poker* by Michael Lewis; *Buffett* by Roger Lowenstein

Moneyball

MICHAEL LEWIS

Reviewed by Jack

Norman Mailer, Tom Wolfe, and Joan Didion. Each is a great contemporary writer of nonfiction, and I contend that Michael Lewis is a writer of the same caliber. He and Malcolm Gladwell have taken narrative nonfiction to new heights. When you put Michael Lewis and an interesting subject together, magic happens.

In 2003, Michael Lewis wrote *Moneyball*, which details the process of Billy Beane's resurrection of the Oakland Athletics baseball organization. If you are a fan of business or a fan of baseball, or simply a sucker for a great underdog success story, this book is essential reading. First, let me tell you how the story ends: from the mid-1990s on, the A's consistently had one of the bottom five payrolls in baseball, and during the same period they were consistently one of the best teams in baseball. What's so interesting about that? Well, put yourself in Billy Beane's shoes. A very young general manager, Beane was put in an untenable position, one destined for failure. He was given no investment, a team of second-stringers, and instructions to improve the team. And he succeeded. If I wanted to use a tired cliché, I would tell you he did it by "thinking outside the box." But what he really did was approach a very traditional game with a fresh attitude and a lot of guts. These are lessons each of us can take into our business. Here's how it went down.

Beane decided that the tried and true statistics used by other teams weren't as valuable or reliable as another set of stats that he had discovered. In the mid-1970s, a baseball fanatic named Bill James had created an alternative way to look at a baseball player's performance. Instead of batting average, he used on-base percentage and slugging percentage as gauges—helpful, but not groundbreaking. James's real breakthrough was realizing that a crucial qualifier was batters with good plate discipline (in other words, they were not swinging at bad pitches). The better the batter worked the pitcher and the more often he walked, the more runs a team scored. And of course, scoring is the real job of a baseball team. Beane applied James's new metrics to the A's organization.

With this data, Beane next went about finding cheap young players or slightly over-the-hill veterans with a couple of years left. Over the course of a few seasons, once the young players reached free agency and moved to another team for big bucks, the A's would get a compensatory first-round draft pick from the acquiring team. Thus, in the 2002 draft, the A's had seven first-round picks (the most in the modern history of the baseball draft), allowing them to pick good, young players who met the radical, new performance stats.

"In what amounted to a systematic scientific investigation of their sport, the Oakland front office had reexamined everything from the market price of foot speed to the inherent difference between the average major league player and the superior Triple-A one."

In addition to using Bill James's alternative statistics, Beane also applied other contrarian ideas. Don't draft high school pitchers (college pitchers are okay, but not usually valuable), don't steal bases, don't bunt. Look at actual numbers and output, not speed and body type. Baseball is a game with a rich history and indoctrinated practices, so with each of these innovative decisions, Beane's approach was viewed as unusual, to say the least.

Beane's negotiations became legendary. Certain general managers from other major league teams would not take calls from him, because they had had their pockets picked by him in the past. Beane's staff took advantage of technology and the proliferation of stats available on the Internet, and tracked every player on every major and minor league team. Because the A's were looking for players with a different skill set than most teams, they were able to "shop the bottom" for a player that fit their profile. Beane had to be careful, however, because if other GMs heard that Beane was interested in a player they currently had on their roster, the player's stock would go through the roof, moving the player out of the A's budget.

Every expert will tell you that the keys to running a successful business are recognizing talent, retaining talent, negotiating, and budgeting. The business of baseball is no different. What Michael Lewis succeeds in doing is telling a fascinating success story that offers insight after business insight. And yet *Moneyball* is more than a tale about a shrewd businessman. Michael Lewis tells a story that will inspire any reader to think creatively and individually, and not be limited by limited resources. The monster takeaway from this book is the need for new metrics. Find a new way to conduct your business that is lean and creative. This atypical business book belongs on every businessperson's bookshelf. **JC**

Moneyball, W. W. Norton Company, Paperback 2004, ISBN 9780393324815

WHERE TO NEXT? « Page 139 for **another great storyteller** « Page 142 for **other great writers** » Page 310 for **another way to look at your talent pool** | EVEN MORE: *Liar's Poker* by Michael Lewis; *Fooled by Randomness* by Nassim Nicholas Taleb; *Shoeless Joe* by W. P. Kinsella

The Lexus and the Olive Tree

THOMAS L. FRIEDMAN
Reviewed by Todd

Published in April 1999, the world of *The Lexus and the Olive Tree* is nearly unrecognizable. September 11, 2001, hasn't happened yet. YouTube doesn't exist. Apple's iProducts are still on the drawing board in Cupertino. The housing market is just starting to heat up. And the dot-com bubble is peaking. Friedman writes to make sense of the limitless possibilities of this post–Cold War, Web-enabled world in the years when we all believed the Internet would change every business model.

Friedman doesn't apply any value judgment to the possibilities themselves. Instead, he walks us back and forth between the good and the bad. At the core of the book are questions of how material fulfillment (the Lexus) and identity, both individual and communal (the Olive Tree), will manifest themselves. Friedman warns that winners will continue to take more and that the gap between haves and have-nots will grow. In the next breath, Friedman says while brutal and challenging, this is precisely what people all over the world are demanding. People don't want to be left behind; they want to be a part of the new system.

Throughout, Friedman writes in first person and present tense. He's on a trip into rural China to monitor elections. Next, he's paying off Iranian customs agents for the privilege to leave the country with all the money he arrived with. One day he is in Silicon Valley interviewing Cisco CEO John Chambers and the next he's strolling through Doha in Qatar lamenting the sudden appearance of a Taco Bell. This style of storytelling gives Friedman "been there, seen that" credibility that is so important to a book like this, structured by story and personal observation. As you walk along with Friedman, you can't help but see how he is one small step from realizing the world *is* flat.

That next book by Friedman, *The World Is Flat*, is one of a handful of business books with a strong sociological bent (like Malcolm Gladwell's *The Tipping Point*) that, in the last decade, entered the popular lexicon and gained near canonical status immediately. In it, Friedman captured a potent combination of our hopes and fears about the growing interconnectedness of people, nations, and markets.

"Thanks to globalization, we all definitely know 'of' one another more than ever, but we still don't know much 'about' each other."

Once you have read *The World Is Flat*, *The Lexus and the Olive Tree* will read like Friedman was warming up for a more far-reaching book. However, *The Lexus and the Olive Tree* is a more personal book than its successor, and the personal is always the most important place to start. While *The World Is Flat* argues that absolute economic equality will remove barriers, *The Lexus and the Olive Tree* makes apparent the tension between acquiring stuff and finding meaning, those individual choices forming the powerful macroeconomic forces we call globalization. **TS**

The Lexus and the Olive Tree: Understanding Globalization, Anchor Books, Paperback 2000, ISBN 9780385499347

WHERE TO NEXT? « Page 221 for **more from a guy who builds big global brands** « Page 253 for **one of the most recognizable global brands** | EVEN MORE: *The World Is Flat* by Thomas L. Friedman; *Redefining Global Strategy* by Pankaj Ghemawat; *The Fortune at the Bottom of the Pyramid* by C. K. Prahalad

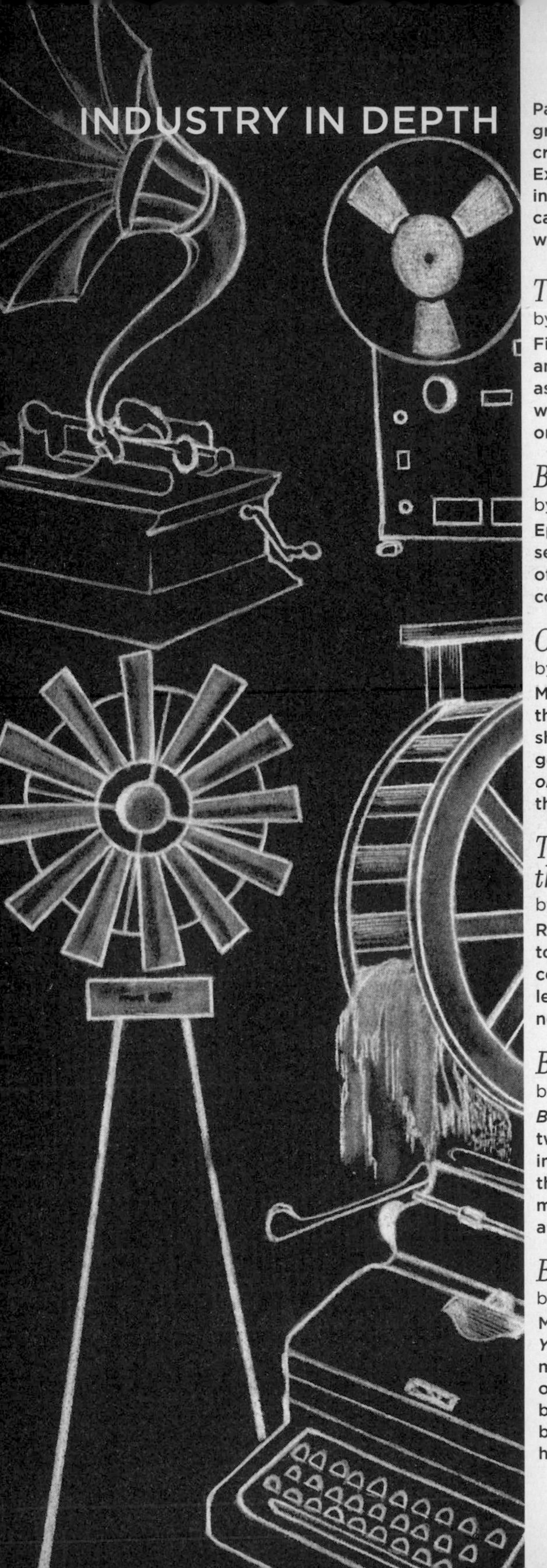

INDUSTRY IN DEPTH

Part investigative journalism, part biography, industry books are the true crime novels of the business book genre. Exposing the inner workings of one industry—and the habits of its consumers—can reveal much about business as a whole and even more about human nature.

The Wal-Mart Effect

by Charles Fishman

Fishman digs deep into the principles and practices of the Bentonville behemoth as it continues to change business as we know it through a persistent focus on cost and efficiency.

Big Picture

by Edward Jay Epstein

Epstein pulls back the curtain on the seldom-seen background operations of Hollywood and the six major media companies that rule the business.

Oil on the Brain

by Lisa Margonelli

Margonelli traces oil from refineries around the world to our gas tanks. Each story sheds light on the complex process that goes into delivering a tank of gas. *Oil on the Brain* is a *How Things Work* book that reads like a Grisham novel.

The Travels of a T-Shirt in the Global Economy

by Pietra Rivoli

Rivoli, an economics professor at Georgetown, set off to discover just how her cotton T-shirt came to be, and learned that the cost of free trade is not as free as she had imagined.

Barbarians at the Gate

by Bryan Burrough and John Helyar

Barbarians at the Gate, written by two former *Wall Street Journal* reporters in 1989, is a still-relevant page-turner that shows how the people behind the money make Wall Street both dramatic and dangerous.

Better

by Atul Gawande

Medicine, acknowledges surgeon and *New Yorker* staff writer Gawande, "requires making a hundred small steps go right—one after the other, no slipups, no goofs," but since perfection is impossible, being better should be everyone's humble goal.

Boeing Versus Airbus

by John Newhouse

Newhouse tells an elegant history of the aircraft industry via the feud between two industry leaders, and spins a tale rife with competition, politics, leadership, and innovation.

The Box

by Marc Levinson

Necessity is the mother of invention, but sometimes the best inventions receive little notice, as evidenced here by the humble shipping container that, according to economist Levinson, did nothing less than launch the start of globalization.

China Shakes the World

by James Kynge

James Kynge was the *Financial Times*'s bureau chief in Beijing and, as such, gives us a detailed, contextual look at this burgeoning powerhouse of a country.

The Emperors of Chocolate

by Joël Glenn Brenner

Brenner dips into the rich world of the American chocolate industry and exposes cutthroat competition, high-level egos, and a history of society-altering practices on par with those of the automotive or pharmaceutical industries.

The Machine That Changed the World

by James P. Womack, Daniel T. Jones, Daniel Roos

Based on a massive MIT study of industrial competition, this book details the automotive industry and lauds Toyota's lean versus mass production system, showing how far-reaching its applications are for every other type of business endeavor.

Where the Suckers Moon

by Randall Rothenberg

A rousing nonfiction tale about advertising and Subaru's effort to change its image in the early 1990s. The lessons in *Where the Suckers Moon* are timeless and tucked in effortlessly amid this detailed story about a company's search for identity.

To read full reviews of these books, go to 100bestbiz.com and download the PDF.

Written by Sally Haldorson, with Kate Mytty & Rebecca Schlei

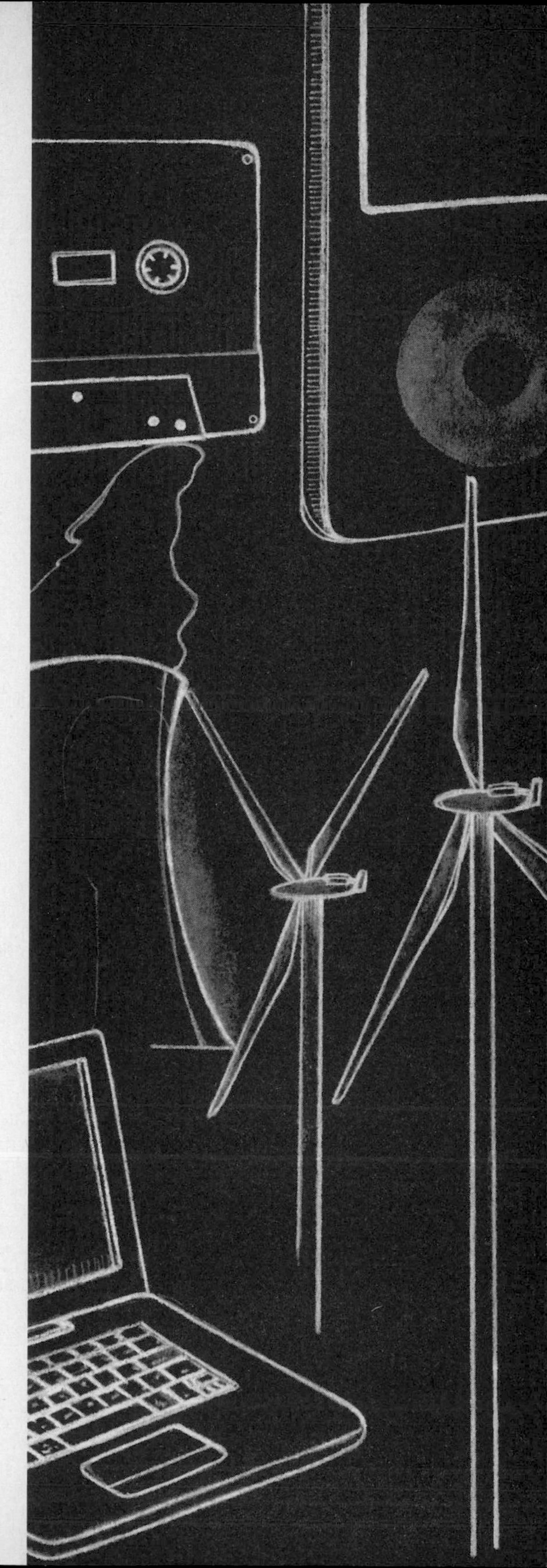

INNOVATION AND CREATIVITY

is about more than painting pictures. And leaving imagination to those in the art department helps no one. Though playwrights and composers have been innovating for several centuries longer than us suits, we would be wise to take some cues. Our picks focus on the inspiration and the process of developing new ideas.

Orbiting the Giant Hairball

GORDON MACKENZIE

Reviewed by Todd

We love to ask readers if they have ever read *Orbiting the Giant Hairball*, because when we get an affirmative answer, it makes asking the question so worthwhile. Their answer starts nonverbally: over the phone, you hear the pause as they recall the experience of reading the book; in person, you can see everything in the person slow down—their shoulders drop slightly, they take a deep breath, and they smile. Only then do they answer verbally with a simple "yes." Few books create such an emotional response.

Gordon MacKenzie opens his book with a story of schoolchildren and creativity. During workshops he holds to show children how he makes his metal sculptures, MacKenzie always asks his classes how many of them are artists. The first graders eagerly raise their hands, but as the children get older fewer hands are raised. The pressure to fit in and "be normal," so common as children age, suppresses their creative genius. And with this anecdote he lays down the bad news—this same suppression of creativity happens in corporations.

MacKenzie explains that the phrase "corporate creativity" is often an oxymoron. He had an early boss who referred to Hallmark's Creative Division, in which they both worked, as "a giant hairball." The description bothered MacKenzie until he pondered the question "Where do hairballs come from?": "Well, two hairs unite. Then they're joined by another. And another. And another. Before long, where there was once nothing, this tangled, impenetrable mass has begun to form."

As the hairball grows, everyone and everything is pulled toward its core. The organizational physics of normalcy and conformity rule the day. MacKenzie admits that this is what allows many organizations to be successful. The problem, though, is that people never reach their full potential nor do the companies that employ them.

MacKenzie's stories and suggestions throughout promote ways of getting and keeping yourself and others in that creative orbit. MacKenzie's solution is not to untangle the hairball but to find a way for individuals to draw from the power of the organization and yet stay in orbit. Some of the topics are surprising. He spends a chapter talking about teasing and how it robs people of the confidence to take risks. Chapter 19 is just one sentence long: "Orville Wright did not have a pilot's license."

In another story, MacKenzie, while furnishing a new set of offices, bought a collection of antique milk cans. When he decided to use them as clever wastebaskets, he was forced to justify his purchase. Accused of procuring unapproved office supplies, he became furious. His clear-headed coworker saved the day by suggesting the items be donated to the corporate art collection and loaned back to the company. Corporate regulations were met and everyone was happy. MacKenzie reflects that letting his anger take hold robbed him of the opportunity to create a solution that worked for everyone—a skill those orbiting the giant hairball need.

"Orville Wright did not have a pilot's license."

His stories are inspirational, but more important, MacKenzie offers a map to the creativity roadblocks inherent in organizations. This is not a common approach. There are plenty of books on how you personally can become more creative or how your team can generate more ideas. The backdrop of a creative person working for a creative organization like Hallmark makes the message real and even more profound ("Wow, if Gordon had these problems, then my journey is going to be even harder").

What makes *Orbiting the Giant Hairball* truly stand apart from any other book in our collection is its perfect fusion of word and image. Many business books have tried to use graphics and pictures to enhance the message, but they often fall short. The visual treatment always seems like an afterthought. MacKenzie uses illustrations to act as signposts throughout the text rather than the usual pulled-out quotes and section headings. His riff on a proposed organizational evolution of Hallmark from pyramid to plum tree appears on yellow ruled paper as scribbled notes, and a crumpled piece of paper at the end of the chapter describes in an instant how the presentation went. MacKenzie's initial choice to self-publish also allowed the book to escape the tendency to normalize by giant publishing hairballs.

The only proper result of this review would be you picking up *Orbiting the Giant Hairball* and being able to answer "yes" when someone asks if you have read it. The inspired smile alone will be worth it. **TS**

Orbiting the Giant Hairball: A Corporate Fool's Guide to Surviving with Grace, Viking, Hardcover 1998, ISBN 9780670879830

WHERE TO NEXT? « Page 78 for **more about hairballs** « Page 264 for **more about dirtballs** « Page 34 for **"the magical things you can do with that ball"** | EVEN MORE: *Rules of the Red Rubber Ball* by Kevin Carroll; *One Great Insight Is Worth a Thousand Good Ideas* by Phil Dusenberry; *Unstuck* by Keith Yamashita and Sandra Spataro

The Art of Innovation

TOM KELLEY WITH JONATHAN LITTMAN
Reviewed by Todd

IDEO, the Silicon Valley's design firm of choice, has brought to life a staggering list of groundbreaking products—the original Apple mouse, the Palm V handheld organizer, Samsung's award-winning monitors—leaving outsiders wondering what IDEO does differently to generate such memorable products and services.

The answer can be found in *The Art of Innovation*, the twenty-first century's hallmark book on how to generate new ideas. The opening pages read more like a company biography than a guide to product transformations, but by chapter 3, *The Art of Innovation* picks up speed and shows why this book is a prime example of what can make a business book so valuable. IDEO opens up its doors and takes the reader on a tour that reveals what makes the studio/firm successful. Author and IDEO general manager Tom Kelley cautions readers against thinking there is a magic formula for generating new ideas—a lesson that exemplifies the kind of honest advice infused throughout the book.

Many of the methods Kelley recommends contain a "best practices" mentality. IDEO's core belief in observation borrows from the field of anthropology. Observation leads to counterintuitive insights: bigger, thicker toothbrushes are better for smaller hands. The company ignores the myth of the individual and embraces the power of teams, pointing to the group of fourteen individuals that enabled Thomas Edison to invent the telephone, phonograph, and lightbulb as exemplars. Prototyping, an activity associated with engineers and technicians, is simply a word for doing; the models become the physical manifestations of their bias for action.

Brainstorming is an essential part of the innovation process at IDEO. Rather than a nebulous gathering over coffee and cake, says Kelley, every "brainstormer" should start a session with a clear, outwardly focused problem statement, with sixty minutes of brainstorming yielding a hundred ideas. To improve group memory, cover everything in the room with paper; it allows plenty of room for ideas and makes it easier to go back and find an idea that needs more development. Numbering each of those ideas is a simple trick IDEO learned to motivate a group and allows for quick movement between ideas without losing the group's place. Best way to prep group members? Send them to a toy store. These best practices show that brainstorming is more than just a tool at IDEO. Kelley elaborates: "It's also a pervasive cultural influence for making sure that individuals don't waste too much energy spinning their wheels. . . ."

"Publicly acknowledge a risk taker, a rule breaker, even a failure, and explain why every successful organization needs them."

The Art of Innovation teaches that the best ideas come from more than daydreaming. Observation trumps conjecture. Teams trounce individuals. And making something happen always beats imagining what it would be like. TS

The Art of Innovation: Lessons in Creativity from IDEO, America's Leading Design Firm, Currency/Doubleday, Hardcover 2001, ISBN 9780385499842

WHERE TO NEXT? » Page 293 for **habits that spark innovation** « Page 186 for **what hinders "doing"** « Page 193 for **how to keep teams talking** | EVEN MORE: *The Ten Faces of Innovation* by Thomas Kelley with Jonathan Littman; *Thoughtless Acts?* by Jane Fulton Suri and IDEO; *Everyday Engineering* by Andrew Burroughs and IDEO

Jump Start Your Business Brain

DOUG HALL
Reviewed by Jack

You may have had the chance to see Doug Hall on television, as one of the judges on a reality show called *American Inventor*. His qualifications for appearing on that show and writing this book include becoming an inventor at age twelve, earning an engineering degree, and putting in years at Procter & Gamble as master marketing inventor, before starting his company called Eureka! Ranch—an organization whose sole purpose, according to its Web site, is to accelerate top-line growth. Hall's book, *Jump Start Your Business Brain*, shares his system of analysis developed at the Ranch; with it he believes you can markedly improve the odds of success of your next project or idea.

Hall's concepts are based on scientific analysis. Sixty thousand data points support his analytic system, along with "[o]ver 1,200,000 customer reactions to new business concepts [that] have been measured and analyzed to identify the core truths that define winning customer ideas." In the first section, "Marketing Physics," Hall asserts that there are three factors that can dramatically improve your chances of success for your next product or idea. In fact, he claims you can improve your percentage of success from the usual 20 percent to well over 40 percent by following these teachings. The three principles are: (1) Overt Benefit—or, What is in it for your customer? Hall teaches that you must be very direct with the overt benefit to break through the clutter in the marketplace; (2) Real Reason to Believe—customer confidence is at an all-time low, and because of that, it is crucial that you are credible and deliver on your promises; and (3) Dramatic Difference—"[w]ithout uniqueness, you have a commodity that sells for commodity-like profit margins." Hall believes this uniqueness, which must be ten times greater than you might think it should be, must also be a function of the Overt Benefit and the Real Reason to Believe. Building on that prior work guarantees relevance for your customer and in turn improves your chances for success. In summary, Hall says the Overt Benefit is *what* you are offering, the Real Reason to Believe is *how* you are going to make good on your promise, and the Dramatic Difference is *why* customers should get excited.

In the next section, "Capitalist Creativity," Hall introduces three fundamental laws for successful idea generation: (1) Explore Stimuli—"stimuli are the fuel that feeds business-growth thinking—or any creative thinking, for that matter"; (2) Leverage Diversity—"diversity is the fuel that turns the spark into a chain reaction of continuous idea creation"; (3) Face Fears—the previous two laws only come alive when you face your fears. The chapter on facing fears is an eye-opener, because you'll discover that while most people use other limitations, such as budget, organizational norms, or passive employees as excuses for limiting creative growth in a company, it is really fear that may be at the root of any imposed limitation. I found this statement in the book from the poet David Whyte especially insightful: "'Creativity is about coming out of hiding and exposing yourself. Practicing creativity is about humiliating yourself in public.'" Hall makes it clear that creativity can sometimes require a person to put ego aside or go against the grain in a meeting. This is an essential, if not comfortable, challenge for most of us.

"The mission of this book is . . . to help managers create products, services and advertising that persuade customers to spend money."

The inspiration for Hall's research came from the work of W. Edwards Deming. Hall recounts what Deming taught:

> [T]he only way to improve manufacturing quality was to improve the process through better systems, worker training and systemic improvement. When the process is improved, Dr. Deming maintained, a chain reaction of reduced waste, less rework and greater customer satisfaction inevitably results. Fix the system, Deming said, and you fix the factory.

Hall took this philosophy and applied it to idea-generation and business-building concepts. Hall believes that Dr. Deming's concept can be applied to any small business or simply to your department and is not limited to factory production systems. The problem may not be your competition or your employees or the marketplace. Instead, Hall believes the cause of much stagnation is the way you choose new ideas or new products. With *Jump Start Your Business Brain*, he supplies us all with the process needed to improve our chances of "winning" our next idea-generation session. **JC**

Jump Start Your Business Brain: The Scientific Way To Make More Money, Emmis Books, Paperback 2001, ISBN 9781578601790

WHERE TO NEXT? « Page 229 for **how to jump-start your start-up** « Page 163 for **more from Deming** » Page 326 for **how to make it memorable** | EVEN MORE: *Jump Start Your Marketing Brain* by Doug Hall; *Cracking Creativity* by Michael Michalko; *Rules for Revolutionaries* by Guy Kawasaki with Michele Moreno

CONFERENCES TO ATTEND

Continuing communication with your peers inspires progress and fosters new ideas. What better place to continue the dialogue than at conferences where you can listen to industry leaders share ideas, and talk through ideas with those around you?

SXSW Interactive

This is where hard-core geeks, serious content creators, new-media entrepreneurs, and creative people gather for five days of provocative panel content and parties. Hundreds of industry experts come to Austin, Texas, to share their expertise. There is no shortage of information at this hip educational conference, which also showcases the tools employed by digital creatives and filmmakers alike. And, of course, there's the music festival.

TED Conference

The TED brand has exploded, creating local and global offshoots featuring the quintessential TED inspiration, but this annual seminal event in California is the granddaddy of TED events. Over five days, speakers get eighteen minutes each to address attendees on science, business, the arts—all aspects of the human experience. Having no breakout groups ensures that everyone shares the same experience. That is why it's so successful—all of the knowledge is connected and shared.

Gel

Short for "Good Experience Live," Gel covers a diverse set of topics—from art to innovation, literature to business. Attendees leave feeling refreshed and inspired after touring New York City art galleries, partaking in technology experiments, and learning through workshops. With a focus on participation and community, Gel is an experience, not just a conference.

PopTech

Every October, visionary thinkers in the sciences, technology, business, design, arts, education, and government gather in Camden, Maine, to explore the cutting-edge ideas, technologies, and forces of change that are shaping our collective future. Attendees then share what they learn with communities throughout the world through books, television, live "satellite" events, and more. Even after the PopTech conference draws to a close, the conversation continues to inspire people around the world.

Written by Aaron Schleicher

A Whack on the Side of the Head

ROGER VON OECH

Reviewed by Jack

All ideas have a life cycle. They are born, live, and die, and new ideas are needed to replace them. But we need a reliable way to generate new ideas, because, unlike good dogs, good ideas don't always come when called. The challenge of being creative is timeless, and when it comes to generating ideas, new technology doesn't necessarily make the challenge any easier. But Roger von Oech's book does. He has taken a potentially complicated issue, because of its subjectivity, and broken it down into stimulating and functional advice.

At the core of the book are ten chapters that detail what von Oech believes to be the biggest mental blocks to creativity: be practical, follow the rules, play is frivolous, avoid ambiguity, don't be foolish. In each chapter, von Oech focuses on the fundamentals of creative thinking. For example, from the "Be Practical" chapter comes this advice: "When you judge new ideas, focus initially on their positive, interesting, and potentially useful features. This approach will not only counteract a natural negative bias, it will also enable you to develop more ideas." As a guy who has always tried to be pragmatic when it comes to new ideas, I have been accused of being negative. This fundamental approach shows that changing the lens through which you first look at an idea can open you up to compromise or even inspiration.

At the end of each chapter is a summary, like this one from "Play Is Frivolous:" If necessity is the mother of invention, play is the father. Use it to fertilize your thinking.

> **TIP:** The next time you have a problem, play with it.
>
> **TIP:** If you don't have a problem, take time to play anyway. You may find some new ideas."

There is often a serious disconnect in using creative thinking to solve business problems. Many of us believe that facts and research will lead to solutions before taking some time to play, thinking that playing isn't serious work.

"By changing perspective and playing with our knowledge, we can make the ordinary extraordinary."

The exercises von Oech uses to stimulate just such creative problem solving are unique. For example, he offers readers the following scenario: You are a marketer given the challenge of promoting a company's $1,000,000 overstock of ball bearings. What do you do? Creative thinking first allows you to search for ideas within your experience, but then you need to try different approaches, one then another and often not getting far. But there should be no limits. "We use crazy, foolish and impractical ideas as stepping stones to practical new ideas," says von Oech. Once you've brainstormed the scenario, he reveals the possibilities, including: use the ball bearings as level testers, sew them into a canvas vest and use them as "weight clothing" for athletes in training, or use them as filler for beanbag chairs or other furniture. The author explains that "[t]he point of this exercise is that an idea, concept, or thing—in this case a ball bearing—takes its meaning from the *context* in which you put it. If you change its context, it will take on a different meaning. For example, transferring a ball bearing from the 'things that reduce friction' context to that of 'shiny and pretty things' gives us all kinds of jewelry and art ideas." This exercise is an effective way to show how even when we are thinking creatively, we often have self-imposed boundaries that actually limit our creativity. Pushing the boundaries, sometimes literally, is a way of opening our eyes to additional possibilities.

It is difficult to convey all of the stimulating information Roger von Oech shares with us in this short review. With every page, you will feel new clarity about how creativity should play a role in your work. He distributes perspective-changing quotes throughout the book, such as, " 'Discovery consists of looking at the same thing as everyone else and thinking something different' " from Albert Szent-Györgyi, and " 'Every act of creation is first of all an act of destruction' " from Pablo Picasso. *A*

Whack on the Side of the Head is a pragmatic guidebook to assist you in unearthing your creative self. **JC**

A Whack on the Side of the Head: How You Can Be More Creative, Business Plus, 25th Anniversary Edition, Paperback 2008, ISBN 9780446404662

WHERE TO NEXT? » Page 299 for **another creativity tool kit** « Page 105 for **getting into someone's head** » Page 298 for **some fresh perspectives** | EVEN MORE: *One Small Step Can Change Your Life* by Robert Maurer; *The Artist's Way* by Julia Cameron; *Creativity* by Mihaly Csikszentmihalyi

The Creative Habit

TWYLA THARP
Reviewed by Todd

My love for big, crazy ideas certainly shades my view, but after reading Twyla Tharp's *The Creative Habit*, I am certain corporate innovation doesn't hold a candle to the challenges of artistic creation. And before you start listing all of the differences, I'd ask you to stop and consider the last marketing campaign or machinery upgrade you were involved with. When you were done, did you measure the results based on how much sales went up and how it compared to your competitors' results . . . or whether it was on par with a Picasso painting or Edison invention? Apple is clearly doing the latter, and maybe it is time for you to do the same.

"Scratching" is the term Tharp, one of America's greatest choreographers, assigns to the initial, exploratory steps of finding a new idea. The primordial matter in which to scratch comes from what we experience—recalling early memories, conversing with friends, observing nature. "Scratch among the best and you will automatically raise the quality of ideas you uncover." For Tharp, the music she chooses makes or breaks the dance she creates, and Mozart, Beethoven, Brahms, and Haydn are her first stops. The companions you choose to accompany you while you scratch shape the entire creative process.

Once those initial creative ideas take flight, you need some way to capture them. For Tharp, every project begins with a simple cardboard box. Everything she acquires during the process goes in the box, much as a musician might capture a melody on composition paper or an illustrator a silhouette in a sketchbook. Whatever the device, the inspirations are gathered in a place without confining the creativity itself. The first item in each of her boxes is a blue index card stating the goal for the project. For her Broadway show *Movin' Out*, one box became eleven boxes. The index cards said " 'tell a story' " and " 'make dance pay for the dancers,' " and items like Billy Joel's entire discography, a copy of the film *Saturday Night Fever*, and a macramé vest filled the boxes.

Tharp discusses creativity using a gracefulness drawn from her career as a choreographer. A natural extension of her eye for art, the book's design is elegant, with oversize text filling oversize pages. Narrative is followed by exercises—more parallels with her life as a dancer. The material throughout reveals more about the author, the creative process, and—we hope—the participating reader. Tharp ends her book with a sense of satisfaction about the life she has chosen: "When it all comes together, a creative life has the nourishing power we normally associate with food, love, and faith."

"Applying algorithms to creativity is like biochemists trying to formulate the chemistry of love. It takes some of the romance out of the enterprise."

Dan Pink, in his book *A Whole New Mind*, says "The new MBA is the MFA [Master of Fine Arts]," and he is right. Artists have long struggled with constant and consistent idea generation for centuries longer than us corporate types. It is about time we use such methods of creativity to enrich our every project. Before the next blank screen or empty page finds you, get a copy of *The Creative Habit* and keep it by your bedside long after you've devoured it the first time. TS

The Creative Habit: Learn It and Use It for Life, Simon & Schuster, Paperback 2006, ISBN 9780743235273

WHERE TO NEXT? « Page 82 for **what happens to industry when inspiration is found** « Page 240 for **how business needs practice too** | EVEN MORE: *The War of Art* by Steven Pressfield; *A Whole New Mind* by Daniel H. Pink; *Bird by Bird* by Anne Lamott

The Art of Possibility

ROSAMUND STONE ZANDER AND BENJAMIN ZANDER

Reviewed by Jack

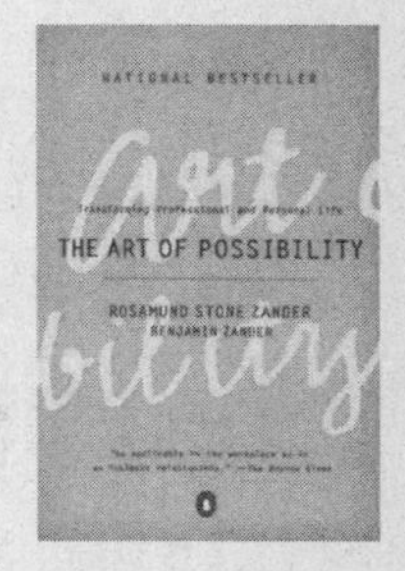

About ten years ago, Harvard Business School Press had Benjamin Zander present to booksellers at its annual convention in preparation for his forthcoming book. I was there that day and he was one of the best motivators I had seen. Zander is the conductor of the Boston Philharmonic as well as a teacher, and, as I saw at the convention, he is a polished communicator. With his wife, Rosamund Stone Zander, an executive coach and a family systems therapist, he has written a book about possibility, using inspirational stories, parables, and fun personal anecdotes. Early on, they write: "Our premise is that many of the circumstances that seem to block us in our daily lives may only appear to do so based on a framework of assumptions we carry with us. Draw a different frame around the same set of circumstances and new pathways come into view." The way to internalize this transformation is, as Zander has learned through his career in music, practice.

The first "practice" in the book is called "It's All Invented." After pages of scientific research showing how animals, insects, and humans perceive their surroundings and make meaning from those sensations, the authors assert that we are confined by the constructs we create. We don't look beyond our assumptions. The practice comes from challenging those assumptions. Since reality is "all invented" anyway, inventing a story or framework of meaning that enhances our quality of life and the lives of those around us is the first step.

Benjamin Zander was teaching a graduate course at the New England Conservatory to instrumentalists and singers. After twenty-five years of teaching, he realized that every year his students so dreaded the performances they had to give for their final grade that they were fearful of taking risks with their playing. So Zander started his next course by telling everyone that they would get an A. The only requirement was that the students write Zander a letter from the future that began, "Dear Mr. Zander,

I got my A because . . ." and include in that letter what they did to deserve the grade. The letters Zander includes in his book are truly amazing in their insight and passion. When you take the pressure of a grade off the table, creativity is allowed free rein. Students discovered the freedom to take risks that they would not have had the courage to attempt if Zander had not removed the usual constraint of academic assessment.

"A shoe factory sends two marketing scouts to a region of Africa to study the prospects for expanding business. One sends back a telegram saying, SITUATION HOPELESS STOP NO ONE WEARS SHOES The other writes back triumphantly, GLORIOUS BUSINESS OPPORTUNITY STOP THEY HAVE NO SHOES"

The simple act of eradicating our rule-bound instincts can change a school classroom or a corporate culture. The Zanders refer to this as "Rule Number 6." The essence of the rule is that there are no rules, and that you should lighten up and stop taking yourself so seriously. When you lighten up, those around you naturally follow suit: "This new universe is cooperative in nature, and pulls for the realization of all our cooperative desires." Shedding self-imposed limitations allows for a deeper level of interaction, and thus new possibilities result.

You can imagine what change the rest of the twelve lessons inspire, with other "practices" like Lighting a Spark, Leading from Any Chair, and The Way Things Are. Reading this book can be revolutionary if you are open to the Zanders' ideas—if you are interested in finding more happiness and satisfaction in your job and your life. *The Art of Possibility* has taught me how to look through a different lens, one that leads to a more humane and satisfying, passion-filled life. **JC**

The Art of Possibility: Transforming Professional and Personal Life, Penguin, Paperback 2002, ISBN 9780142001103

WHERE TO NEXT? « Page 284 for **the art of innovation** « Page 245 for **the art in small business** « Page 51 for **how leadership is an art** | EVEN MORE: *Are You Ready to Succeed?* by Srikumar S. Rao; *What Got You Here Won't Get You There* by Marshall Goldsmith with Mark Reiter; *Leadership and the New Science* by Margaret J. Wheatley

There are a number of international business titles worth a read that you won't stumble upon in your local bookstore. Each book is radically different from a traditional business book, unique in format and chock-full of pictures. If you're looking for fresh perspectives, you'll find them in these books.

Fresh Perspectives
not in a bookstore near you.

Creativity Today
by Igor Byttebier and Ramon Vullings, Netherlands

Byttebier and Vullings believe that creativity is important in every career, and that you are responsible for the development of your personal creativity. They help foster creativity with case studies, exercises, and various challenges such as finding solutions to traffic jams and waiting in lines.

The Idea Book
by Fredrik Härén, Sweden

A good idea is often inspired by something external. To that end, *The Idea Book* has 150 pages saturated with ways to learn about creativity through various activities, stories, and quotations from famed thinkers like Albert Einstein and IKEA founder Ingvar Kamprad, interspersed with 150 blank pages for jotting down new ideas as they come.

Life's a Pitch
by Stephen Bayley and Roger Mavity, United Kingdom

Two separate books are bound together in *Life's a Pitch.* Both are about presentation. Mavity argues that people respond more readily to emotion than to logic, and that how you pitch yourself is more important than what you're pitching. Bayley sees life itself as theater, and writes on how to be a better actor.

KaosPilot A-Z, 2nd Edition
by Uffe Elbæk and friends, Denmark

In 1991, Elbæk founded a revolutionary business university called KaosPilot, with an education program based on creativity, projects, and business design. This book embodies that education. Contributors include the late Anita Roddick of The Body Shop, Kevin Kelly of *Wired* magazine, and more. Elbæk explains, "And just so you're warned, *KaosPilot A-Z* is a book full of values, beliefs and critical orientation, full of life, references and tips, full of flashbacks, visions and jumping up and down . . . and not least full of pictures."

Written by Kate Mytty and Dylan Schleicher

Thinkertoys

MICHAEL MICHALKO
Reviewed by Jack

When your organization has a problem, whether it is how to reduce expenses, increase revenue, or design a new logo, and you swear you have thought of all the different scenarios possible but nothing seems to move the needle, you need to turn your thinking around and apply some creativity to the problem. After all, as Albert Einstein stated, the definition of insanity is doing the same thing over and over again and expecting different results. Enter Michael Michalko's masterpiece on creative thinking, *Thinkertoys*.

Michael Michalko is a renowned creativity specialist and frequent speaker on creativity issues to the corporate world. Michalko developed the ideas on creative thinking presented in *Thinkertoys* while an officer in the U.S. Army assigned to NATO. There he established a team that researched creative thinking methods and applied those innovative ideas to military, political, and economic problems. After he left the military, he was asked to develop think tanks for the CIA on creative thinking.

So what are Thinkertoys? Remember those brainteaser books we played with as children? (Or perhaps you still have a game magazine tucked somewhere in your car for long lines at the drive-through.) *Thinkertoys* employs those same kinds of visual games to help you understand how it is possible to solve problems or change perspectives creatively. Michalko divides the book into a linear techniques section and an intuitive section for generating new ideas.

Within the thirty-nine chapters, the author scatters puzzles, games, and visual riddles to illustrate his lessons. He explains, "You can best profit by playing with these toys, in your own unique style, to stimulate ideas from your imagination. . . . You might be tempted to just use one or more Thinkertoys you like best, but playing with a variety will be more productive." From imagining your own "personal Hall of Fame" of admired people, real or fictional, who can act as a sounding board for your ideas, to brainwriting and scribbling, and even creating a Murder Board like the CIA uses to evaluate and criticize ideas before implementation, every Thinkertoy can be implemented when you most need them.

"Creativity is not an accident, not something that is genetically determined."

While *Thinkertoys* activities can shape the way you think ("Give your mind a workout every day"), Michalko is not content to wax episodic on creativity. He is conscious throughout that creativity is nothing without productive implementation.

> When your idea feels final, implement it. Do not spend days, weeks, or months refining it. If you delay, you may find yourself in a situation like that of the Victorian portrait painter who chose not to seek immediate benefits from his talents. Instead, he spent years refining his craft and art until he finally reached a pitch of dazzling brilliance—just in time to be rendered obsolete by photography.

In these pages, Michalko's exercises will help you teach yourself how to be creative and fine-tune your ability to generate ideas, but the very fact that they are action-laden will, in turn, help you create action. Now go and fix that which needs fixing: the tools are right here. **JC**

Thinkertoys: A Handbook of Creative-Thinking Techniques, Second Edition, Ten Speed Press, Paperback 2006, ISBN 9781580087735

WHERE TO NEXT? « Page 290 for **more help with your creativity challenges** « Page 193 for **another way to ignite creativity** | EVEN MORE: *Thinkpak: A Brainstorming Card Deck* by Michael Michalko; *How to Get Ideas* by Jack Foster; *Creative Whack Pack* by Roger von Oech

BIG IDEAS These books take you to unexplored crossroads, connecting common knowledge with the most advanced understandings of the world. New insights appear at these intersections when the walls of academic discipline are removed. The future of business books lies here.

The Age of Unreason

CHARLES HANDY

Reviewed by Jack

When I ran my record store, I knew my product better than anyone who crossed the threshold because I have an innate passion for music. But when I moved on to selling business books, truth be told, I bluffed my way through conversations by detailing information about publishers or reciting an author's track record. I would talk about anything but the content of the book because I didn't have the academic background or the personal experience to discuss the merits of a particular book. *The Age of Unreason* was the first business book that spoke my language. And through it, Charles Handy offered me a way into business books.

Born and raised in Ireland, the son of an archdeacon and educated at Oxford, Handy spent over ten years with Shell International. During the 1960s, he attended the Sloan School of Business and met Warren Bennis and other cutting-edge leadership and management people who sparked in him an interest in organizations and how they work. He then taught at the London Business School for almost three decades, wrote eighteen books, and penned numerous articles. Handy calls himself a "social philosopher," and from that perspective he advocates the humanistic approach to business that first appealed to me. In *The Age of Unreason*, Handy writes about changing, living, and working—the essentials to leading our best lives.

At the time of this book's publication, in 1989, Handy declared that "the Age of Unreason is upon us," that "discontinuous" change, change that is irregular and unpredictable, had become the norm. Handy provides the following insightful example of discontinuous change. When he started working at a young age, he was expected to work 47 years, 47 weeks per year, and 47 hours per week, or a total of a little over 100,000 hours. The generation following his works half those hours, entering the workforce after graduate school and working 37 hours a week, 37 weeks a year (due to training and extended time off), equaling only 50,000 hours over a lifetime. All that changed in one generation. Imagine the sorts of effects this has had on leisure, education, family life, and generally on how society ends up spending its time.

Handy says, "Now, for the first time in the human experience, we have a chance to shape our work to suit the way we live instead of our lives to fit our work. We would be mad to miss the chance." To accomplish this we need to take the job outside the organization, because that allows us more control and we can make our work our own. With the change to 50,000 hours comes more time to take that control, and Handy reminds us to spend this time learning new talents, meeting new people, and learning new skills.

"The purpose of this book is to promote a better understanding of the changes which are already about us, in order that we may, as individuals and as a society, suffer less and profit more."

Handy is not opposed to organizations, though he sees a gradual shift to a "shamrock"-shaped organization. Within this structure, there are three distinct groups of people who are "managed differently, paid differently, organized differently," and are held to different expectations. The first of the three groups is the "core"—the qualified professionals, managers, and technicians. The second leaf of the shamrock includes the outside contractors who perform specialized but nonessential work, and the members of the third leaf are the temporary or part-time people. Handy believes that this third group is the fastest growing section as business changes to a service economy. Handy's shamrock organization, visualized almost twenty years ago, is proving to be true today.

In keeping with his self-defined role as social philosopher, he applies the "shamrock" concept to schools. In addition to the existing schools, another lobe would feature an education manager who would create an appropriate educational program for each student. And the third lobe would contain a host of minischools teaching a specialized curriculum (independent art schools, language schools, computing). This type of school would be small, flexible, and focused on the needs of the student.

It is difficult for me to express how affected I am by Handy's writing. Because there are so many books that cross my desk and populate the shelves of our warehouse, I rarely keep books on my own personal shelves. But I keep Charles Handy front and center. Tom Peters captured my feelings about Handy when, in March 2007, he wrote on his blog, "Put simply, he is one of the most decent and thoughtful and profound people-professionals I have ever known. We agree on many-most-almost all-virtually everything when it comes to the 'important stuff.'" I certainly could not have said this better myself. Many years ago, I had the real honor of sharing a dinner with Handy. Here is your opportunity to meet him through this insightful, timeless book. **JC**

The Age of Unreason: Reflections of a Reluctant Capitalist, Harvard Business School Press, Paperback 1990, ISBN 9780875843018

WHERE TO NEXT? « Page 61 for **how to implement your Unreason** « Page 67 for **how to communicate your Unreason** « Page 256 for **a business that lived through Unreason** | EVEN MORE: *Myself and Other More Important Matters* by Charles Handy; *The Age of Discontinuity* by Peter Drucker; *Nuts!* by Kevin Freiberg and Jackie Freiberg

Out of Control

KEVIN KELLY
Reviewed by Todd

The continuing development of human civilization has been predicated on our ability to control nature. The development of agriculture and domestication of animals typify the early grasp we gained over plants and animals. Mendel's cross-pollination of peas in 1866 shows even greater control, the first step toward the bioengineering of today. Kevin Kelly, in his 1994 book *Out of Control*, challenges the very notion of control and argues that the biggest advances in science, economics, and social systems will come through letting go.

Now that is not to say that control doesn't lead to progress, just that we need to change our perception of it. Kelly believes step-function changes have come with advances in automatic controls. For example, the steam engine converted superheated water into mechanical power, but it wasn't until James Watt added a centrifugal governor that the machinery could regulate itself. The control of energy was followed by the control of materials. The feedback mechanisms available to fabricators make possible the creation of almost anything. Kelly imagines, "Cameras the size of molecules? Sure, why not? Crystals the size of buildings? As you wish. . . . Matter—in whatever shape we want—is no longer a barrier. Matter is almost 'free.' " The new regime of automatic control is that of information, a paradigm we are only beginning to understand but one that Kelly believes will usher in an era of self-evolving machines capable of making their own decisions.

In 1990, graduate students at Carnegie Mellon designed a six-legged robot named Ambler. The designers of Ambler labored to create a machine that could act autonomously with capabilities needed for a fictional trip to Mars. But the two-ton creation could barely navigate the test area. The flaw was Ambler's centralized brain and its need to consider every choice before even the smallest movement. At MIT, Rodney Brooks approached the problem differently, inspired by the construction of insects. His robot Genghis had a tiny microprocessor to run each of its six legs, mimicking the neurons ants and cockroaches have in their legs. Each leg looked at what the other legs were doing and acted accordingly, and with a little fiddling by Rodney, Genghis was scampering across the floor. Brooks slowly taught the machine how to climb and navigate over more complex environments, one simple routine built upon another.

"Complexity must be grown from simple systems that already work," Kelly writes. With the recent discovery of neurons on the heart and taste buds in the stomach, we are coming to realize that human life too is actually quite decentralized, more akin to the chaotic, swarming fields of individual agents, each playing their own small part in the manifestation of a greater whole. We seem to accept this functionality from a beehive or an ant colony, but shudder at the thought that life may be nothing more than subroutines built upon subroutines. Control resembles multifaceted reflex rather than some highly structured consciousness.

"The song goes: No one is in charge. We can't predict the future. Now hear the flip side of the album: We're all steering. And we *can* learn to anticipate what is immediately ahead. To learn is to live."

And machines, whether mechanical or biological, only begin to scratch the surface of complexity. Consider the scale of many human organizations and how individuals are now acting as the smaller subroutines. Financial markets, with their multitudes of traders, each acting independently, signal economic meaning through price while computers ironically curb their erratic behavior. The Internet is showing the first signs of intelligence as participants provide Amazon reviews, del.icio.us links, and Digg votes that filter and illuminate greater meaning to the cacophony of random bits and bytes.

I cannot come close in this review to covering everything that Kelley does in 472 pages. The author's survey is wide and deep, drawing on history to build readers' appreciation and on science fiction to feed their imagination. Though written in 1994, *Out of Control* still possesses a prescient quality, because we still struggle to accept and internalize a world that is complex and out of our control by design. Kelly writes, "What little time left in this century is rehearsal time for the chief psychological chore of the 21st century: letting go, with dignity." **TS**

Out of Control: The New Biology of Machines, Social Systems, and the Economic World, Basic Books, Paperback 1994, ISBN 9780201483406

WHERE TO NEXT? » Page 322 for **crowd control** « Page 58 for **corporate control** « Page 18 for **self-control** | EVEN MORE: *Emergence* by Steven Johnson; *Sync* by Steven H. Strogatz

In August 2004, Seth Godin and his team of interns built a distribution hub for world-changing ideas, where everyday people could find an audience for their ideas, and the audience had a say in which ideas would be published. Those fresh ideas would be ahead of the curve—they'd push people to action.

And so was born ChangeThis, a Web site that publishes four to six essays, called manifestos, monthly. Some manifestos begin as idea proposals, submitted by people from around the world. These ideas are voted on by the reading public; the most popular become published manifestos. Other manifestos are sought out and written by well-known thinkers, including Tom Peters, Donna Brazile, Malcolm Gladwell, Michael Pollan, Al Gore, and Seth himself. Topics range from corporate sustainability to creativity to nutrition. Each manifesto is free to read and distribute.

Whether it's how to better manage e-mail to free up time, or how to manage communal space to benefit the community, ChangeThis endeavors to spread ideas that make peoples' lives better.

"You don't know if your idea is any good the moment it's created. Neither does anyone else. The most you can hope for is a strong gut feeling that it is. And trusting your feelings is not as easy as the optimists say it is. There's a reason why feelings scare us." Hugh MacLeod, "How to Be Creative" Issue 6.05, 10/19/2004

"Companies that strive for a higher purpose . . . often find that customers, vendors, suppliers and employees naturally root for its success. A well-defined cause can change the world, no matter how big or small." Ben McConnell and Jackie Huba, "The Customer Evangelist Manifesto" Issue 1, 8/13/2004

"Henry Ford could have said, 'We're all manufacturers' and been right. Today, we can say, 'We're all marketers,' and we will be just as right." Seth Godin, "Marketing Mismatch: When New Won't Work With Old" Issue 42.01B, 1/16/2008

Go to changethis.com for more.

The Rise of the Creative Class

RICHARD FLORIDA
Reviewed by Todd

If you are reading our book, there is a good chance you are a member of Richard Florida's Creative Class. Engineers, writers, actresses, and architects make up the core of this new economic segment, and it expands further when you include occupations like lawyers, accountants, and managers, who all use creativity to solve problems. *The Rise of the Creative Class* is as much about finding out who we are as it is about hearing Florida's intriguing theories on creativity's role in economic development.

Florida's research shows that roughly 30 percent of America's workforce falls squarely in the Creative Class, rising from 20 million people in 1980 to over 38 million in 1999. The average salary of a Creative Class member is $48,750, roughly double that of those working in manufacturing or service industries, and that sum accounts for one-half of all salary and wage income in United States. But the differences appear in more than just numbers.

Florida tells us that the Creative Class shuns conformity and prefers to express its individuality. For example, during interviews, the Creative Class will ask potential employers about same-sex partner benefits, independent of their own orientation, to test a company's openness to diversity. This bohemian mind-set is not new for artisans, but these values have now been adopted by a much wider group. And yet the Creative Class believes in the rewards earned through hard work, with goal-setting and achievement among their criteria for success, which is what sets this group apart from the bohemian. The adoption of these values by the Creative Class explains a variety of worldwide trends, ranging from casual Fridays to corporate interest in employees' personal fitness and health.

The social contract between the Creative Class and its employers has changed as well. Workers expect to be treated like individuals, demanding flexible work schedules and an even more flexible dress code. Managers are left to customize their approach to each employee, but companies have also gained in this changed relationship. Because the Creative Class is intrinsically motivated by challenge, companies hook their employees with a cadence of new products and demanding release schedules, and in turn get a high level of devotion. In this arrangement, the compensation is not in dollars but recognition from peers and industry leaders.

"The best cities, like the best companies, do many things well, offering something for everybody."

If the Creative Class expects different rules in the workplace, it is because members live by different ones in their personal pursuits. "Creative work is largely intellectual and sedentary; thus Creative Class people seek to recharge through physical activity." Florida believes the meteoric rise in health-club memberships and the upswing in adventure sports, from rock climbing to snowshoeing, reveals a group of people pursuing a creative, active lifestyle. He further emphasizes that their activities come in the form of individual sports like running, biking, and swimming, pursuits that again match personal interests and flexible work schedules. This lifestyle trend drives to the core of Florida's research and conclusions.

In the past, access to water or other natural resources determined the economic potential of a region. But Florida believes that the Creative Class is the new resource for economic growth. When choosing where to live, the Creative Class looks for "thick labor markets" that allow for easy horizontal moves from one company to another. Some choose cities with easy access to outdoor recreation, allowing daily engagement to match unpredictable work schedules. As a result of Florida's conclusions and with the publication of *The Rise of the Creative Class*, regional economic development has been turned on its ear. Spending by state and city governments to attract corporations or finance professional sports arenas was proved useless by Florida's research. Instead, his 3T's—technology, talent, and tolerance—are the new blueprint many areas are using to grow creative capital.

Florida says that there is much for the Creative Class to do. To begin, its members must recognize their common values of individuality and meritocracy and shed their dated differences of artist versus engineer or liberal versus conservative. The next step is to take a leadership role in growing creative capital through investing in research and development, both public and private, and supporting multidimensional and varied forms of local culture.

The regional economic issues for business leaders make the book alone worth reading, but it is Florida's naming of a new tribe that many readers will identify with and find most encouraging: Who doesn't want to be part of the Creative Class? **TS**

The Rise of the Creative Class: And How It's Transforming Work, Leisure, Community and Everyday Life, Basic Books, Paperback 2004, ISBN 9780465024773

WHERE TO NEXT? « Page 281 for **the tension between creativity and organizations** « Page 179 for **the connection between management and retention** « Page 279 for **innovation and creativity** | EVEN MORE: *The Death and Life of Great American Cities* by Jane Jacobs; *The World Is Flat* by Thomas L. Friedman; *Bowling Alone* by Robert D. Putnam

Emotional Intelligence

DANIEL GOLEMAN
Reviewed by Todd

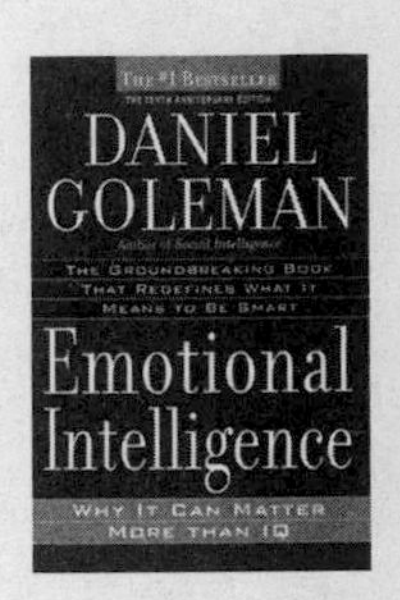

We are a society fixated on testing for intelligence. But as we lament reading about how our community or country is lagging in the latest reading and arithmetic scores, author Daniel Goleman tells us that one's Intelligence Quotient, or IQ, doesn't predict much of anything. IQ tests are a relic of World War I, when they were used by the armed forces to filter millions of recruits into the appropriate positions. Study after study since shows IQ is a poor predictor of eventual success in the real world.

Instead, Goleman asserts, it is *emotion* that plays a greater role in our ability to learn, act, and relate to others. Goleman put the term "emotional intelligence" (EI) into our collective vocabulary by popularizing the work of researchers John Mayer and Peter Salovey. Published in 1995, *Emotional Intelligence* is the broadest of Goleman's books and provides the best survey of how EI plays into all aspects of our lives.

Goleman begins with a discussion of self-awareness, the first of five competencies identified in the original research on EI. One's ability to deal with emotion falls somewhere on a continuum: from a healthy conscious ability to detect and alter one's mood, to an in-between level that brings awareness but accepts a mental state whether good or bad, to a stormy, uncontrollable cocktail of emotion that engulfs the individual. Goleman offers examples of the detriment caused when people handle emotions poorly: Gary is unable to sense his fiancée's emotions nor describe his own, while Elliot, after the removal of a brain tumor severed a neural connection that allows people to place emotional value on alternative choices, loses the ability to reach decisions. In both cases, without the ability to determine one's emotional state, it is impossible to handle the emotions themselves and managing them is no small feat.

The brain leaves us with "little or no control over *when* we are swept up by emotion, nor over *what* emotion it will be." Therefore, being able to control these emotions once they're present, the second competency, is essential. Anger, anxiety, and melancholy have all developed through human evolution to deal with danger, uncertainty, and loss. The mild forms of these emotions are what most of us struggle with on a daily basis and Goleman draws on research to suggest coping mechanisms to manage them. He suggests watching television or reading as a way to minimize anger and anxiety, and, when melancholy and withdrawn, to get out of the house to spend time with friends.

Empathy is just as important as emotional self-awareness, says Goleman, going on to describe the third competency of emotional intelligence. Many of our emotional cues come from the 90 percent of communication that is nonverbal. Babies from an early age look for cues that their expressions are being understood and will mimic the moods of their parents. One-year-olds will cry in reaction to another child's tears, and by age two, the toddler can separate his or her feelings from others, offering the appropriate consolation for upset playmates. Teenagers who develop a natural aptitude for empathy are more popular, more outgoing, and have better luck dating. Empathy is not easy to practice and requires the ability to set aside one's own emotions to perceive the feelings being transmitted by those around him or her.

"Emotional self-control—delaying gratification and stifling impulsiveness—underlies accomplishment of every sort."

The fourth competency Goleman identifies, managing relationships, is the art of managing the emotions of those around you. Actors are masters at playing with the emotions of their audiences. Politicians and business leaders use the same skills to motivate and persuade their constituents. Goleman suggests that studying children at play provides some interesting insights. Researchers find that everyone, popular and unpopular alike, gets rejected by the group at one point or another, but rather than pushing their way in and drawing attention to themselves, the popular kids observe and then imitate what the group is doing in order to be included.

Finally, harnessing emotion can also be a powerful force in the pursuit of success in relationships. This starts with our ability to control impulses that might distract us. In the 1960s, psychologist Walter Mischel developed a test in which four-year-olds were given the choice between eating one puffy treat immediately or waiting several minutes to be rewarded with two treats. The level of restraint foreshadowed social competence as the children were tracked into adolescence. The teenagers who showed restraint as youngsters embraced challenges, were self-reliant, and took initiative, while their impatient counterparts were shy, indecisive, and tended to overreact with a quick temper. Forgoing immediate gratification, reining in that emotional instinct, is a key difference between excellent and world-class performers. Goleman also suggests that optimism and creating a positive state of mind are the answers to connecting emotion to successful efforts. In fact, MetLife now uses optimism as the key determinant for new sales hires.

Emotional Intelligence presents a case that compels the reader to reconsider a whole range of situations from work to home, containing chapters on marriage, management, and ways to teach children about EI. For most, the message will be how to increase awareness of emotions, which results in making relationships healthier. For many, it will be hard not to see personal demons, past or present, in what Goleman describes. TS

Emotional Intelligence: Why It Can Matter More Than IQ, Bantam, Paperback 10th Anniversary Edition 2006, ISBN 9780553383713

WHERE TO NEXT? « Page 264 for **some folks who thought they were smart** » Page 316 for **how emotions manifest from our primal drives** « Page 56 for **how love and leadership go together** | EVEN MORE: *Frames of Mind* by Howard Gardner; *Why Marriages Succeed or Fail* by John Gottman; *Executive* by Harry Levinson

Driven

PAUL R. LAWRENCE AND NITIN NOHRIA
Reviewed by Todd

My wife and I have this running joke that when we witness some human behavior we don't understand, we ask, "What would a caveman do?" We ask this question most often when observing our young children in their daily routines, but recently our reflection on behavior has widened to include our own habits and associated motives. As much as we think we have evolved into refined humans, our basic drives are the same as our ancestors from 70,000 years ago.

And Harvard Business School professors Paul Lawrence and Nitin Nohria agree. In *Driven*, the authors hypothesize that the actions of today's homo sapiens are based on a set of genetically programmed drives. If you think sex and hunger are on that list, you'd be misled by a purely biological point of view. The authors took on the role of academic outsider, trying to connect the realms of biologists and social scientists. The authors lament that the compartmentalization of knowledge within psychology, anthropology, sociology, and the popular ideologies within these disciplines makes it difficult to propose a unified theory for human behavior. But that is the quest in *Driven*.

In many ways, *Driven* is a survey of evolutionary theory proposed over the last forty years, and Lawrence and Nohria do more than an adequate job of describing the terrain. The authors begin with an idea proposed by psychologist Steven Pinker: the human mind has a wide set of preprogrammed skills ranging from basic concepts of quantity, the ability to select suitable habitats, and a moral code and sense of what's right. They continue with archeologist Steven Mithen's postulation that it was the intermingling of these skills that lead to the species' large cognition leap 50,000 years ago.

Lawrence and Nohria then hypothesize that, during this time, human behavior came to be driven by one of four sources: acquiring, bonding, learning, and defending. On the surface, these ring with truth, certainly, but the authors are careful to show these four as primary sources and other motives that we may attach instinctively to the four as just derivatives. For example, the drive to acquire is most often associated with ambition and envy, but at its most basic, this drive is for long-term survival. The drive to bond, again in evolutionary terms, led us to form tribes, further improving the likelihood of survival, but it also sits at the base of atrocities such as genocide. It is the drive to learn which best explains how humans singularly evolved beyond their primate cousins, with the persistence of religion and art in all known human cultures filling in the gaps of our understanding. The drive to defend protects possessions, relationships, even ideologies and leads to, at one end, disagreements, and at the other extreme, war.

"Humans seem to have a predisposition to be open and curious about new theories, but it also seems true that they do not abandon old theories until convinced the new ones are better—that is, more useful, compact, and accurate."

Lawrence and Nohria take the final portion of their book to apply their own expertise with organizations, using the four-driver lens. They start with an almost utopian description of workers naturally bonding with one another, the drive to acquire tempered by well-communicated company goals, and teams defending themselves both internally and externally for needed resources. Then the authors use two U.S. companies as case studies for the four-drive organizational design. First, General Motors is compared to Japanese auto companies. The authors conclude that the company's rise under Alfred Sloan came from the emphasis on the drive to acquire, pitting managers and their divisions against one another for the allocation of resources. This drive has become even more prominent in the company's relationship with suppliers and unions in recent years and contrasts with their Japanese competitors, who foster bonding through company-wide consensus and learning through their religious devotion to continuous improvement. Conversely, in the eyes of the authors, Hewlett-Packard is the exemplar company who got it right from the start. The evidence they provide shows careful consideration by founders Bill Hewlett and David Packard to embrace a set of values that allows employees to engage in all four drives. The result is an almost unparalleled ability to adapt to changes in economic climate and technological products.

In the effort to better understand human behavior, *Driven* provides an illuminating blueprint for parenting and relating for my wife and me. For example, the effectiveness of giving our children "time-outs" to correct bad behavior is explained by their temporary isolation and resulting inability to bond with the rest of the family while in the temporary isolation. The usefulness of Lawrence and Nohria's four drivers can explain the rising credit card debt in America due to the easy means by which those plastic cards fulfill our drive to acquire. Whether your application is personal or societal, appreciating and understanding these basic drives provides another view into the strengths and weakness of our species. **TS**

Driven: How Human Nature Shapes Our Choices, Jossey-Bass, Paperback 2002, ISBN 9780787963859

WHERE TO NEXT? « Page 209 for **an organization that satisfied the drives** « Page 204 for **an organization that did not satisfy the drives** « Page 208 for **more on Darwin, who inspired the drives** | EVEN MORE: *Consilience* by Edward O. Wilson; *The Third Chimpanzee* by Jared M. Diamond; *The Origin of Wealth* by Eric D. Beinhocker; *Descartes' Error* by Antonio Damasio; *How the Mind Works* by Steven Pinker; *Survival of the Sickest* by Sharon Moalem and Jonathan Prince

To Engineer Is Human

HENRY PETROSKI
Reviewed by Todd

Everything fails; it is just a matter of when.

Parents forewarn their children that failure is common, even likely, through the nursery rhymes of "Humpty Dumpty" and "Jack and Jill." Our first steps and first bike rides without the training wheels give us an idea of what failure feels like, literally. As we find our balance, scraped-up knees and bruised pride happen less frequently. Henry Petroski begins his book, *To Engineer Is Human*, by revisiting these same children's tales, cautioning us again, and, with an engineer's eye, describing a world more reminiscent of London Bridge.

Due to their design, the pen on your desk is likely to last for months while your automobile will likely get you from point A to B for many years, their life spans governed by a balance between function, aesthetic, and economy. Engineers arbitrate those competing forces when bringing an idea into the material world. This arbitration, as Petroski describes it, is something closer to art than science. But sometimes, Petroski warns, art comes at the expense of sound engineering and construction.

The construction of the Hyatt Regency Hotel in Kansas City called for a grand atrium with two walkways suspended from the ceiling by a set of rods that ran through both structures. The single rod mechanism was replaced, during early planning, with two separate rods to simplify construction and utilize standard fabrication techniques. This small change left the system with barely enough strength to support the walkway; adding people proved disastrous. On July 17, 1981, the walkway collapsed, killing 114 people and injuring 200 others.

Petroski uses the Hyatt Regency story to illustrate several nuances of engineering. Many parties were simply negligent: an early ceiling collapse and comments from construction workers about instability gave engineers ample warning to reexamine the walkway plans; no changes were made. Letters to the editors of trade publications following the accident also suggested what seemed like obvious engineering alternatives.

But that is the trick. Knowing the nature of a failure provides paths to the core problem, but this is a hindsight luxury the original engineers didn't have. And there we return back to the idea of engineering as art. The unique design and construction of these walkways left engineers working in a thought space that was dangerous, more so than they realized.

As much as the field of study seems to be based in fact and formula, engineering is better described as grounded in hypothesis, a working practice of individuals developing ideas that tentatively describe phenomena but need constant reevaluation. Engineers spend enormous amounts of time studying the mistakes made by their colleagues. Petroski points to an Egyptian pyramid in Dahshur, with its sudden change to a more shallow angle midway up, as an early example of a trial and error method of construction. Flying buttresses on European cathedrals indicate a similar postconstruction epiphany. Computer-aided three-dimensional drafting and finite element analysis do not protect today's engineers from failure as new designs further strain the tensions between competing factors. While unequivocally a tragedy, the Hyatt Regency walkway collapse becomes a valuable case study from which future engineers can learn.

"Engineering, like poetry, is an attempt to approach perfection."

Petroski's expertise in failure analysis provides important lessons for those in business. Formulas for organizational success, whether self-determined or suggested, are, like design, better described as hypothesis, accurate under some conditions and always open for reexamination. What engineers call "a factor of safety" and inventory analysts call "safety stock" deals with the parallel uncertainty of real world conditions on a rope or a distribution system. Businesses have their own versions of engineering's "factor of safety," whether it concerns extra boxes of inventory under the expeditor's desk or adding a few days to a customer promise for variation in the distribution center, but they'd better make sure those safety factors don't inflate and allow sloppy business practices.

Much lip service is given to accepting failure in business as a natural phase in the learning process, yet internalizing the idea seems a little more difficult. Shareholders don't show sympathy for failed products. Customers expect their product to arrive when promised and in pristine condition. Most of the other books featured in these pages detail the workings of successful companies, while Petroski's book tells a more complicated tale of failure, one in which business practitioners can find wisdom. The most important lesson has to be appreciating failure as a learning opportunity. Failure is common. Not learning from failure forces companies to repeat the same mistakes. In engineering, that repetition can cost lives; in business, our livelihood. **TS**

To Engineer Is Human: The Role of Failure in Successful Design, Vintage Books, Paperback 1992, ISBN 9780679734161

WHERE TO NEXT? « Page 65 for **more subtle forms of failure** « Page 268 for **how genius can fail** « Page 173 for **operational failure** | EVEN MORE: *The Evolution of Useful Things* by Henry Petroski; *The Logic of Failure* by Dietrich Dorner; *Mistakes Were Made (But Not By Me)* by Carol Tavris and Elliot Aronson

The Wisdom of Crowds

JAMES SUROWIECKI

Reviewed by Todd

The field of nonfiction narratives was a crowded one in 2006, with a number of books published examining varying aspects of decision making. Steven Levitt and Stephen Dubner's immensely popular *Freakonomics* takes the tools of the dismal science of economics and applies it unexpectedly to things like the housing decisions of drug dealers (many, it turns out, choose to live with their mothers). Malcolm Gladwell's sophmore effort, *Blink*, explores the subtle nuances of intuition. While the previous two books looked at decision making by individuals, James Surowiecki took a decidedly different approach in examining the decision-making power of groups in his book *The Wisdom of Crowds*.

Surowiecki offers copious examples to show when groups solve problems better than individuals. When contestants on the TV game show *Who Wants to Be a Millionaire?* use their phone-a-friend lifeline, the likelihood of a right answer stands at 65 percent, while asking the audience delivers the correct response 91 percent of the time. The Iowa Electronic Markets bring together individuals who make trades based on what they think will happen in a variety of political elections. This market-based method is more accurate than voter polls 75 percent of the time and predicts actual election outcomes within a few percentage points.

This is not to say that group decision making is superior in all instances. Surowiecki proposes three conditions that must be satisfied in order for masses to outperform their members. First, the group must be diverse, a condition that ensures a wide sourcing of ideas and perspectives. The members of the group must have a certain level of independence, a tougher constraint given our social nature and natural tendency to follow the crowd. Finally, there must be a method to aggregate the differing opinions of the group. For example, markets use price to pull together all of the opinions of buyers and sellers and determine value.

When these conditions are satisfied, groups prove well suited to tackling three categories of problems. The phone-a-friend example or making election predictions are what Surowieicki refers to as *cognitive* problems, those questions which have definitive answers. The problem of *coordination* finds a solution in the stock market, in this case matching supply with demand. Organizations do much the same in organizing individuals in the pursuit of a purpose. The toughest of the three problems requires *cooperation* to reach a solution. Individuals have a hard time looking past their own self-interests and adopting a broader view. Paying taxes or curbing pollution are among the many problems that fall into this category.

"What I think we know now is that in the long run, the crowd's judgment is going to give us the best chance of making the right decision, and in the face of that knowledge, traditional notions of power and leadership should begin to pale."

The second half of the book is devoted to cases, three of which deal specifically with business issues. "Committees, Juries, and Teams: The *Columbia* Disaster and How Small Groups Can Be Made to Work" is the best example of Surowiecki's ability to synthesize issues of economics, sociology, and psychology with real-world storytelling. In this case, the focus is on the dysfunction present in NASA's Mission Management Team during the ill-fated flight of the space shuttle *Columbia* in 2003. From the start, team leader Linda Ham worked from a preset conclusion that the foam debris that struck the shuttle on liftoff was not a risk, ignoring inquiries and statements to the contrary. The absence of questioning by Ham's team in the face of further evidence confirms studies conducted by political scientist Charlan Nemeth, who found that juries that consider a minority opinion produce more nuanced decisions and used a more rigorous process for reaching their conclusions. Transcripts of the NASA team meetings show Ham did not allow minority opinion. Surowiecki also uses social psychologist Garold Stasser's research to illustrate some of the problems of small teams like this one. In Stasser's experiment, all members of a team are given the same two pieces of information, while a few of the members are given one or two additional pieces of information. Consistently, teams deliberated on the common information, not the unique knowledge held by the minority. The *Columbia* tragedy could have been avoided with a broader decision-making process that brought all team members to the table, allowing their information to be shared and integrated into the deliberations.

Companies are already utilizing *The Wisdom of Crowds*. Companies like Hewlett-Packard, Google, and Microsoft are using internal-decision markets to predict customer demand for their products. Spanish-based clothing retailer Zara is using real-time feedback from its thousand-plus stores worldwide and its three-week concept-to-product cycle to introduce twenty thousand new products each year and produce the exact type and quantity needed for each outlet, replenishing stock twice weekly. But the widespread use of teams requires leaders to understand the pitfalls in group dynamics and ensure that the overall organization and its subcomponents are making the best decisions possible.

When next posed with the question "How do we solve this problem?" the answer should be clear—listen to the crowd. They make better decisions, period. TS

The Wisdom of Crowds, Anchor Books, Paperback 2005, ISBN 9780385721707

WHERE TO NEXT? « Page 196 for **the nuts and bolts of small groups** « Page 193 for **working well in small groups** « Page 306 for **complex group dynamics** | EVEN MORE: *Flavor of the Month* by Joel Best; *Super Crunchers* by Ian Ayres; *Smart Mobs* by Howard Rheingold

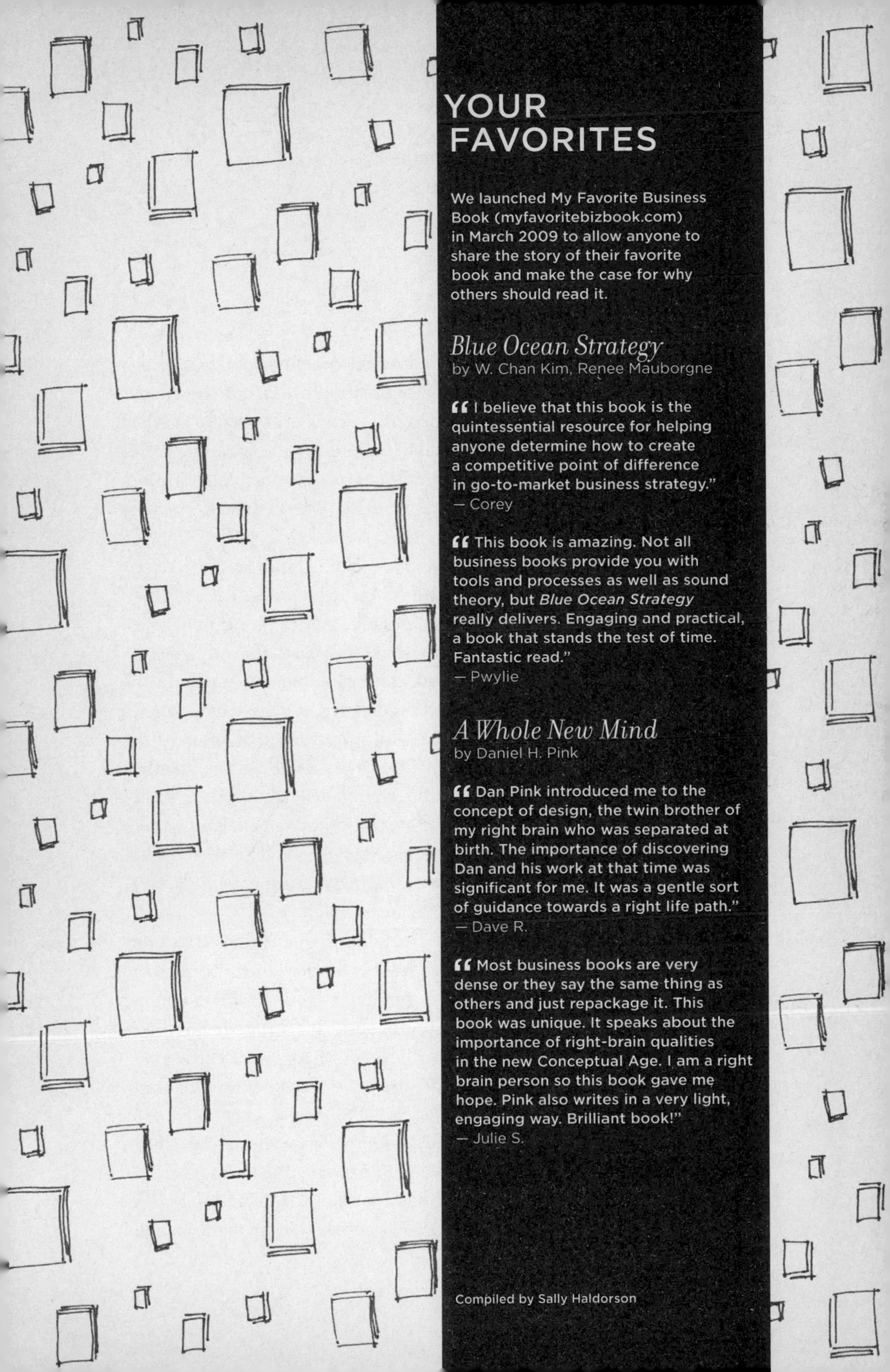

YOUR FAVORITES

We launched My Favorite Business Book (myfavoritebizbook.com) in March 2009 to allow anyone to share the story of their favorite book and make the case for why others should read it.

Blue Ocean Strategy
by W. Chan Kim, Renee Mauborgne

"I believe that this book is the quintessential resource for helping anyone determine how to create a competitive point of difference in go-to-market business strategy."
— Corey

"This book is amazing. Not all business books provide you with tools and processes as well as sound theory, but *Blue Ocean Strategy* really delivers. Engaging and practical, a book that stands the test of time. Fantastic read."
— Pwylie

A Whole New Mind
by Daniel H. Pink

"Dan Pink introduced me to the concept of design, the twin brother of my right brain who was separated at birth. The importance of discovering Dan and his work at that time was significant for me. It was a gentle sort of guidance towards a right life path."
— Dave R.

"Most business books are very dense or they say the same thing as others and just repackage it. This book was unique. It speaks about the importance of right-brain qualities in the new Conceptual Age. I am a right brain person so this book gave me hope. Pink also writes in a very light, engaging way. Brilliant book!"
— Julie S.

Compiled by Sally Haldorson

Made to Stick

CHIP HEATH AND DAN HEATH
Reviewed by Todd

Ideas are slippery. Yet each day, we are called upon to communicate our ideas to others—to our employees, our clients, our spouses, our children. Often the words and images used to communicate ideas fade, and with them the ideas' intent, as our listeners' brains filter the endless stream of fact and opinion, notion and conclusion. The challenge lies in how to get your idea not to slip, but to stick.

Your childhood home, Kennedy's challenge to put humans on the moon, a moral lesson from one of Aesop's Fables. Each of these ideas possesses identifiable qualities that make it stick in our memories. Chip Heath, a professor at Stanford, has been intrigued for over a decade by the phenomenon of how many bad ideas gain traction, many in the form of urban myths. Dan Heath cofounded a company that produces video-based textbooks, and he found while working with some of the most-loved professors in the country that they used almost identical teaching methodologies. The two brothers brought together their interests, theories, and experiences to write *Made to Stick*, a book that will help anyone with a message make it memorable and effective. Dan and Chip lay out six key principles of sticky ideas: simplicity, unexpectedness, concreteness, credibility, emotion, and stories.

Human memory excels at remembering identifiable "things" like one-room apartments or midcentury ranch houses. Concreteness trumps the abstract. This explains why it is easy to remember your childhood home. We also care about events from our childhood, associating birthday parties and broken bones with the places where they happened. Those emotions trigger strong memories and make them even stickier. Concreteness and emotion are hallmarks of a sticky idea.

Chip and Dan use President John F. Kennedy's State of the Union speech in 1961 to illustrate another principle of stickiness: unexpectedness. Kennedy covered most of what was expected for that era: the Cold War, NATO, and civil defense. The speech's conclusion, though, changed the course of American history. He declared, "This nation should commit itself to achieving the goal, before this decade is out, of landing a man on the moon and returning him safely to Earth. . . ." The declaration was unexpected, and the call for serious space exploration caught the attention of the American public. More important, the challenge created a "knowledge gap," as a nation asked itself how it would do that. That curiosity—the gap between what we know and what we want to know—is what propelled the United States to put Neil Armstrong on the moon in 1969.

THE SIX PRINCIPLES OF STICKY IDEAS:

- Simplicity
- Unexpectedness
- Concreteness
- Credibility
- Emotions
- Stories

Proverbs are the quintessential sticky ideas. The proverb "A bird in the hand is worth two in the bush" is full of concreteness in its reference to clearly understandable objects. A complex philosophical idea with wide applicability is communicated simply, with no wasted words. A similar sentiment can be found in Spanish, Polish, and medieval Latin. This idea appears to have originated in Aesop's "The Hawk and the Nightingale," written in 570 BC. Now, *that* is a sticky idea.

"We wanted to take apart sticky ideas—both natural and created—and figure out what made them stick."

Like all great books, business or otherwise, stories are the backbone of *Made to Stick*. They bring ideas—both the Heath brothers' and ours—to life. Stories, the authors say, act as flight simulators for the mind. Xerox repairmen frequently share stories with their cohorts over lunch. What at first might look like the sharing of gripes among coworkers is actually a rich learning environment. As each repairman tells his tale of some unexpected machine malfunction, the other lunchmates visualize those same problems, preparing themselves for a future encounter. These Xerox technicians' tales contain most of the Heaths' principles of stickiness. In each, you'll find concrete descriptions of copier components, unexpected problems, and emotional frustration. The trick is keeping the story simple enough that it retains its essence and its impact.

What do Fortune 500 CEOs and health-care workers in Africa have in common? Both have the formidable challenge of selling ideas to thousands of people. Whether communicating a strategic course correction or advocating healthy behaviors that can save lives, making their ideas sticky is what will make their efforts successful. It's the same for teachers, tool-and-die makers, managers, marketers . . . and, well, you. Everybody is selling something (and I mean that in the most positive of terms). *Made to Stick* gives you the tools to find more traction for your ideas. **TS**

Made to Stick: Why Some Ideas Survive and Others Die, Random House, Hardcover 2007, ISBN 9781400064281

WHERE TO NEXT? « Page 139 for **the Heaths' inspiration** « Page 108 for **becoming top of mind** « Page 136 to **get people talking** | EVEN MORE: *Words That Work* by Frank Lutz; *Story* by Robert McKee; *Start-up* by Jerry Kaplan

More Than You Know

MICHAEL J. MAUBOUSSIN

Reviewed by Todd

Michael Mauboussin is chief investment strategist at Legg Mason Capital. He, like everyone else in the stockbroking trade, spends his days researching companies and industries in search of insights that can lead to buy and sell recommendations for his clients. As you can imagine, this is a tough business. Everyone is looking at the same data yet needs to conclude something different. The only way to be original is to take a different approach and that is exactly what Mauboussin does in his work and in this book, *More Than You Know*.

Mauboussin believes in knowing a little about a lot, and that through this diversity of thought, we become better problem solvers. The original versions of the thirty-eight essays in *More Than You Know* were originally written while Mauboussin worked at the Credit Suisse Group, a Swiss financial service company, and released under that company's newsletter column, "The Consilient Observer." Consillience—the idea that all knowledge can be unified into a single working system—has heavily influenced Mauboussin's investing philosophy. Breadth of knowledge creates, rather than opposes, depth of knowledge.

Each essay ties an accessible metaphor to a piece of specific research and its implications for investors. Don't be scared off by the financial angle. The essence of Mauboussin's work lingers on investigating how humans can make better decisions—something we can all use help with. To dismiss the work as not in your purview would be to miss the richness of sources Mauboussin draws from and miss the very point of using a broader base of knowledge to make better decisions.

Mauboussin's essay "From Honey to Money" draws on research into the collective intelligence observed in bees and ants. The author marvels at the ability for these colonies to generate "complex, adaptive, and robust results" with decentralized decision making that works against much of the command and control structure we have built into our organizations. Looking to examples that mimic this organization and behavior,

Mauboussin focuses on the decision markets. Iowa Electronics has accurately predicted elections at a variety of government levels, and the Hollywood Stock Exchange has shown amazing accuracy for predicting both box office receipts and Oscar nominees. The individuals in these markets closely resemble the ant or bee with their self-determined actions, the motivation to be right (earning money), and active feedback through the pricing on the markets themselves.

The last step of Mauboussin's analysis is to ask if the jump from hive to decision market to stock market holds true. "Hives don't have prices," he says, and this makes decision making in nature less susceptible to the positive feedback loops that send market prices soaring (or crashing). He also points out that in decision markets the bet is always placed on a specific outcome and this eliminates some of the strategies available to stock traders, such as following momentum.

Mauboussin unveils other unpredictable musings through the book: What can Tupperware parties teach us about influence? What can the evolution of Tiger Woods's golf swing say about finding optimal solutions? The breadth of subjects Mauboussin draws from and his central message that we should never put limits on what we know should inspire each of us to develop more numerous sources of inspiration as we try to make better sense of what we do and of the greater world around us. TS

"There are too many layers of interactions in the brain. The parts don't explain the whole."

More Than You Know: Finding Financial Wisdom in Unconventional Places, Updated and Expanded, Columbia Business School Publishing, Hardcover 2007, ISBN 9780231143721

WHERE TO NEXT? « Page 27 for **why stock traders trounce Marines in trading pits and war games** « Page 271 for **why understanding baseball statistics can help with decision making** | EVEN MORE: *Consilience* by Edward O. Wilson; *Creative Destruction* by Richard Foster and Sarah Kaplan; *Fooled by Randomness* by Nassim Nicholas Taleb

THE LAST WORD Thanks for reading *The 100 Best Business Books of All Time*. We wrote the book to help people find solutions to their business problems. We hope you found that and more. Visit 100bestbiz.com for more on all of the books we featured here, including chapter excerpts, interviews with the authors, videos about the books, and more.

—Jack and Todd

How to Read a {Business} Book

BY TODD SATTERSTEN

During my sophomore year of high school, a family moved into our rural, southeastern Wisconsin school district. The two kids had been educated in the private schools in the inner suburbs of Chicago, which was immediately evident by the books they were reading.

The son was a year older than I was, and our only daily interaction took place during band class when he pulled his French horn from the instrument locker next to the one where my baritone was stored. He was always reading until the last possible moment before class started. His selections of Poe, Twain, and Fitzgerald were distantly familiar, but one day he entered reading Mortimer Adler's *How to Read a Book.* You can imagine the number of times he was sarcastically asked, "How do you read a book about reading books if you don't know how to read a book?" Everyone took his or her shot. The cheap and easy laughs at his expense showed just how insecure the rest of my classmates and I were in the face of his perceived superiority.

I might have been one of the kids mocking that boy, but twenty years later, my view could not be more different. During the year it took to write *The 100 Best Business Books of All Time,* Jack and I had to start reading a new book at the beginning of each week and compose a thoughtful review of the book's premise and arguments by week's end to reach our contractual deadline. While we had both reviewed books for years, the pace of the book project made it essential for us to discover a set of reading rules that could be used to save time and improve comprehension as we navigated the thousands of business books that are published each year. Here are some of the things we learned along the way.

Get a Recommendation

Publishers are very good marketers. They spend enormous amounts of time constructing clever titles and designing shiny dust jackets in the hopes you will pick up—and ultimately buy—their books. This is precisely the point where most readers make their first mistake.

Think about the first business book you read. It was probably *Seven Habits of Highly Effective People* by Stephen Covey or *Good to Great* by Jim Collins, or maybe *In Search of Excellence* by Tom Peters and Bob Waterman. In any case, I bet you read that first book because someone you trusted recommended it, and reading that first book was likely a meaningful experience for you. It shook your world up just enough that you saw things a little differently.

After your experience with that first valuable business book, you likely logged on to Amazon or ran down to Barnes & Noble in search of more solutions and good reads. And this is where things go bad for most business book readers. Undoubtedly, your second book purchase was a less satisfying experience than your first.

The problem? 11,000. That is the number of business books published in the United States every year. Recommendations reduce the noise. Suggestions from friends and colleagues are best, because they know you and your circumstances. Reliable media sources that regularly review business books, like the *Wall Street Journal* and *BusinessWeek,* are also a great source for slimming the pile. Blogs, tweets, and Facebook statuses can be just as valuable. Online booksellers offer customer reviews on their product pages, and physical bookstores have employees who can help you find a book.

Worthwhile as they are, recommendations merely reduce the size of the pile. The next step is to determine which book is the right one.

The Promise

Books that are worthy of your time deliver a clear promise. The author and publisher use several mechanisms to make that promise clear and, when well executed, these cues align to show the reader what they'll get from their time spent with the book.

Start with the cover. The title gives the book a name. The subtitle tells you what the book is about. Observe the colors used and the fonts chosen. Most business book covers are simple with only text. Sometimes you'll see an image or author photograph that provides additional clues to the promise. Again, this is all marketing, but if executed properly, the covers tell you what you are getting yourself into.

Next, quickly scan the table of contents. The authors provide the outline of the book in a couple of pages. You can see clearly the topics and arguments the authors intend to make. You might be surprised how often a scan of the table of contents will rule out a book and send you on to the next.

The introduction is THE most important part of any book. Seriously. I am always amazed by the number of people who tell me they skip the introduction and jump right to the first chapter. In business books, the introduction sets the tone and pace of the book. Most authors use a story to illustrate the difficulty or challenge they are going to tackle. More important, the introduction should provide an explicit promise and the path by which it will be delivered. If you can't make it through the introduction, and if it doesn't leave you intrigued, chances are the book isn't going to turn you on either.

In the introduction to *The 100 Best Business Books of All Time,* we said:

"The endless stream of new books requires a filter to help discern the good and the better from the absolute best. The solution to that problem is this book, *The 100 Best Business Books of All Time.*"

We hoped to make it very easy for you to discern whether our book was written for you in mind, or if you were one of the few business readers for whom choosing a good book comes easily.

Let's look at a few other introductory promises from some very good business books:

From *The Art of Woo* by G. Richard Shell & Mario Moussa:
"Our attention in this book is squarely on the problems you face when you must persuade others who are, at least nominally, on your team."

They are saying clearly to the reader, "If you were looking for car salesperson skills, perhaps another book would be more up your alley."

From *The Halo Effect* by Phil Rosenzweig:
"Think of it as a guide for the reflective

manager, a way to separate the nuggets from the nonsense. . . . The central idea in this book is that our thinking about business is shaped by a number of delusions. . . . The ones that distort our understanding of company performance, that make it difficult to know why one company succeeds and another fails."

If you are in the market for a "how to" guide to business success, Rosenzweig is telling you to look elsewhere because he intends to puncture our false hopes that there is just such a guide.

Read the whole introduction—generally only around ten pages. Once you combine your impression of the introduction with the cover and content elements, you can determine if a given work is the right book for your problem. If the promise is unclear, or if there is a conflict between cover and copy, move on. If no promise can be found, run as fast as you can the other way, because murky intentions lead to murky execution.

Starting at the End

Several years ago, Les Tuerk—the cofounder of the speaker's bureau, BrightSight Group—told me that he started every book at the end. Not at the last chapter or couple of pages, but in the index. Les said that all the key concepts included in the book were easily recognizable, from companies mentioned and famous people cited, to preexisting concepts specifically called out. The citations show you exactly where they can be found.

That insight struck me as novel. And, as I began to apply that advice myself, I found the chances are good that if there is some version of the problem you are wrestling with described in the index, you are holding the right book in your hands.

Chapter summaries have a similar and equally valuable potential to show you where the meat of the material lies within the book. With the exception of CEO biographies and business narratives, business books need not be read from cover to cover. Skimming is a perfectly acceptable method of reading this genre and chapter summaries can make the process go even faster. More and more books are including short, bulleted lists at the end of every chapter to improve memory retention. These summary points also act as a substitute for intensive reading. Most people argue that they don't have time to read business books, so don't think of it as cheating, but instead as the time-saver that it is.

Whether you start at the end of a chapter or the end of the book, you will still need to read the book. The good news is that you will want to once you've found the books that are really for you.

It Is Not About You

Congratulations! You are done with the tough part of sorting through the pile of recommended reading and have found the book that is best for you.

Now, while you may think this is finally the moment when you can settle into your comfy chair at home and soak up the solution to your problem, I want you to stop and do something a little counterintuitive: I want you to think about someone else while you're reading.

One of the best ways to improve retention of the material you are about to read is to imagine yourself having to tell someone else about it. That act of imagining yourself as teacher completely changes the way you read. As you turn the pages, you start to anticipate what would be most interesting and applicable to your "class." You begin to organize the structure by which you are going to share this new information. The logical result of this strategy is to record memorable and valuable highlights.

Leave Your Mark

Recording what you learn from reading a book should happen both inside and outside that book.

Get over any fear you have of writing in a book. Business books are meant to be interacted with. Take a pen and leave notes in the margins. Grab that pink highlighter you used in college and mark up passages that capture your attention. Tim Sanders, in his book *Love Is the Killer App*, suggested that important learning points be written on the first blank page in the front of the book and great quotes for future presentations be recorded on the inside back cover. Personally, I became a fan of 3M Post-it Flags in writing *The 100 Best* for quickly marking pages that I needed to return to later.

Now you need to share what you have learned with the world. It doesn't matter how. Pick a form and a medium and go with it. Steve Cunningham at readitfor.me decided videos were the best way to share his passion for business books. Chris Yeh builds book outlines on the aptly titled wiki Book Outlines. Sean wrote short reviews and provided mind maps drawn on brown paper bags at stickybusinessbooks.com. John Moore at brandautopsy.com uses SlideShare and creates quick presentations with the "money quotes."

Just write a review—one hundred characters or one thousand words—and give it to someone to read. You get the idea.

Leaving marks in the book and leaving your own mark about what you learned will help you solve your problem and, in tandem, help others solve theirs.

Choose Your Own Path

Many people take pride in being able to speed-read. Others flaunt it when they read a book cover-to-cover in one day. Many books are recommended with the following sentiment: "you won't be able to put it down!"

But that's not the way to read a business book. Instead, set at least fifteen minutes aside to read and don't read for longer than forty-five minutes in a stretch. Too short a time and you can't get your brain calmed down enough to pay attention to what you are reading. Too long and you will exceed your cranial buffer and start to forget important pieces. One of the common excuses executives give for not reading more business books (which are the most economical way to get new ideas) is not having enough time. Reading for less than an hour at a time means you can move through a chapter in one or two sittings, and an entire book in about a week. Just think of the inspiration and information you can gather reading fifty-two books a year.

If the book isn't working for you, stop reading it and choose another. It doesn't matter if you are twenty pages in or two hundred pages. Ignore the $20 and couple hours you've invested and move on. Don't bother to fool yourself into thinking you will return to the book at some later date. There will always be another book on the same subject worth more in its unexpectedness and execution. Always remember that if you took the time and care to choose the right book to solve your problem, the reading should be enjoyable too.

Connect the Dots

Remember those summer book reading challenges staged by your elementary teachers in which you got a star sticker for every book you completed? Since the third grade, you have been told you should read more. It's still great advice for adults.

Books are about context, the greater meaning. Being able to connect multiple books improves our ability to compare and contrast approaches and philosophies.

Professor Albert Madansky at the University of Chicago says, "You can only truly comprehend and evaluate a business book after you have read many of them. Fortunately, as you become better at reading them, you also become better at selecting them."

You Need Only One Idea

I've been a passionate advocate of business books for years, way before I worked for a business book retailer. I've argued that business books offer the solutions to your business problems. But now I want to lower your expectations as to what business books can deliver. You will still occasionally read books that don't deliver on their promise, even if you follow this advice in selecting books. You will spend some money and time on unfulfilling reads. There is nothing you can do about it.

So let's set the goal as something very modest: one good idea. That's all you need.

Let's do the math to prove it. Many books are priced at around $25 and the time you spent reading the book is worth $400; let's round it up to $500. I can guarantee that you will find at least one idea in each book you carefully choose and sit down to read that can deliver $500 worth of benefits.

Let's summarize how to read a business book:

- ➔ Spend more time choosing books to avoid reading the wrong books.
- ➔ Search for the promise the author makes.
- ➔ The end can be a great place to start.
- ➔ Read as much for others as for yourself.
- ➔ More books read means more understanding gained.
- ➔ You only need one good idea.

These guidelines will help you orient your expectations from the start and spend more time reading great books.

ACKNOWLEDGMENTS

Our first thank you goes out to Sally Haldorson. She was conspicuously hiding in our customer services group for eight years with a master's degree in creative writing. Sally's roles included editor, cheerleader, psychologist, humorist, and referee. The book would have never happened without you, Sally.

We next have to thank Joy Panos Stauber. Everything (and we mean everything) about the way this book looks is owed to Joy. She has been our designer, art director, and brand creator for several years. Joy is also our friend, which makes it even better.

Kate Mytty was our air traffic controller. This was a massive project, and there were a lot of moving parts. Imagine tracking down the permissions to use every book cover. Kate made all the little things that make all the difference happen.

Rebecca Schlei Hartman made sure everything was right. She checked quotations and page numbers. She questioned word usage. She kept an eye out for things we never would have caught. Rebecca kept us aware that details do matter.

The words of a number of our staff appear on the pages of this book. In addition to the folks above, Todd Lazarski, Jon Mueller, Roy Normington, Aaron Schleicher, and Dylan Schleicher all contributed to making this book what it is.

When we signed the contract, we told everyone that this book wasn't about Jack or Todd, but about 800-CEO-READ. We need to thank Meg Bacik, Jake Cohen, Scott Kopf, Shane Muellemann, Mel Koenig, and Shawn Quinn, along with everyone mentioned earlier, whose hard work kept the company engine running smoothly and efficiently while we were working on this project.

We need to thank Carol Grossmeyer, Rebecca Schwartz, and Daniel Goldin from our parent company, Dickens Books, for their support. The publication of this book is a big deal for the entire company.

We also need to thank the folks at Portfolio. Will Weisser read our first proposal and challenged us to go back to the drawing board. Adrian Zackheim helped us see the audience for this book. Adrienne Schultz provided the support and the guidance every book (and author) needs. There was no better cheerleader than Deb Lewis. We also want to thank Maureen Cole and Jeffrey Krames for their support through the whole process. Thank you also goes out to Brooke Carey and Natalie Horbachevsky for guiding us through the paperback process.

We send our love out to Barbara Cave Henricks and Sara Schneider, who helped get the word out for the book. Ray Bard read early drafts and helped us think about how to better market the book. Charles Fishman gets kudos for delivering the subtitle. Nick and Nikki Smith Morgan helped us hone the message for the whole book as we got out and started talking to others about it.

We need to acknowledge all the authors whose works are included in the book. We are merely summarizing your hard work. All of your thoughts and ideas have made our business better. Thank you!

And finally, we must thank our families. It was hard—much harder than either of us expected—to write this book. Jack says: "Ann, thank you for being there for the past forty years. And also thanks to my granddaughters for giving me joy and happiness. There were times during this process when your delight put this all in the right perspective." Todd says: "Amy, thanks for your patience and understanding. To Ethan, Zach, and Alexa—you *do* have a father."

Thanks for reading.

INDEX

Grateful acknowledgment is made to the following for permission to reproduce the following book jackets and book covers:

Anchor Books, a division of Random House, Inc.: *The Wisdom of Crowds* by James Surowiecki. Used by permission of Anchor Books.

Bantam, a division of Random House, Inc.: *Emotional Intelligence* by Daniel Goleman; *McDonald's: Behind the Arches* by John F. Love; and *Sam Walton: Made in America* by Sam Walton and John Huey.

Bard Press: *Little Red Book of Selling* by Jeffrey Gitomer.

Basic Books, a member of the Perseus Books Group: *On Becoming a Leader* by Warren G. Bennis; *Out of Control* by Kevin Kelly; *Partnership Charter* by David Gage; *The Rise of the Creative Class* by Richard Florida; and *The Story Factor* by Annette Simmons. Used by arrangement with Basic Books. All rights reserved.

Clerisy Press: *Jump Start Your Business Brain* by Doug Hall. Courtesy of Clerisy Press Inc., Cincinnati, Ohio.

Collins Business, an imprint of HarperCollins Publishers: *Control Your Own Destiny or Someone Else Will* by Noel M. Tichy and Stratford Sherman; *Crossing the Chasm* by Geoffrey A. Moore; *The Effective Executive* by Peter F. Drucker; *The E-Myth Revisited* by Michael E. Gerber; *The Essential Drucker* by Peter F. Drucker; *Good to Great* by Jim Collins; *The HP Way* by David Packard; *In Search of Excellence* by Thomas J. Peters and Robert H. Waterman; *Influence* by Robert B. Cialdini; *The Innovator's Dilemma* by Clayton M. Christensen; *Moments of Truth* by Jan Carlzon; *Reengineering the Corporation* by Michael Hammer and James Champy; *Swim with the Sharks without Being Eaten Alive* by Harvey B. Mackay; and *Who Says Elephants Can't Dance?* by Louis V. Gerstner, Jr.

Columbia University Press: *More Than You Know* by Michael J. Mauboussin. Used with permission of Columbia University Press.

Crown Business, a division of Random House, Inc.: *Execution* by Larry Bossidy and Ram Charan; *How to Be a Star at Work* by Robert E. Kelley; *The Leadership Moment: Nine True Stories of Triumph and Disaster and Their Lessons for Us All* by Michael Useem; *Losing My Virginity* by Richard Branson; and *What the CEO Wants You to Know* by Ram Charan. Used by permission of Crown Business.

Doubleday, a division of Random House, Inc.: *The Art of Innovation* by Tom Kelley with Jonathan Littman; *The Great Game of Business* by Jack Stack with Bo Burlingham; *Leadership is An Art* by Max Depree; *My Years with General Motors* by Alfred Sloan; *Only the Paranoid Survive* by Andrew S. Grove; *The Power of Intuition* by Gary Klein; and *The Republic of Tea* by Mel Ziegler, Bill Rosenzweig, and Patricia Ziegler. Used by permission of Doubleday.

Farrar, Straus, Giroux: *The Lexus and the Olive Tree* by Thomas L. Friedman.

The Free Press, a division of Simon & Schuster Adult Publishing Group: *Discovering the Soul of Service* by Leonard L. Berry, copyright © 1999 by Simon & Schuster, Inc.; and *Now, Discover Your Strengths* by Marcus Buckingham and Donald O. Clifton, copyright © 2001 by Simon & Schuster, Inc. Used with the permission of The Free Press. All rights reserved.

Grand Central Publishing, a division of Hachette Book Group USA, Inc.: *Selling the Invisible* by Harry Beckwith and *A Whack on the Side of the Head* by Roger von Oech.

Harper Perennial, a division of HarperCollins Publishers: *Flow* by David Packard.

Harvard Business School Publishing: *The Age of Unreason* by Charles Handy, 1990; *Balanced Scorecard* by Robert S. Kaplan and David P. Norton, 1996; *Beyond the Core* by Chris Zook, 2004; *Competing for the Future* by Gary Hamel and C.K. Prahalad, 1996; *The Experience Economy* by B. Joseph Pine II and James H. Gilmore, 1999; *Financial Intelligence* by Karen Berman and Joe Knight, with John Case, 2006; *First 90 Days* by Michael Watkins, 2003; *The Knowing-Doing Gap* by Jeffrey Pfeffer and Robert I. Sutton, 2000; *Leading Change* by John P. Kotter, 1996; *The Monk and the Riddle* by Randy Komisar with Kent Lineback, 2001; and *Questions of Character* by Joseph L Badaracco, Jr., 2006. © Copyright Harvard Business School Publishing. All rights reserved.

Houghton Mifflin Company: *Guerilla Marketing, 4th Edition* by Jay Conrad Levinson.

Hyperion: *How to Become a Rainmaker* by Jeffrey J. Fox, cover copyright © 2000 Hyperion and *Never Give In!* by Winston S. Churchill, cover copyright © 2003 Hyperion.

Jossey-Bass, A Wiley Imprint: *Driven* by Paul R. Lawrence and Nitin Nohria; *The Five Dysfunctions of a Team* by Patrick Lencioni; *Leadership Challenge* by James M. Kouzes and Barry Z. Posner; and *Up the Organization* by Robert Townsend.

Kaplan Publishing, a division of Kaplan, Inc.: *The Radical Leap* by Steve Farber. Published with permission from Kaplan Publishing, a division of Kaplan, Inc.

Little, Brown and Company, a division of Hachette Book Group USA, Inc.: *Six Thinking Hats* by Edward de Bono and *The Tipping Point* by Malcolm Gladwell.

McGraw-Hill, a division of The McGraw-Hill Companies: *A Business and Its Beliefs* by Thomas J. Watson, 2003; *Chasing Daylight* by Eugene O'Kelly, 2007; and *Positioning* by Al Ries and Jack Trout, 2000. Reproduced with permission of The McGraw-Hill Companies.

The MIT Press: *Out of the Crisis* by W. Edwards Deming.

Nigel Parry/Creative Photographers inc.: *The Creative Habit* by Twyla Tharp, Simon & Schuster. Cover image reprinted with the permission of © Nigel Parry/CPi.

North River Press: *The Goal* by Eliyahu M. Goldratt and Jeff Cox.

Oriel Incorporated: *The Team Handbook, Third Edition* by Peter R. Scholtes, Brian L. Joiner and Barbara J. Streibel, © 2003 Oriel Incorporated. All rights reserved.

Pearson Education: *Zag: Number One Strategy of High-Performance Brands* by Marty Neumeier. Reproduced by permission of Pearson Education, Inc. All rights reserved.

Penguin Books, a member of Penguin Group (USA) Inc.: *The Art of Possibility* by Rosamund Stone Zander and Benjamin Zander; *Getting Things Done* by David Allen; and *A New Brand World* by Scott Bedbury and Stephen Fenichell.

Pocket Books, an imprint of Simon & Schuster Adult Publishing Group: *How to Win Friends and Influence People* by Dale Carnegie. Copyright © 1998 by Simon & Schuster, Inc. Used with the permission of Pocket Books. All rights reserved.

Portfolio, a member of Penguin Group (USA) Inc.: *The Art of the Start* by Guy Kawasaki; *Purple Cow* by Seth Godin; and *The Smartest Guys in the Room* by Bethany McLean and Peter Elkind.

Random House, Inc.: *The Force* by David Dorsey; *Lucky or Smart?* by Bo Peabody; *Made to Stick* by Chip Heath and Dan Heath; *Titan* by Ron Chernow; *What Should I Do With My Life?* by Po Bronson; and *When Genius Failed* by Roger Lowenstein. Used by permission of Random House, Inc.

Random House Children's Books, a division of Random House, Inc.: *Oh, The Places You'll Go!* by Dr. Seuss. Used by permission of Random House Children's Books.

Revell, a division of Baker Publishing Group: *Secrets of Closing the Sale* by Zig Ziglar.

Simon & Schuster Adult Publishing Group: *The 7 Habits of Highly Effective People* by Stephen Covey, copyright © 2004 by Simon & Schuster, Inc.; *American Steel* by Richard Preston, copyright © 1991 by Simon & Schuster, Inc.; *First, Break All the Rules* by Marcus Buckingham and Curt Coffman, copyright © 1999 by Simon & Schuster, Inc.; *Growing a Business* by Paul Hawken, copyright © 1988 by Simon & Schuster, Inc.; and *Why We Buy* by Paco Underhill, copyright © 2000 by Simon & Schuster, Inc. Used with the permission of Simon & Schuster Adult Publishing Group. All rights reserved.

Taylor and Francis Group, LLC, a division of Informa plc.: *Toyota Production System* by Taiichi Ohno. Reproduced by permission of Taylor and Francis Group, LLC.

Ten Speed Press: *Thinkertoys* by Michael Michalko. Used with permission of Ten Speed Press, Berkeley, CA. www.tenspeed.com.

Viking Penguin, a member of Penguin Group (USA) Inc.: *Orbiting the Giant Hairball* by Gordon MacKenzie.

Vintage Books, a division of Random House, Inc.: *Personal History* by Katharine Graham and *To Engineer is Human* by Henry Petroski. Used by permission of Vintage Books.

W.W. Norton & Company, Inc.: *Moneyball* by Michael Lewis and *Naked Economics: Undressing the Dismal Science* by Charles Wheelan. Used by permission of W. W. Norton & Company, Inc.

SIDEBARS

"Sidebars" designed by Joy Panos Stauber

Images thanks to:
The Best Route to an Idea: Sign drawn by Joy Panos Stauber
Best-selling Business Books: Cash register drawn by Dylan Schleicher
Business Books for Kids of All Ages: Image by ©iStockphoto.com/GildedCage
Classics: Image by ©iStockphoto.com/Anna Ceglinska
Conferences to Attend: Image by ©iStockphoto.com/Ingmar Wesemann

The Economist logo used with permission from *The Economist* magazine.
>1000 Words: Graphics drawn by Joy Panos Stauber
Found in Fiction: Typewriter drawn by Dylan Schleicher
Fresh Perspectives Not in a Bookstore Near You: Heads by Joy Panos Stauber; Gears by ©iStockphoto.com/Julie Felton
1982: Waking a Giant (Genre): Photo by Joy Panos Stauber
Globalization of Manners: Image by ©iStockphoto.com/Scott Dunlap
Industry in Depth: "Industries" drawing by Dylan Schleicher
Jack Covert Selects: Photo by Karen Sherlock from the *Milwaukee Journal Sentinel* 8/171995, © 1995 Journal Sentinel Inc., reproduced with permission.
Leadership in Movies: Image by ©iStockphoto.com/Michael Kurtz
Your Favorites: Sketches by Joy Panos Stauber
Selling on the Silver Screen: Image by ©iStockphoto.com/Michael Kurtz
Making Choices: Copyright © 2011 Veer.com/hoch2wo
How to Read a Business Book: Image composition and retouching by Richard Paul Studios

**FOR MORE ON
THE 100 BEST BOOKS,
VISIT**

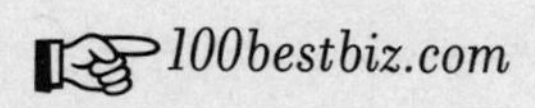

- The 7 Habits of Highly Effective People
- The Age of Unreason
- American Steel
- The Art of Innovation
- The Art of Possibility
- The Art of the Start
- The Balanced Scorecard
- Beyond the Core
- A Business and Its Beliefs
- Chasing Daylight
- Competing for the Future
- Control Your Destiny or Someone Else Will
- The Creative Habit
- Crossing the Chasm
- Discovering the Soul of Service
- Driven
- The Effective Executive
- Emotional Intelligence
- The E-Myth Revisited
- The Essential Drucker
- Execution
- The Experience Economy
- Financial Intelligence
- The First 90 Days
- First, Break All the Rules
- The Five Dysfunctions of a Team
- Flow
- The Force
- Getting Things Done
- The Goal
- Good to Great
- The Great Game of Business
- Growing a Business
- Guerrilla Marketing
- How to Be a Star at Work
- How to Become a Rainmaker
- How to Win Friends and Influence People
- The HP Way
- In Search of Excellence
- Influence
- The Innovator's Dilemma
- Jump Start Your Business Brain
- The Knowing-Doing Gap
- The Leadership Challenge
- Leadership Is an Art
- The Leadership Moment
- Leading Change
- The Lexus and the Olive Tree
- Little Red Book of Selling
- Losing My Virginity
- Lucky or Smart?
- Made to Stick
- McDonald's
- Moments of Truth
- Moneyball
- The Monk and the Riddle
- More Than You Know
- My Years with General Motors
- Naked Economics
- Never Give In!
- A New Brand World
- Now, Discover Your Strengths
- Oh, the Places You'll Go!
- On Becoming a Leader
- Only the Paranoid Survive
- Orbiting the Giant Hairball
- Out of Control
- Out of the Crisis
- The Partnership Charter
- Personal History
- Positioning: The Battle for Your Mind
- The Power of Intuition
- Purple Cow
- Questions of Character
- The Radical Leap
- Reengineering the Corporation
- The Republic of Tea
- The Rise of the Creative Class
- Sam Walton: Made in America—My Story
- Secrets of Closing the Sale
- Selling the Invisible
- Six Thinking Hats
- The Smartest Guys in the Room
- The Story Factor
- Swim with the Sharks without Being Eaten Alive
- The Team Handbook
- Thinkertoys
- The Tipping Point
- Titan
- To Engineer Is Human
- Toyota Production System
- Up the Organization
- A Whack on the Side of the Head
- What Should I Do with My Life?
- What the CEO Wants You to Know
- When Genius Failed
- Who Says Elephants Can't Dance?
- Why We Buy
- The Wisdom of Crowds
- Zag